Fundamentals of Investment Management

Published by Willford Press,
118-35 Queens Blvd., Suite 400,
Forest Hills, NY 11375, USA

ISBN: 978-1-68285-983-4

Cataloging-in-Publication Data

Fundamentals of investment management / Henry Stamp.
p. cm.
Includes bibliographical references and index.
ISBN 978-1-68285-983-4
1. Portfolio management. 2. Investments. 3. Investment analysis.
I. Stamp, Henry.

HG4529.5 .F86 2022
332.6--dc23

For information on all Willford Press publications
visit our website at www.willfordpress.com

Willford Press

Contents

Preface

Investment management refers to the professional asset management of various securities such as shares and bonds as well as other assets like real estate. It aims to meet the specified investment goals for benefitting the investors. Institutions such as insurance companies, pension funds, corporations and charities can be investors. People who invest directly or through investment contracts and through collective investment schemes are termed as private investors. The investment management of investment funds is referred to as asset management or fund management. Some of the major areas of focus within this field are asset allocation, diversification and long-term returns. This textbook attempts to understand the multiple branches that fall under the discipline of investment management and how such concepts have practical applications. It explores all the important aspects of this field in the present day scenario. This book will provide comprehensive knowledge to the readers.

Given below is the chapter wise description of the book:

Chapter 1- The professional handling of various assets such as shares, real estate and bonds for the purpose of meeting specified investment goals to benefit investors is known as investment management. This is an introductory chapter which will introduce briefly all the significant aspects of the different types of investments, the objectives behind them and their management.

Chapter 2- The set of behaviors, rules or procedures which have been designed to assist an investor in selecting an investment portfolio is known as investment strategy. There are various kinds of investment strategies such as liability driven, insider driven and benchmark-driven investment strategy. The topics elaborated in this chapter will help in gaining a better perspective about these investment strategies.

Chapter 3- The science of allocating assets for institutions and individuals, making decisions about investment mix and policy, balancing risk against performance and matching investments to objectives is known as portfolio management. This chapter discusses in detail the theories and methodologies related to management of portfolio as well as the strategies which are involved in it.

Chapter 4- Any resource which is owned by the business, and which is expected to generate cash flow in the future is known as an asset. Assets are usually classified on the basis of their convertibility, usage and physical existence. The chapter closely examines these key concepts of assets and their allocation to provide an extensive understanding of the subject.

Chapter 5- The fixed income instrument which represents a loan made by an investor to a borrower is known as a bond. A bond can be issued by a government or a corporation. Some of the important types of bonds are investment-grade corporate bonds, high-yield bonds treasury bonds and foreign bonds. This chapter has been carefully written to provide an easy understanding of these types of bonds as well as bond valuation and bond strategies.

Chapter 6- The probability of the occurrence of a loss relative to the expected return on an investment is known as an investment risk. The efficiency of an investment is evaluated using a performance measure known as Return on Investment (ROI). The topics elaborated in this chapter will help in gaining a better perspective about the branches of different types of investment risks as well as the Risk-Return Ratio.

Indeed, my job was extremely crucial and challenging as I had to ensure that every chapter is informative and structured in a student-friendly manner. I am thankful for the support provided by my family and colleagues during the completion of this book.

Henry Stamp

1

Understanding Investment Management

The professional handling of various assets such as shares, real estate and bonds for the purpose of meeting specified investment goals to benefit investors is known as investment management. This is an introductory chapter which will introduce briefly all the significant aspects of the different types of investments, the objectives behind them and their management.

Investment Management

Investment management refers to the handling of financial assets and other investments—not only buying and selling them. Management includes devising a short or long-term strategy for acquiring and disposing of portfolio holdings. It can also include banking, budgeting, and tax services and duties, as well.

The term most often refers to managing the holdings within an investment portfolio, and the trading of them to achieve a specific investment objective. Investment management is also known as money management, portfolio management, or wealth management.

Professional investment management aims to meet particular investment goals for the benefit of clients whose money they have the responsibility of overseeing. These clients may be individual investors or institutional investors such as pension funds, retirement plans, governments, educational institutions, and insurance companies.

Investment management services include asset allocation, financial statement analysis, stock selection, monitoring of existing investments, and portfolio strategy and implementation. Investment management may also include financial planning and advising services, not only overseeing a client's portfolio but coordinating it with other assets and life goals. Professional managers deal with a variety of different securities and financial assets, including bonds, equities, commodities, and real estate. The manager may also manage real assets such as precious metals, commodities, and artwork. Managers can help align investment to match retirement and estate planning as well as asset distribution.

In corporate finance, investment management includes ensuring a company's tangible and intangible assets are maintained, accounted for, and well-utilized.

According to an annual study by research and advisory firm Willis Towers Watson and the financial newspaper Pensions & Investments, the investment management industry is growing. When based on the combined holdings of the 500 biggest investment managers, the global industry had approximately US$93.8 trillion assets under management (AUM) in 2018. This figure is up from an estimated $79 trillion in 2017.

Running an investment management business involves many responsibilities. The firm must hire professional managers to deal, market, settle, and prepare reports for clients. Other duties include conducting internal audits and researching individual assets—or asset classes and industrial sectors.

Aside from hiring marketers and training managers who direct the flow of investments, those who head investment management firms must ensure they move within legislative and regulatory constraints, examine internal systems and controls, account for cash flow and properly track record transactions and fund valuations.

In general, investment managers who have at least $25 million in assets under management (AUM) or who provide advice to investment companies offering mutual funds are required to be registered investment advisors (RIA). As a registered advisor, they must register with the Securities and Exchange Commission (SEC) and state securities administrators. It also means they accept the fiduciary duty to their clients. As a fiduciary, these advisors promise to act in their client's best interests or face criminal liability. Firms or advisors managing less than $25 million in assets typically register only in their states of operation.

Investment managers are usually compensated via a management fee, usually a percentage of the value of the portfolio held for a client. Management fees range from 0.35% to 2% annually. Also, fees are typically on a sliding scale—the more assets a client has, the lower the fee they can negotiate. The average management fee is around 1%.

Pluses and Minuses of Investment Management

Though the investment management industry may provide lucrative returns, there are also key problems that come with running such a firm. The revenues of investment management firms are directly linked to the market's behavior. This direct connection means that the company's profits depend on market valuations. A major decline in asset prices can cause a decline in the firm's revenue, especially if the price reduction is great compared to the ongoing and steady company costs of operation. Also, clients may be impatient during hard times and bear markets, and even above-average fund performance may not be able to sustain a client's portfolio.

- Pros:
    - Professional analysis.
    - Full-time diligence.

  - Ability to time or outperform market.
  - Ability to protect portfolio in down times.

- Cons:
  - Sizeable fees.
  - Profits fluctuate with market.
  - Challenges from passively managed vehicles, robo-advisors.

Since the mid-2000s, the industry has also faced challenges from two other sources.

- The increase of robo-advisors digital platforms that provide automated, algorithm-driven investment strategies and asset allocation.
- The availability of exchange traded funds, whose portfolios mirror that of a benchmark index.

The latter hinderance exemplifies passive management since few investment decisions have to be made by human fund managers. The former challenge does not use human beings at all—other than the programmer writing the algorithm. As a result, both can charge far lower fees than human fund managers can charge. However, according to some surveys, these lower-cost alternatives will often outperform actively managed funds—either outright or in terms of overall return—primarily due to them not having heavy fees dragging them down.

The pressure from this dual competition is why investment management firms must hire talented, intelligent professionals. Though some clients look at the performance of individual investment managers, others check out the overall performance of the firm. One key sign of an investment management company's ability is not just how much money their clients make in good times—but how little they lose in the bad.

Real World Example of Investment Management

The top 20 investment management firms control a record 43% of all the global assets under management, according to the Willis Towers Watson report mentioned earlier—some $40.6 trillion worth. In the U.S., the five leading firms include, in descending order:

- Bank of America Global Wealth & Investment Management which, as of 2008, includes Merrill Lynch ($1.25 trillion in AUM).
- Morgan Stanley Wealth Management ($1.1 trillion in AUM).
- J.P. Morgan Private Bank ($677 billion in AUM).

- UBS Wealth Management ($579 billion in AUM).
- Wells Fargo ($564 billion in AUM).

Basic Investment Objectives

The options for investing savings are continually increasing, yet every investment vehicle can be categorized according to three fundamental characteristics: safety, income, and growth.

Those options also correspond to investor objectives. While an investor may have more than one of these objectives, the success of one comes at the expense of others. We examine these three types of objectives, the investments used to achieve them, and the ways investors can incorporate them into a strategy.

Safety

There is truth to the axiom that there is no such thing as a completely safe and secure investment. However, we can get close to ultimate safety for our investment funds through the purchase of government-issued securities in stable economic systems or through the purchase of corporate bonds issued by large, stable companies. Such securities are arguably the best means of preserving principal while receiving a specified rate of return.

The safest investments are found in the money market. In order of increasing risk, these securities include: Treasury bills (T-bills), certificates of deposit (CD), commercial paper or bankers' acceptance slips or, in the fixed-income (bond) market, in the form of municipal and other government bonds and corporate bonds. As they increase in risk, these securities also increase in potential yield.

There's an enormous range of relative risk within the bond market. At one end are government and high-grade corporate bonds, which are considered some of the safest investments around. At the other end are junk bonds, which have a lower investment grade and may have more risk than some of the more speculative stocks. In other words, corporate bonds are not always secure although most instruments from the money market are considered safe.

Objective of basic Investment

Income

The safest investments are those likely to have the lowest rate of income return or yield. Investors must inevitably sacrifice a degree of safety if they want to increase their yields. As yield increases, so does the risk.

To increase their rate of investment return and take on risk above that of money market instruments or government bonds, investors may choose to purchase corporate bonds or preferred shares with lower investment ratings. Investment grade bonds rated at A or AA are slightly riskier than AAA bonds but typically also offer a higher income return than AAA bonds. Similarly, BBB-rated bonds carry medium risk, but they offer less potential income than junk bonds, which offer the highest potential bond yields available but at the highest possible risk. Junk bonds are the most likely to default.

Most investors, even the most conservative-minded ones, want some level of income generation in their portfolios, even if it is just to keep up with the economy's rate of inflation. But maximizing income return can be an overarching principle for a portfolio, particularly for individuals who require a fixed sum from their portfolio every month. A retired person who requires a certain amount of money every month is well served by holding reasonably safe assets that provide funds over and above other income-generating assets, such as pension plans.

Capital Growth

This discussion has thus far been concerned only with safety and yield as investment objectives and has not considered the potential of other assets to provide a rate of return from an increase in value, often referred to as a capital gain.

Capital gains are entirely different from yield in that they are only realized when the security is sold for a price that is higher than the price at which it was originally purchased. Selling at a lower price is referred to as a capital loss. Therefore, investors seeking capital gains are likely not those who need a fixed, ongoing source of investment returns from their portfolio, but rather those who seek the possibility of longer-term growth.

Capital growth is most closely associated with the purchase of common stock, particularly growth securities, which offer low yields but a considerable opportunity for an increase in value. For this reason, common stock ranks among the most speculative of investments as the return depends on what will happen in an unpredictable future. Blue-chip stocks can potentially offer the best of all worlds by possessing reasonable safety, modest income, and potential for capital growth generated by long-term increases in corporate revenues and earnings as the company matures. Common stock is rarely able to provide the safety and income generation of government bonds.

Funds that are garnered through common stock offerings, for example, are often geared toward the growth plans of small companies, a process that is extremely important for the overall economy. To encourage investment in these areas, governments choose to tax capital gains at a lower rate than income. This strategy encourages entrepreneurship and the founding of new businesses that boost the economy.

Secondary Objectives

Tax Minimization: An investor may pursue certain investments to leverage tax minimization as part of their investment strategy. A highly paid executive, for example, may seek investments with favorable tax treatment to lessen his or her overall income tax burden. Making contributions to an IRA or another tax-sheltered retirement plan, such as a 401(k), can be an effective tax minimization strategy.

Marketability/Liquidity: Many of the investments we have discussed are reasonably illiquid, which means they cannot be immediately sold and easily converted into cash. Achieving a degree of liquidity, however, requires the sacrifice of a certain level of income or potential for capital gains.

Common stock is often considered the most liquid of investments because it can be sold within a day or two. Bonds are also marketable, but some bonds are highly illiquid or non-tradable with a fixed term. Similarly, money market instruments may only be redeemable at the precise date at which the fixed term ends. If an investor seeks liquidity, money market assets and non-tradable bonds are not likely to be held in their portfolio.

The Bottom Line

The advantages of one investment often come at the expense of another. If an investor desires growth, for instance, they must often sacrifice some income and safety. Therefore, most portfolios have one pre-eminent objective with all other potential objectives carrying less weight in the overall scheme.

Choosing a single strategic objective and assigning weightings to all other possible objectives is a process that depends on such factors as the investor's temperament, his or her stage of life, marital status or family situation. Each investor can determine an appropriate mix of investment opportunities. But you need to spend the appropriate amount of time and effort in finding, studying, and selecting the opportunities that match your objectives.

Investment Objective

Objectives may be driven by any number of things, including personal risk tolerance, life circumstances, tax considerations and relative time horizon of the investment. What follows are a few descriptions of various, common investment objectives, including the incentives and rationale behind them.

Growth Investors

Typical growth investors seek high rates of growth and capital appreciation. They are willing to tolerate more risk and will invest in growth stocks that have high P/E (price-to-earnings) ratios. Companies with high P/E ratios are typically looking for future performance to make up the price premium on the current earnings. If the company fails to create the expected earnings growth couched in the P/E ratio, then the share price will fall. Growth companies can see wild downward swings in the value of their stock when this occurs. Growth investors are not after the income from dividend-paying stocks, but are more interested in capital appreciation and capital gains as the profits from these types of businesses are plowed back in to facilitate more rapid growth.

Aggressive Growth Investors

Similar to growth investors, Aggressive Growth Investors focus on companies that have high P/E ratios, but they are looking for the very highest growth potential possible. These types of investments are reminiscent of venture capital investors. Aggressive growth stocks typically couple the highest growth rates with very risky companies. In some cases (especially in instances where earnings do not yet exist), these types of stocks have ridiculously-high P/E ratios. Those seeking an Aggressive Growth strategy typically need a very high tolerance for risk.

Capital Appreciation Investors

Capital Appreciation Investors are long-term investors. They seek capital appreciation growth over a very long and extended period of time. Appreciation in this case could be deemed "increase in value." Many such investors are not interested in growth per se, but are looking to build value over the long haul. An example of this type of investment could include money placed in a 401(k) or IRA plan.

Value Investors

"Value investing" is a term often attributed to the late Ben Graham (venerable sage to billionaire investor Warren Buffet). A value investor seeks stocks whose value is often underpriced in the market. The types of stocks invested in by value investors typically have low P/E ratios and tend to be overlooked by the market. Another key component of value investing is to go after investments whose underlying business assets are extremely sound. Value stocks do not necessarily simply have a low price, but will have a low price relative to the earnings they produce (when compared with other possible investments). Value investors are under the assumption that the market will eventually take notice of the undervaluation and the stock will subsequently rise.

Growth at Reasonable Price (GARP) Investors

GARP investors combine some of the aspects of value investing and growth investing. That is, they seek high potential for growth while maintaining a reasonable P/E ratio. This is more difficult than it sounds, particularly if one assumes there is very little room for arbitrage opportunities. Stocks that appearl to GARP investors are typical in the middle of the road, however. That is, they may have slightly higher P/E ratios than value stocks and slightly lower expected growth rates than your typical growth stock. They will have vague characteristics of both, however. Put differently, GARP investors are typically looking for stocks with low PEG (price-to-earnings growth) ratios.

Income Investors

Income investors are likely the most risk averse of all those listed here. They typically seek reliable income and capital preservation. They will generally pick "blue chip" stocks that pay reliable dividends. In general, income stocks are typically less volatile than growth stocks are are more interesting to those seeking reliable regular payments. In fact, many retirees have interest in income-generating stocks. These types of investors will often invest in bonds or investments that are perceived as relatively stable with less risk. Due to their lack of relative volatility and stable payments, income stocks/bonds are typically referred to as defensive investments.

Determinants of Investment

Interest rates play a key role in the determination of the desired stock of capital and thus of investment. Because investment is a process through which capital is increased in one period for use in future periods, expectations play an important role in investment as well.

Capital is one factor of production, along with labor and natural resources. A decision to invest is a decision to use more capital in producing goods and services. Factors that affect firms' choices in the mix of capital, labor, and natural resources will affect investment as well.

Interest Rates and Investment

We often hear reports that low interest rates have stimulated housing construction or that high rates have reduced it. Such reports imply a negative relationship between interest rates and investment in residential structures. This relationship applies to all forms of investment: higher interest rates tend to reduce the quantity of investment, while lower interest rates increase it.

To see the relationship between interest rates and investment, suppose you own a small factory and are considering the installation of a solar energy collection system to heat your building. You have determined that the cost of installing the system would be $10,000 and that the system would lower your energy bills by $1,000 per year. To simplify the example, we shall suppose that these savings will continue forever and that the system will never need repair or maintenance. Thus, we need to consider only the $10,000 purchase price and the $1,000 annual savings.

If the system is installed, it will be an addition to the capital stock and will therefore be counted as investment. Should you purchase the system?

Suppose that your business already has the $10,000 on hand. You are considering whether to use the money for the solar energy system or for the purchase of a bond. Your decision to purchase the system or the bond will depend on the interest rate you could earn on the bond.

Putting $10,000 into the solar energy system generates an effective income of $1,000 per year—the saving the system will produce. That is a return of 10% per year. Suppose the bond yields a 12% annual interest. It thus generates interest income of $1,200 per year, enough to pay the $1,000 in heating bills and have $200 left over. At an interest rate of 12%, the bond is the better purchase. If, however, the interest rate on bonds were 8%, then the solar energy system would yield a higher income than the bond. At interest rates below 10%, you will invest in the solar energy system. At interest rates above 10%, you will buy a bond instead. At an interest rate of precisely 10%, it is a toss-up.

If you do not have the $10,000 on hand and would need to borrow the money to purchase the solar energy system, the interest rate still governs your decision. At interest rates below 10%, it makes sense to borrow the money and invest in the system. At interest rates above 10%, it does not.

In effect, the interest rate represents the opportunity cost of putting funds into the solar energy system rather than into a bond. The cost of putting the $10,000 into the system is the interest you would forgo by not purchasing the bond.

At any one time, millions of investment choices hinge on the interest rate. Each decision to invest will make sense at some interest rates but not at others. The higher the interest rate, the fewer potential investments will be justified; the lower the interest rate, the greater the number that will be justified. There is thus a negative relationship between the interest rate and the level of investment.

In figure "The Investment Demand Curve" shows an investment demand curve for the economy—a curve that shows the quantity of investment demanded at each interest rate, with all other determinants of investment unchanged. At an interest rate of 8%, the level of investment is $950 billion per year at point A. At a lower interest rate of 6%, the investment demand curve shows that the quantity of investment demanded will rise to $1,000 billion per year at point B. A reduction in the interest rate thus causes a movement along the investment demand curve.

The investment demand curve shows the volume of investment spending per year at each interest rate, assuming all other determinants of investment are unchanged. The curve shows that as the interest rate falls, the level of investment per year rises. A reduction in the interest rate from 8% to 6%, for example, would increase investment from $950 billion to $1,000 billion per year, all other determinants of investment unchanged.

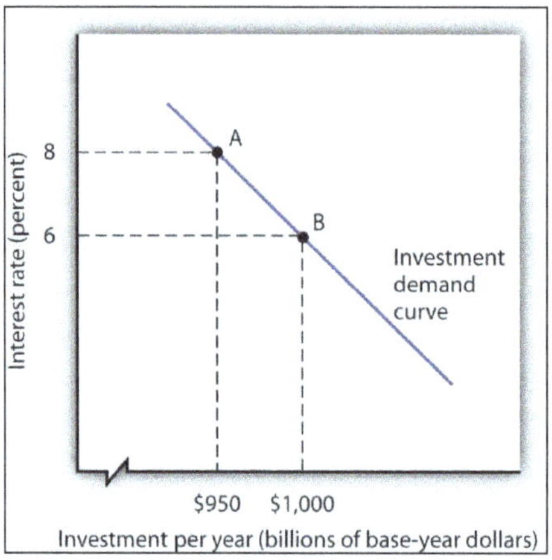

Figure: The Investment Demand Curve.

Other Determinants of Investment Demand

Perhaps the most important characteristic of the investment demand curve is not its negative slope, but rather the fact that it shifts often. Although investment certainly responds to changes in interest rates, changes in other factors appear to play a more important role in driving investment choices.

This topic examines eight additional determinants of investment demand: expectations, the level of economic activity, the stock of capital, capacity utilization, the cost of capital goods, other factor costs, technological change, and public policy. A change in any of these can shift the investment demand curve.

Expectations

A change in the capital stock changes future production capacity. Therefore, plans to change the capital stock depend crucially on expectations. A firm considers likely future sales; a student weighs prospects in different occupations and their required educational and training levels. As expectations change in a way that increases the expected return from investment, the investment demand curve shifts to the right. Similarly, expectations of reduced profitability shift the investment demand curve to the left.

The Level of Economic Activity

Firms need capital to produce goods and services. An increase in the level of production is likely to boost demand for capital and thus lead to greater investment. Therefore, an increase in GDP is likely to shift the investment demand curve to the right.

To the extent that an increase in GDP boosts investment, the multiplier effect of an initial change in one or more components of aggregate demand will be enhanced. We have already seen that the increase in production that occurs with an initial increase in aggregate demand will increase household incomes, which will increase consumption, thus producing a further increase in aggregate demand. If the increase also induces firms to increase their investment, this multiplier effect will be even stronger.

The Stock of Capital

The quantity of capital already in use affects the level of investment in two ways. First, because most investment replaces capital that has depreciated, a greater capital stock is likely to lead to more investment; there will be more capital to replace. But second, a greater capital stock can tend to reduce investment. That is because investment occurs to adjust the stock of capital to its desired level. Given that desired level, the amount of investment needed to reach it will be lower when the current capital stock is higher.

Suppose, for example, that real estate analysts expect that 100,000 homes will be needed in a particular community by 2010. That will create a boom in construction—and thus in investment—if the current number of houses is 50,000. But it will create hardly a ripple if there are now 99,980 homes.

How will these conflicting effects of a larger capital stock sort themselves out? Because most investment occurs to replace existing capital, a larger capital stock is likely to increase investment. But that larger capital stock will certainly act to reduce net investment. The more capital already in place, the less new capital will be required to reach a given level of capital that may be desired.

Capacity Utilization

The capacity utilization rate measures the percentage of the capital stock in use. Because capital generally requires downtime for maintenance and repairs, the measured capacity utilization rate typically falls below 100%. For example, the average manufacturing capacity utilization rate was 79.7% for the period from 1972 to 2007. In November 2008 it stood at 72.3.

If a large percentage of the current capital stock is being utilized, firms are more likely to increase investment than they would if a large percentage of the capital stock were sitting idle. During recessions, the capacity utilization rate tends to fall. The fact that firms have more idle capacity then depresses investment even further. During expansions, as the capacity utilization rate rises, firms wanting to produce more often must increase investment to do so.

The Cost of Capital Goods

The demand curve for investment shows the quantity of investment at each interest rate, all other things unchanged. A change in a variable held constant in drawing this curve shifts the curve. One of those variables is the cost of capital goods themselves. If, for example, the construction cost of new buildings rises, then the quantity of investment at any interest rate is likely to fall. The investment demand curve thus shifts to the left.

The $10,000 cost of the solar energy system in the example given earlier certainly affects a decision to purchase it. We saw that buying the system makes sense at interest rates below 10% and does not make sense at interest rates above 10%. If the system costs $5,000, then the interest return on the investment would be 20% (the annual saving of $1,000 divided by the $5,000 initial cost), and the investment would be undertaken at any interest rate below 20%.

Other Factor Costs

Firms have a range of choices concerning how particular goods can be produced. A factory, for example, might use a sophisticated capital facility and relatively few workers, or it might use more workers and relatively less capital. The choice to use capital will be affected by the cost of the capital goods and the interest rate, but it will also be affected by the cost of labor. As labor costs rise, the demand for capital is likely to increase.

Our solar energy collector example suggests that energy costs influence the demand for capital as well. The assumption that the system would save $1,000 per year in energy costs must have been based on the prices of fuel oil, natural gas, and electricity. If these prices were higher, the savings from the solar energy system would be greater, increasing the demand for this form of capital.

Technological Change

The implementation of new technology often requires new capital. Changes in technology can thus increase the demand for capital. Advances in computer technology have encouraged massive investments in computers. The development of fiber-optic technology for transmitting signals has stimulated huge investments by telephone and cable television companies.

Public Policy

Public policy can have significant effects on the demand for capital. Such policies typically seek to affect the cost of capital to firms. The Kennedy administration introduced two such strategies in the early 1960s. One strategy, accelerated depreciation, allowed firms to depreciate capital assets over a very short period of time. They could report artificially high production costs in the first years of an asset's life and thus report lower profits and pay lower taxes. Accelerated depreciation did not change the actual rate at which assets depreciated, of course, but it cut tax payments during the early years of the assets' use and thus reduced the cost of holding capital.

The second strategy was the investment tax credit, which permitted a firm to reduce its tax liability by a percentage of its investment during a period. A firm acquiring new capital could subtract a fraction of its cost—10% under the Kennedy administration's plan—from the taxes it owed the government. In effect, the government "paid" 10% of the cost of any new capital; the investment tax credit thus reduced the cost of capital for firms.

Though less direct, a third strategy for stimulating investment would be a reduction in taxes on corporate profits (called the corporate income tax). Greater after-tax profits mean that firms can retain a greater portion of any return on an investment.

A fourth measure to encourage greater capital accumulation is a capital gains tax rate that allows gains on assets held during a certain period to be taxed at a different rate than other income. When an asset such as a building is sold for more than its purchase price, the seller of the asset is said to have realized a capital gain. Such a gain could be taxed as income under the personal income tax. Alternatively, it could be taxed at a lower rate reserved exclusively for such gains. A lower capital gains tax rate makes assets subject to the tax more attractive. It thus increases the demand for capital. Congress reduced the capital gains tax rate from 28% to 20% in 1996 and reduced the required holding period in 1998. The Jobs and Growth Tax Relief Reconciliation Act of 2003 reduced the capital gains tax further to 15% and also reduced the tax rate on dividends from 38% to 15%. A proposal to eliminate capital gains taxation for smaller firms was considered but dropped before the stimulus bill of 2009 was enacted.

Accelerated depreciation, the investment tax credit, and lower taxes on corporate profits and capital gains all increase the demand for private physical capital. Public policy can also affect the demands for other forms of capital. The federal government subsidizes state and local government production of transportation, education, and many other facilities to encourage greater investment in public sector capital. For example, the federal government pays 90% of the cost of investment by local government in new buses for public transportation.

Types of Investments

Think of the various types of investments as tools that can help you achieve your financial goals. Each broad investment type—from bank products to stocks and bonds—has its own general set of features, risk factors and ways in which they can be used by investors.

Learn more about the various types of investments below.

- Stocks

When you buy shares of a company's stock, you own a piece of that company. Stocks come in a wide variety, and they often are described based the company's size, type, performance during market cycles and potential for short- and long-term growth.

- Investment Funds

Funds—such as mutual funds, closed-end funds and exchange-traded funds—pool money from many investors and invest it according to a specific investment strategy.

Funds can offer diversification, professional management and a wide variety of investment strategies and styles. But not all funds are the same.

- Options

Options are contracts that give the purchaser the right, but not the obligation, to buy or sell a security, such as a stock or exchange-traded fund, at a fixed price within a specific period of time. It pays to learn about different types of options, trading strategies and the risks involved.

- Retirement

Numerous types of investments come into play when saving for retirement and managing income once you retire. For saving, tax-advantaged retirement options such as a 401(k) or an IRA can be a smart choice. Managing retirement income may require moving out of certain investments and into ones that are better suited to a retirement lifestyle.

- Alternative and Complex Products

These products include notes with principal protection and high-yield bonds that have lower credit ratings and higher risk of default than traditional investments, but offer more attractive rates of return.

- Commodity Futures

Commodity futures contracts are agreements to buy or sell a specific quantity of a commodity at a specified price on a particular date in the future. Commodities include metals, oil, grains and animal products, as well as financial instruments and currencies. With limited exceptions, trading in futures contracts must be executed on the floor of a commodity exchange.

- Bonds

A bond is a loan an investor makes to an organization in exchange for interest payments over a specified term plus repayment of principal at the bond's maturity date.

- Bank Products

Banks and credit unions can provide a safe and convenient way to accumulate savings—and some banks offer services that can help you manage your money. Checking and savings accounts offer liquidity and flexibility. Find out more about these and other bank products.

- Annuities

An annuity is a contract between you and an insurance company, in which the company promises to make periodic payments, either starting immediately—called an immediate annuity—or at some future time a deferred annuity.

- Saving for Education

Funding education begins with savings.

- Initial Coin Offerings and Cryptocurrencies

These are speculative investments that come with significant uncertainty and many risks. Before you consider an investment in ICOs or cryptocurrencies, learn more.

- Security Futures

Federal regulations permit trading in futures contracts on single stocks, also known as single stock futures, and certain security indices.

- Insurance

Life insurance products come in various forms, including term life, whole life and universal life policies. There also are variations on these—variable life insurance and variable universal life—which are considered securities.

Most Common Types of Investments

Stocks and Bonds

Without a doubt, owning stocks has been the best way historically to build wealth. And for more than a century, investing in bonds has been considered one of the safest ways to make money. But how do these investments work?

Stocks are pretty simple: they're shares of ownership in a specific company. When you own a share of Apple, for example, you own a tiny piece of that company. Stock prices fluctuate with a company's fortunes, and also with the economy at large.

When you buy a bond, meanwhile, you are lending money to the company or institution that issued it. In the case of a school bond, for instance, you are lending money to the school district to build a new high school or improve classroom conditions. Buying a bond issued by a company means you're lending money to that company, which it can use to grow the business.

Investing in Mutual Funds

One of the most popular ways to own stocks and/or bonds is through mutual funds. In fact, most people are statistically less likely to own individual investments than they are shares of companies through mutual funds held in their 401(k) or Roth IRA.

Mutual funds offer many benefits to investors, particularly to beginners who are just mastering investing basics. They're pretty easy to understand and allow you to diversify your investments over more companies. However, mutual funds also have a few serious drawbacks: they charge fees, which can eat into your profits, and they may boost your tax bill, even in a year when you don't sell shares.

Real Estate Investments

The world is full of people who are convinced that real estate is the only investment that makes sense. Whether you subscribe to that philosophy or not, there are more ways than ever to add real estate to your portfolio.

Yes, you can buy a home for yourself, or properties to rent. But you also can purchase a security called a real estate investment trust (REIT), which combines the benefits of stocks with the tangible property of land, shopping malls, apartment buildings, or almost anything else you can imagine.

Investing Structures and Entities

When you move beyond stocks, bonds, mutual funds, and real estate, you encounter different types of investment entities. For example, millions of people will never own a share of stock or a bond. Instead, they invest their money in a family business, such a restaurant, retail shop, or rental property. Yes, these are businesses, but you also should consider them investments, and treat them accordingly.

More experienced investors likely will invest in hedge funds or private equity funds at some point in their life, while others will buy shares of publicly traded limited partnerships through their broker. These special legal structures can have big tax implications for you, and it is important you understand how investing through them can both benefit, and potentially harm your pocketbook.

Investing in a Bad Economy

It's the nature of the world that sometimes bad things happen. When they happen to your investments or savings, you don't need to panic. Sometimes, you need to take a hit before you can make some money again, and holding on until the recession ends is the best plan.

Traditional Investments

Traditional Investments: Stocks and Bonds

As an investor, you have a variety of options to choose from, including stocks and bonds. The investment you select depends on your financial goals, your investment preferences, and your tolerance for risk.

These options represent traditional investments: You put your money down and hold on. Although you want to make changes as necessary to protect your investment, these types of investments can add stability to more aggressive — and riskier — investment strategies (like trading and hedging).

Investing in Stocks

When you buy stock, you're buying ownership in a corporation (or company). The benefit of owning stock in a corporation is that whenever the corporation profits, you profit as well. Typically, investors buy stocks and hold them for a long time, making decisions along the way about reallocating investment capital as financial needs change, selling underperformers, and so on.

As an investor, you want to make sure that your stock portfolio is carefully balanced among the different types of stocks (growth, value, domestic, international, and so on) and your other investments. A well-balanced traditional portfolio (which includes stocks and long-, short-, and intermediate-term bonds) generally offers a steady return of between 5 and 12 percent, depending on the specific investments and the amount of risk you're willing to assume.

Investing in Bonds

To raise money, governments, government agencies, municipalities, and corporations can sell bonds. When you buy a bond, you're essentially lending money to this entity for the promise of repayment in addition to a specified annual return. In that sense, a bond is really nothing more than an IOU with a serial number. Some people, to sound impressive, call bonds debt securities or fixed-income securities.

Although some entities are more reliable than others, bonds generally offer stability and predictability well beyond that of most other investments. Because you are, in most cases, receiving a steady stream of income (the annual returns, for example), and because you expect to get your principal back in one piece (at the end of the bond's life), bonds tend to be more conservative investments than stocks, commodities, or collectibles.

Alternative Investment

Alternative investments are those asset classes that vary from traditional investments on grounds on complexity, liquidity, regulatory mechanism and mode of fund management. But that is too theoretical isn't it. Different types of alternative investments include Private Equity, Hedge Funds, Venture Capital, Real Estate/ Commodities and Tangibles like Wine/ Art/Stamps.

Let us delve a little further and understand what actually differentiates Alternative investments from the traditional ones.

Alternative Investments vs. Traditional Investments

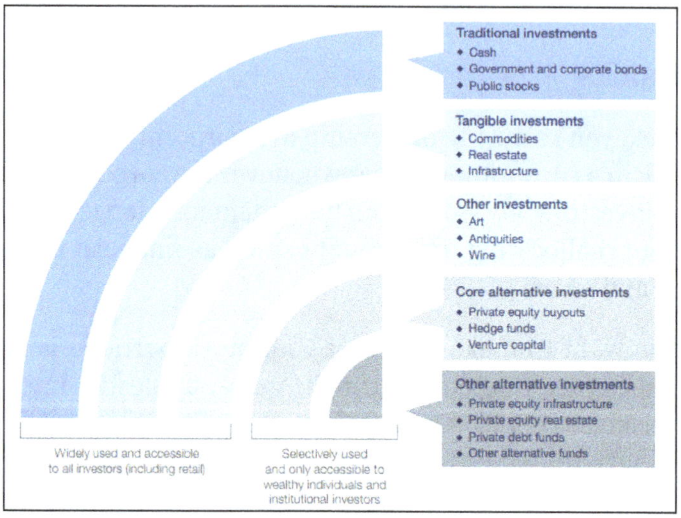

Illiquidity in Nature

As these are assets with a niche investor base, the trading in these are infrequent as compared to the traditional investments. Due to the low volume of trading and absence of public market, these investments cannot be sold off quickly. There is also a sheer lack of buyers who want to readily purchase the investments. This is in total contrast with the publicly traded stocks, mutual funds and fixed securities which are constantly being bought and sold due to a much wider investor base.

Less Transparency and Lower Regulations

While the investments are heavily regulated under the Dodd-Frank Wall Street Reform and Consumer Protection Act, they are not directly covered by the Securities and Exchange Commission (SEC) and the Financial Industry Regulatory Authority (FINRA). While few of the Anti-fraud norms are applicable on alternative investments, there is no single agency that has defined regulatory norms for the Alternative space and monitors activities of the fund managers.

Limited Performance Indicators

Due to lower volume of trading, the data, facts and figures pertaining to alternative Investments are difficult to obtain. While there are many sources floating in the internet, determining their credibility is a task. Investors of traditional investments have wider access to data, news and research which helps him take decisions and formulate strategies, but for alternative investments, limited access to information and historical trends increase dependency on fund managers.

Close-ended Funds

Alternative investments are mainly close-ended funds with an investment horizon of 10-15 years. Hedge Funds are the only exception of this and similar to traditional investments in this respect. In alternative investments, funds are not automatically reinvested but returned back to the investors after the time frame, who can then chose to invest it somewhere else.

Preference of Alternative Investments

Now the question arises, if these are investments with an air of ambiguity, why would high net worth investors want to have them in their portfolios and how would it benefit them?

Alternative investments as a domain is still evolving and maturing. While it is mainly considered to be a prerogative of the High Net Worth investors, there are also retail investors who are showing keen interest in them. After the financial crisis in 2008, where even the best of the diversified portfolios were swayed by extreme volatility, alternative investments proved their worth.

The major reasons why they score brownie points over traditional investments are:

Low Co-relation with Markets

Low correlations to traditional asset classes like equity markets and fixed income markets act as a major advantage for alternative investments. These asset classes usually have a co-relation between -1 to 0 which make them less susceptible to systematic risk or market-oriented risk element. However, a catch in this scene is the upside is also capped due to low co-relation with market.

A Strong Tool for Diversification

Alternative investments by virtue of their lower co-relation co-efficient offers better diversification benefits with enhanced returns. These assets perfectly complement the traditional investments and when a stock or bond underperforms, a hedge fund or private equity firms can cushion the extent of losses over the long term. One can add or replace the alternative assets based on individual investment goals and risk appetite.

Active Management

As compared to passive indexed investment, alternative investment calls for active management of funds. The complex nature of the assets, volatility and elevated risk level of these investments required constant monitoring and recalibration of investment strategies as needed. Moreover, the wealthy investors for whom high management fees is not a concern, would definitely want to reap the benefits of high-end expertise.

There various types of Alternative investments. Few are well-structured, while few follow instinctiveness of the investors. Let us try to understand the structure and underlying philosophies behind these asset types.

Alternative Investments Types

Private Equity

Not all equities are listed on stock exchanges. Private Equity refers to funds that institutional investors or high net worth investors directly place in private companies or in the process of buyout of public companies. Usually these private companies then utilize the capital for their organic and inorganic growth. It can be for expanding their footprint, increasing the marketing operations, technological advancement or making strategic acquisitions.

Mostly the investors lack expertise to select companies which suits their investment goals, thus they prefer investing through Private Equity Firms rather than direct mode. These firms raise funds from high net worth investors, endowments, insurance companies, pension funds etc.

A quick look at Private Equity Fund structure:

Limited Partner	General Partner	Compensation Structure
They are the institutional or high net worth individuals who invest in these funds.	The General Partners are the ones responsible for managing the investments in the fund.	The General Partners receive management fees as well as a share of profits on the investment. This is known as Carried Interest and ranges between 8% to 30%.

The private equity industry was out of regulatory supervision since its birth in 1940s, however after the 2008 financial crisis, it falls under the purview of Dodd–Frank Wall Street Reform and Consumer Protection Act. In the recent times, there is increased call for transparency and the US Securities and Exchange Commission (SEC) has started collecting data on the private equity firms.

When it comes to judging the performance of Private Equity, measures like IRR (Internal rate of Return) were widely used, but it has certain limitations. IRR did not address the reinvestment element for interim cash flows or negative flows. Thus, evolved the Modified IRR. A more practical and holistic tool than the traditional IRR, the modified IRR or MIRR is main measure to quantify the Private Equity performance these days.

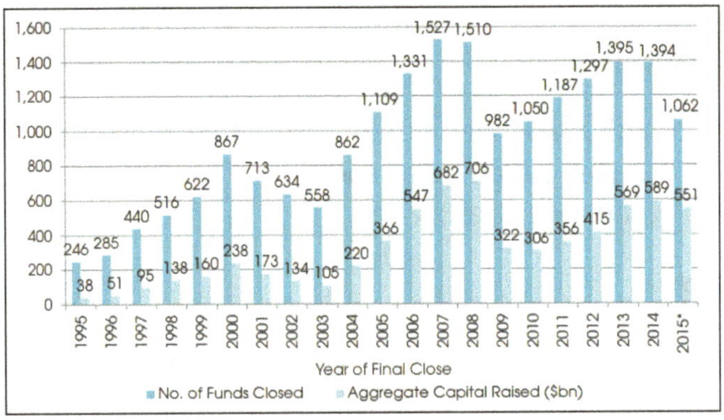

Private Capital will refer to the broader spectrum of private closed-end funds, including private equity, private debt, private real estate, infrastructure and natural resources.

Hedge Funds

Mutual Funds are quite popular, but, Hedge Funds, its distant cousin, still belongs to a lesser known territory. This is an alternative investment vehicle, which only caters to investors with ultra-deep pockets. As per US laws, hedge fund should cater only to "accredited" investors. This implies that they must possess a net worth of more than $1 million and also earn a minimum annual income. According to World Economic Forum (WEF), Hedge funds have more than $3 trillion Assets under management (AUM), which represents 40% of total alternative investments.

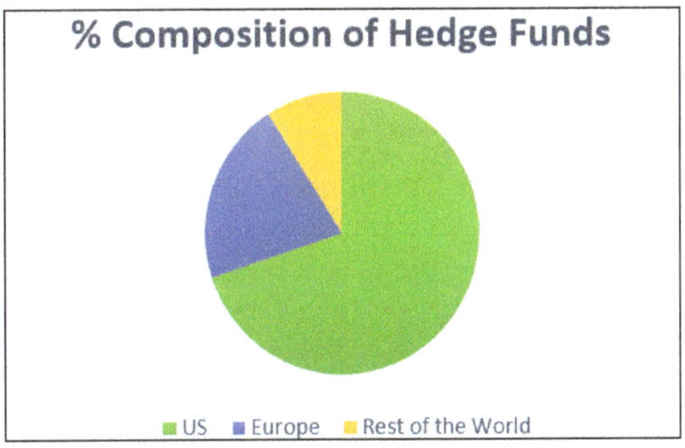

These funds derived this name due to their core idea to generate consistent return and preserve capital, instead of focusing on the magnitude of returns.

With minimal co-relation to equity markets, most hedge funds have been able to diversify portfolio risks and reduce volatility.

Hedge funds are also pool of underlying assets but they differ from Mutual Funds on a number of grounds. They are not regulated as Mutual Funds and hence have the leeway to invest in broader range of securities. Hedge funds are best known for investments in risky assets and derivatives. When it comes to investment techniques, hedge funds prefer to take a more high-end complex approach calibrated to varied levels of risk and return. Many of them also resort to "Leveraged" investment, which means using borrowed money for investment.

One factor that distinguishes Hedge Funds from other alternative investments is its liquidity quotient. These funds can take as low as a few minutes for sell-off due to increased exposure to liquid securities.

Venture Capital

We live in the age of entrepreneurship. New ideas and technological advancements have led to proliferation of start-up ventures across the globe. But ideas aren't enough for a firm to survive. To sustain, a firm needs capital. Venture Capital is an alternative asset class that invests equity capital in private start-ups and show exceptional potential of growth.

Doesn't it sound familiar to Private Equity? No it doesn't. Private Equity invest equity capital into mature companies, while Venture Capital is mainly for startups.

Venture Capital usually invests at seed and early stage businesses while some invest at expansion stage. The investment horizon is typically between 3-7 years and venture capitalists expect returns to the tune of >8x-10x the invested capital. This high rate of return is a natural outcome owing to the risk quotient associated with the investment. While some ideas might appear lackluster in the inception stage, who knows, they may turn out to be the next Facebook or Apple? Investors who have the caliber to shoulder this level of risk and believe in the underlying potential of the idea are the ideal venture capitalists.

With the growth in entrepreneurship, this is the time for Venture Capital to thrive. From 2013 to 2015, the deals have grown 54% YoY. Geographically, Venture Capital investments are concentrated mostly in the US, followed by Europe and China.

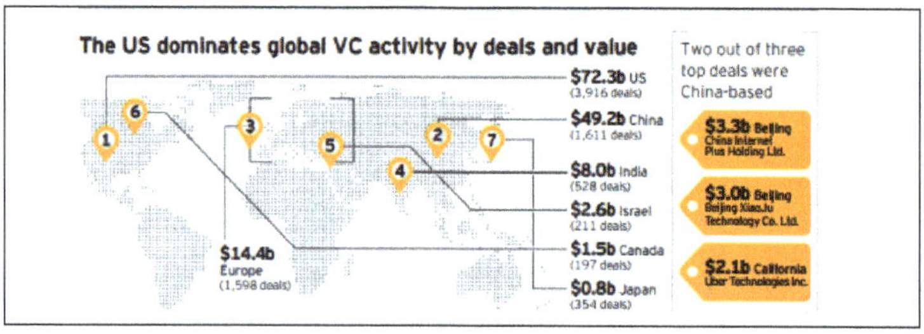

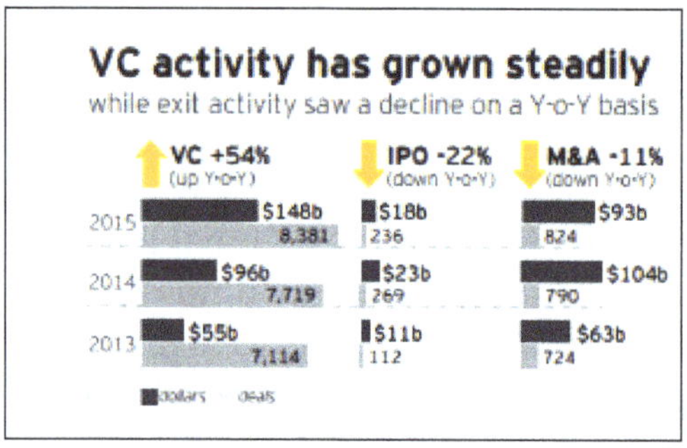

Investing in new ventures involves a high degree of risk peppered with uncertainty. There is high possibilities of negative outcomes and this justifies the risk quotient. Each stage of Venture Capital investment presents a new risk, however, the returns generated are directly proportional to the quantum of risk, and that's what lures the Venture Capitalists.

The risk/Return element for Venture Capital according to the stage of investment.

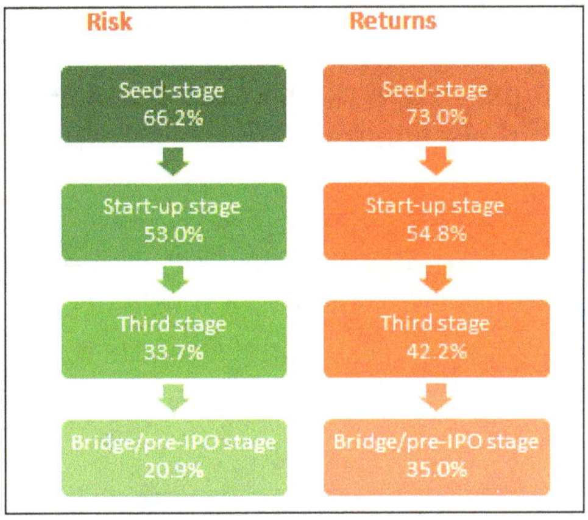

The risk is highest at the seed stage (66%) and reduces till the pre-IPO stage (20%).

Returns at seed stage are as high as 73%, and declines as the risk phases out till the pre-IPO stage.

Real Assets

Not all investments are towards businesses or pool of funds. Some of them are towards real assets like precious metals or natural resources. Investing money in gold, silver or other precious metal have been there since times immemorial. They have always been known to be the best hedge against market movements and currency fluctuations due to their inverse relationship with the US Dollar. Investors can invest in gold through gold coins, bullions, or indirectly through sector traded funds or exchange-traded funds.

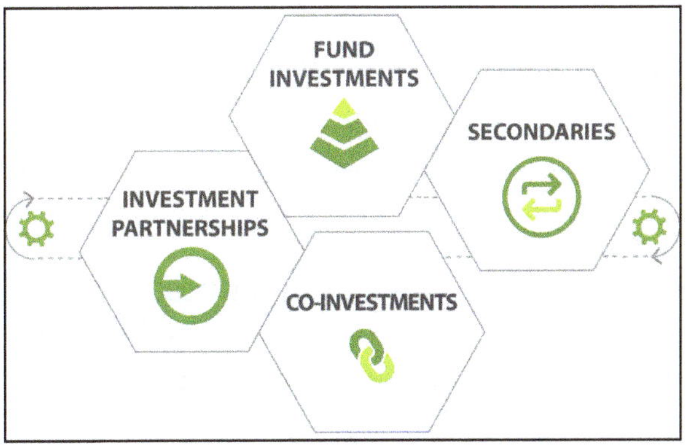

Real estate is also one of the avenues that has caught the fancy of investors since long. Investing in plots, houses and reaping rental yields or commercial assets are some of the direct ways of investing in real estate. Indirect ways through which retail investors can park their money in real estate are through Real estate Investment trusts (REITs). Once again, the low co-relationship between equity markets and real estate has branded real estate as an ideal hedge against inflation.

Collectibles Like Wine, Art, Stamps or Vintage Cars

For those who thought stamps, art work and vintage wine are just prestigious souvenirs, think again. Hidden in these connoisseurs are astute investors who know the real value of these collectibles.

Classic cars like 1950 Ferrari 166 Inter Vignale Coupe and Ferrari 250 GTO Berlinetta tops the list, while investment-grade wines like Bordeaux come a close second. Coins, art and stamp are some of the other luxury investments that also preferred options.

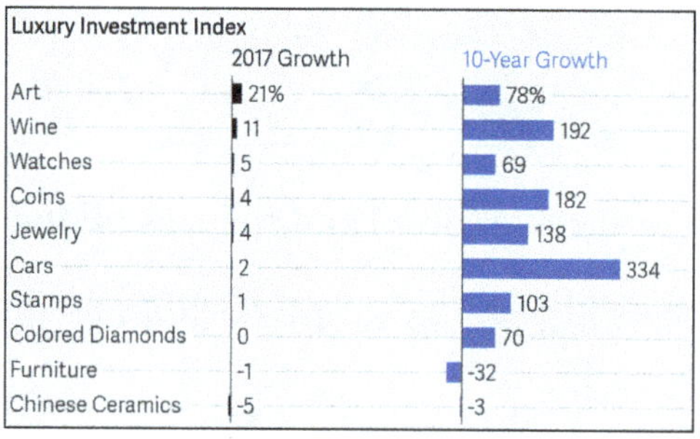

According to Knight Frank, the Knight Frank Luxury Investment Index (KFLII) rose by 7% in 2015 as compared to a 5% drop in the value of the FTSE 100 equities index and a mere 1% rise for the high-end housing market in London. However, the value for collectibles are unpredictable and can be impacted by forces of supply and demand, prevailing economic conditions, willingness of buyers and the physical state of the prestigious collection.

Investment Outsourcing

This is the process of hiring someone else to manage your investment portfolio. It's usually done by institutional investors, organisations that invest money on behalf of their members.

It's becoming increasingly common, not only for institutional investors but also among families with a very high net worth. You might also have heard of large companies such as Russell Investments and SEI, both based in the US, which provide outsourcing for their clients.

There are a growing number of companies working in outsourced investment management worldwide. The trend originally began among smaller firms, who were either unwilling or unable to set up their own internal investment teams. The most common model is to use an outsourced chief investment officer, who is employed by a family or organisation who do not have fully-staffed investment departments. The process of investment outsourcing is evolving as it becomes more popular, but usual practice is to hand over all decision-making - including asset allocation and monitoring.

Investment Control

This can refer to the process of monitoring the performance of an asset management firm. The aim is to ensure that standards are high and the client's money is being invested correctly.

An investor may perform a form of investment control to ensure that their portfolio is being managed in a way they are happy with. An asset management firm may also do this to ensure their clients are satisfied.

There are many benefits to this process taking place. Such scrutiny should ensure that best practice is being followed by a manager, as well as clarifying that all relevant laws and regulations are being followed. Another key aim is to analyse past investment decisions objectively, which should help improve decision-making in the future and therefore lead to stronger investment returns. It also improves transparency, and allows risk and return data to be analysed. One potential benefit is to identify performance dispersion in investments.

Investment Demand

Investment demand refers to the demand by businesses for physical capital goods and services used to maintain or expand its operations. Think of it as the office and factory space, machinery, computers, desks, and so on that are used to operate a business. It is important to remember that investment demand here does not refer to financial investment. Financial investment is a form of saving, typically by households that wish to maintain or increase their wealth by deferring consumption till a later time.

In this model, investment demand will be assumed to be exogenous. This means that its value is determined outside of the model and is not dependent on any variable within the model. This assumption is made primarily to simplify the analysis and to allow the focus to be on exchange rate changes later. The simple equation for investment demand can be written as,

$$I^D = I_0,$$

where the "o," or naught, subscript on the right side indicates that the variable is exogenous or autonomous. In words, the equation says that investment demand is given exogenously as I_0.

Admittedly, this is not a realistic assumption. In many other macro models, investment demand is assumed to depend on two other aggregate variables: GNP and interest rates. GNP may affect investment demand since the total demand for business expansion is more likely the higher the total size of the economy. The growth rate of GNP may also be an associated determinant since the faster GNP is growing, the more likely companies will predict better business in the future, inspiring more investment.

Interest rates can affect investment demand because many businesses must borrow money to finance expansions. The interest rate is the cost of borrowing money; thus, the higher the interest rates are, the lower the investment demand should be, and vice versa.

If we included the GNP and interest rate effects into the model, the solution to the extended model later would prove to be much more difficult. Thus we simplify things by assuming that investment is exogenous. Since many students have learned about the GNP and interest rate effect in previous courses, you need to remember that these effects are *not* a part of this model.

Investment Demand Curve and its Importance

The Investment Demand Curve is a graphical representation that illustrates the fact that investors will invest less when capital costs more and how they will be willing to invest more when the capital costs less.

To elaborate, investors exhibit a certain demand that varies by cost just as the buyers of any commodity exhibit a certain cost-sensitive demand for the goods they seek. Given a lower cost, the typical buyer would demand a greater quantity. We should conceptualized this demand curve in much the same way as that which we would use to graph the demand for other commodities, but with a slight change. Instead of saying that a certain quantity is demanded at a given price, we say that a certain investment volume is demanded when the cost of investment capital weighs in at a certain rate.

This is necessary because with the basic demand curve for other commodities, units of currency are used on the y-axes. When investments (quantified in dollars/ euros/ yen/ etc.) are the commodity, we value them as rates.

The investment demand curve depicts the dollar value of investment projects demanded for every given interest rate. It slopes downward because as the interest rate increases demand for investment decreases. This is because the interest rate measurers the cost of borrowing money. As the cost of borrowing money increases, fewer investment projects will be profitable.

The Investment demand curve or simply the investment schedule is a locus of points each representing a combination of gross investment demand (I) and the rate of interest (r) within a given time period. It is a downward sloping curve depicting a negative correlation between gross investment and the (lending) rate of interest. As the rate of interest increases, the gross investment demand falls since higher rate of interest implies higher rental to be paid on the capital borrowed by the firms. The rate of interest (lending) is generally increased by the central bank of an economy in order to curb the inflationary trend (contractionary monetary policy).

No matter what you decide to pursue in life, you will be making investment decisions of some kind - buying stock, real estate (your home, office, etc.), or maybe investing in a start up like InstaEDU as an owner. The downward sloping Investment Demand Curve shows the simple relationship between the level of investments and interest rates in the economy. As the interest rates rise, the level of investments reduces since the cost of financing increases and vice versa. This is why the study of Investment Demand Curve is useful.

Examples of Demand Curves

Rate of Interest and Investment Demand Curve

The marginal efficiency of capital is estimated. We can represent diminishing marginal efficiency of capital in general by a curve which will slope downward. This has been done in figure in which along the X-axis investment in capital assets is measured and along the X-axis marginal efficiency of capital in general is shown. It will be seen from the figure that when investment in capital asset is equal to 07, marginal efficiency of capital is i,. When the investment is increased to OI_2, marginal efficiency of capital falls to i_2. Likewise, when investment rises to OI_3, marginal efficiency of capital further diminishes to i_3.

Inducement to invest depends upon the marginal efficiency of capital and the rate of interest. With the given particular rate of interest and given the curve of marginal efficiency of capital in general we can show what will be the equilibrium level of investment in the economy. If in figure below along the Y-axis, rate of interest is also shown, then level of investment can be easily determined.

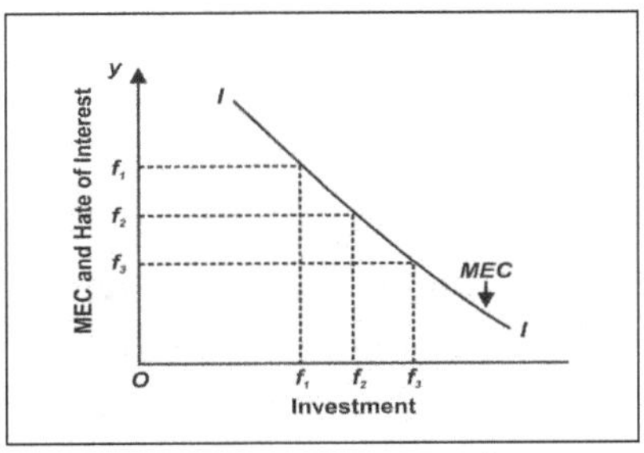

Figure: Investment Demand Curve.

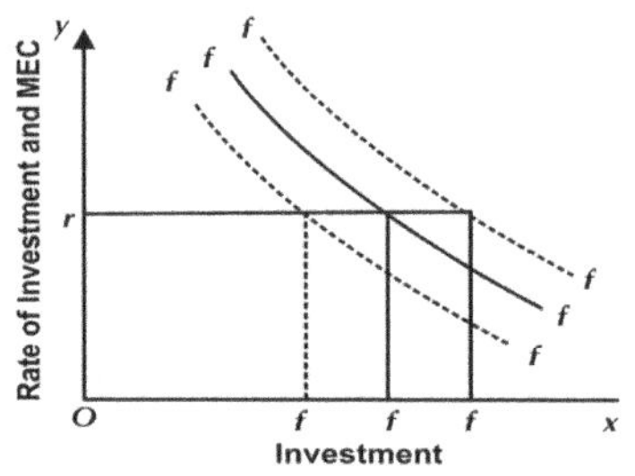

Figure: Shifts in Investment Demand Curve due to Changes Marginal Efficiency of Capital.

The equilibrium level of investment will be established at the point where marginal efficiency of capital becomes equal to the given current rate of interest. Thus, if the rate of interest is $i_1$then I_1 investment will be undertaken. Since at OI_1 level of investment marginal efficiency of capital is equal to the rate of interest i_1. If the rate of interest falls to i_2, investment in the capital assets will rise to OI_2, since at OI_2 level of investment the new rate of interest i_2 is equal to the marginal efficiency of capital. Thus, we see that the curve of marginal efficiency of capital in general shows the demand for investment or inducement to invest at various rates of interest.

Hence marginal efficiency of capital curve represents the investment demand curve. This investment demand curve shows how much investment will be undertaken by the entrepreneurs at various rates of interest. If the investment demand curve is less elastic, then investment demand will not increase much with the fall in the rate of interest. But if the investment demand curve or marginal efficiency of capital curve is very much elastic, then the changes in the rate of interest will bring about large changes in investment demand.

Business Expectations and Investment Demand Curve

The marginal efficiency of capital depends upon the supply price of capital on the one hand and prospective yields on the other. It is important to note here that the prospective yields are greatly affected by the expectations of the entrepreneurial class regarding profit making. These expectations generally change very frequently. Indeed, it is the profit expectations of the entrepreneur which determine the level of investment. When the expectations of the entrepreneur regarding profit making become dim, the marginal efficiency of capital declines and as a result demand for investment falls.

The occurrence of depression is mainly due to the pessimistic expectations of the entrepreneurial class regarding profit making. On the contrary, when the expectations of the entrepreneurs regarding profit opportunities increase, their inducement to invest rises. As a result of the increase in investment, aggregate demand in the economy increases and levels of income and employment increase. We thus see that profit expectations of entrepreneurs greatly affect investment demand and consequently the level of income and employment.

We have explained above that, according to Keynes, marginal efficiency of capital along with rate of interest determines the level of investment and therefore of the levels of income and employment. A significant contribution of Keynes is that he emphasized the important role that business expectations play in determining the prospective yield from assets on which marginal efficiency of capital and therefore the level of investment depends. He drew distinctions between short-term expectations and long-term expectations.

Keynes thought that prospective yields of capital assets depended on partly existing facts which we can assume to be known with a fair degree of certainty and partly on future events which can be predicted with a degree of uncertainty and involves greater risk. It is the existing facts which are known almost with certainty that determine short-term expectations.

The short-term business expectations about prospective yields from investment depend on (i) the existing stock of capital assets and (ii) the strength of consumer demand for goods which require a good deal of those assets for their production. The investors think that the current consumption demand will continue in immediate future too and base their expectations of prospective yield from investment in capital assets on it.

As regards the state of long term expectations, Keynes emphasized future changes in the stock of capital assets and changes in the level of aggregate demand during the entire future life of the assets whose prospective yields are being estimated.

Business men acquiring new assets which have long life for production of goods are more concerned with long-run forces on which future earnings from capital assets depend. It is these long-run forces which make long-run expectations about future yields that make them quite uncertain. Changes in these long term expectations make investment quite volatile. Therefore, Keynes gave great importance to the state of confidence for determining investment.

It should be carefully noted that when the expectations regarding prospective yields change, the whole curve of the marginal efficiency of capital will shift. If profit expectations fall, the marginal efficiency of capital curve, that is, investment demand curve will shift downward to left, as shown by the shift of the curve from II to I'I' in figure. On the other hand, when the profit expectations of the entrepreneurial class become better than before, the marginal efficiency of capital curve will shift upward to the right, as shown by the marginal efficiency of capital curve I'I'. Downward shift in the marginal efficiency of capital curve indicates that at the given rate of interest, less investment will be undertaken than before.

And upward shift in the marginal efficiency of capital curve indicates that more will be invested at the given rate of interest than before. When in the beginning, investment demand curve, that is, marginal efficiency of capital curve is represented by II, at the rate of interest r, demand for investment is OI, As a result of downward shift in the marginal efficiency of capital curve to I"I", investment demand at the rate of interest r falls to OI". When the marginal efficiency of capital shifts upward to I'I', investment demand at the given rate of interest r rises to OI'.

It follows, therefore, that the rate of investment depends on marginal efficiency of capital and the rate of interest. If investment demand is interest-elastic, a reduction in rate of interest tends to stimulate investment. But it may fail to do so, if marginal efficiency of investment is already lower than the rate of interest (as may well happen during a depression). Of the two determinants of the rate of investment, marginal efficiency of investment is more volatile than the rate of interest.

The rate of interest is usually 'sticky' in the short run, while marginal efficiency of investment can fluctuate from one extreme to another. If there is a divergence between the two, usually the marginal efficiency of investment will adjust to the rate of interest. If, for example, the marginal efficiency of investment is 20 per cent, while the current rate of interest is 12 per cent, forces will be set in motion so as to bring the former to the level of the latter.

In such a situation, there will be more investment because marginal efficiency of investment is greater than the rate of interest, and with the increase in investment, marginal efficiency of investment will fall. At the point where it is just reduced to the level of the current rate of interest, further investment will cease.

Inflation

Inflation is a sustained rise in overall price levels. Moderate inflation is associated with economic growth, while high inflation can signal an overheated economy.

As an economy grows, businesses and consumers spend more money on goods and services. In the growth stage of an economic cycle, demand typically outstrips the supply of goods, and producers can raise their prices. As a result, the rate of inflation increases. If economic growth accelerates very rapidly, demand grows even faster and producers raise prices continually. An upward price spiral, sometimes called "runaway inflation" or "hyperinflation," can result.

In the U.S., the inflation syndrome is often described as "too many dollars chasing too few goods;" in other words, as spending outpaces the production of goods and services, the supply of dollars in an economy exceeds the amount needed for financial transactions. The result is that the purchasing power of a dollar declines.

In general, when economic growth begins to slow, demand eases and the supply of goods increases relative to demand. At this point, the rate of inflation usually drops. Such a period of falling inflation is known as disinflation. A prominent example of disinflation in an economy was in Japan in the 1990s. As figure below shows, inflation fell from over 3% at the start of the decade to below zero by the end. This was driven by the sharp slowdown in economic growth that followed the bursting of an asset price bubble. Disinflation can also result from a concerted effort by government and policy-makers to control inflation; for example, for much of the 1990s, the U.S. enjoyed a long period of disinflation even as economic growth remained resilient.

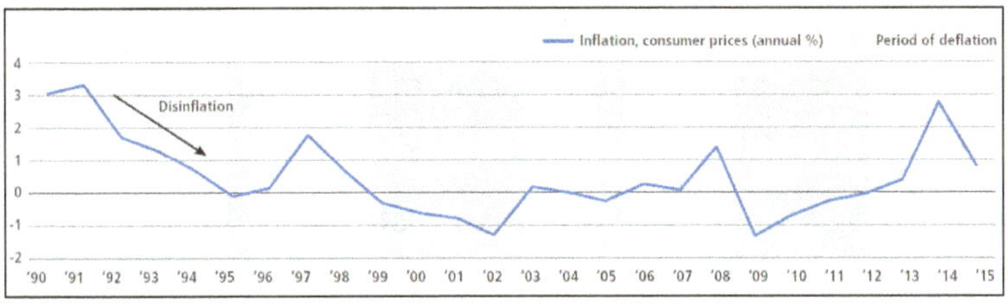

When prices actually fall, deflation has taken root. This occurred in Japan in 1995, from 1999 to 2003, and more recently from 2009 to 2012. Often the result of prolonged weak demand, deflation can lead to recession and even depression.

Measurment Inflation

There are several regularly reported measures of inflation that investors can use to track inflation. In the U.S., the Consumer Price Index (CPI), which reflects retail prices of goods and services, including housing costs, transportation, and healthcare, is the most widely followed indicator, although the Federal Reserve prefers to emphasize the Personal Consumption Expenditures Price Index (PCE). This is because the PCE covers a wider range of expenditures than the CPI. The official measure of inflation of consumer prices in the UK is the Consumer Price Index (CPI), or the Harmonized Index of Consumer Prices (HICP). In the eurozone, the main measure used is also called the HICP.

When economists and central banks try to discern the rate of inflation, they generally focus on "core inflation", for example "core CPI" or "core PCE". Unlike the "headline," or reported inflation, core inflation excludes food and energy prices, which are subject to sharp, short-term price swings, and could therefore give a misleading picture of long-term inflation trends.

Causes of Inflation

Economists do not always agree on what spurs inflation at any given time, but in general they bucket the factors into two different types: cost-push inflation and demand-pull inflation.

Rising commodity prices are an example of cost-push inflation. They are perhaps the most visible inflationary force because when commodities rise in price, the costs of basic goods and services generally increase. Higher oil prices, in particular, can have the most pervasive impact on an economy. First, gasoline, or petrol, prices will rise. This, in turn, means that the prices of all goods and services that are transported to their markets by truck, rail or ship will also rise. At the same time, jet fuel prices go up, raising the prices of airline tickets and air transport; heating oil prices also rise, hurting both consumers and businesses.

By causing price increases throughout an economy, rising oil prices take money out of the pockets of consumers and businesses. Economists therefore view oil price hikes as a "tax," in effect, that can depress an already weak economy. Surges in oil prices were followed by recessions or stagflation – a period of inflation combined with low growth and high unemployment – in the 1970s.

In addition to oil, rising wages can also cause cost-push inflation, as can depreciation in a country's currency. As the currency depreciates, it becomes more expensive to purchase imported goods, so costs rise; which puts upward pressure on prices overall. Over the long term, currencies of countries with higher inflation rates tend to depreciate relative to those with lower rates. Because inflation erodes the value of investment returns over time, investors may shift their money to markets with lower inflation rates.

Unlike cost-push inflation, demand-pull inflation occurs when aggregate demand in an economy rises too quickly. This can occur if a central bank rapidly increases the money supply without a corresponding increase in the production of goods and service. Demand outstrips supply, leading to an increase in prices.

Measures to Control Inflation

Central banks, such as the U.S. Federal Reserve, European Central Bank (ECB), the Bank of Japan (BoJ) or the Bank of England (BoE) attempt to control inflation by regulating the pace of economic activity. They usually try to affect economic activity by raising and lowering short-term interest rates.

Lowering short-term rates encourages banks to borrow from a central bank and from each other, effectively increasing the money supply within the economy. Banks, in turn, make more loans to businesses and consumers, which stimulates spending and overall economic activity. As economic growth picks up, inflation generally increases. Raising short-term rates has the opposite effect: It discourages borrowing, decreases the money supply, dampens economic activity and subdues inflation.

Management of the money supply by central banks in their home regions is known as monetary policy. Raising and lowering interest rates is the most common way of implementing monetary policy. However, a central bank can also tighten or relax banks' reserve requirements. Banks must hold a percentage of their deposits with the central bank or as cash on hand. Raising the reserve requirements restricts banks' lending capacity, thus slowing economic activity, while easing reserve requirements generally stimulates economic activity.

A government at times will attempt to fight inflation through fiscal policy. Although not all economists agree on the efficacy of fiscal policy, the government can attempt to fight inflation by raising taxes or reducing spending, thereby putting a damper on economic activity; conversely, it can combat deflation with tax cuts and increased spending designed to stimulate economic activity.

Effect of Investment Returns on Inflation

Inflation poses a "stealth" threat to investors because it chips away at real savings and investment returns. Most investors aim to increase their long-term purchasing power. Inflation puts this goal at risk because investment returns must first keep up with the rate of inflation in order to increase real purchasing power. For example, an investment that returns 2% before inflation in an environment of 3% inflation will actually produce a negative return (–1%) when adjusted for inflation.

If investors do not protect their portfolios, inflation can be harmful to fixed income returns, in particular. Many investors buy fixed income securities because they want a stable income stream, which comes in the form of interest, or coupon, payments. However, because the rate of interest, or coupon, on most fixed income securities remains the same until maturity, the purchasing power of the interest payments declines as inflation rises.

In much the same way, rising inflation erodes the value of the principal on fixed income securities. Suppose an investor buys a five-year bond with a principal value of $100. If the rate of inflation is 3% annually, the value of the principal adjusted for inflation will sink to about $83 over the five-year term of the bond.

Because of inflation's impact, the interest rate on a fixed income security can be expressed in two ways:

- The *nominal*, or *stated, interest rate* is the rate of interest on a bond without any adjustment for inflation. The nominal interest rate reflects two factors: The rate of interest that would prevail if inflation were zero and the expected rate of inflation, which shows that investors demand to be compensated for the loss of return due to inflation. Most economists believe that nominal interest rates reflect the market's expectations for inflation: Rising nominal interest rates indicate that inflation is expected to climb, while falling rates indicate that inflation is expected to drop.

- The *real interest rate* on an asset is the nominal rate minus the rate of inflation. Because it takes inflation into account, the real interest rate is more indicative of the growth in the investor's purchasing power. If a bond has a nominal interest rate of 5% and inflation is 2%, the real interest rate is 3%.

Unlike bonds, some assets rise in price as inflation rises. Price rises can sometimes offset the negative impact of inflation.

- Equities have often been a good investment relative to inflation over the very long term, because companies can raise prices for their products when their costs increase in an inflationary environment. Higher prices may translate into higher earnings. However, over shorter time periods, stocks have often shown a negative correlation to inflation and can be especially hurt by unexpected inflation. When inflation rises suddenly or unexpectedly, it can heighten uncertainty about the economy, leading to lower earnings forecasts for companies and lower equity prices.
- Prices for commodities generally rise with inflation. Commodity futures, which reflect expected prices in the future, might therefore react positively to an upward change in expected inflation.

Protection of Fixed Income from Inflation

To combat the negative impact of inflation, returns on some types of fixed income securities are linked to changes in inflation:

- Inflation-linked bonds issued by many governments are explicitly tied to changes in inflation. In the 1980s, the U.K. was the first developed country to introduce "linkers" to the market. Several other countries followed, including Australia, Canada, Mexico and Sweden. In 1997, the U.S. introduced Treasury Inflation-Protected Securities (TIPS), now the largest component of the global ILB market.
- Floating-rate notes offer coupons that rise and fall with key interest rates. The interest rate on a floating-rate security is reset periodically to reflect changes in a base interest rate index, such as the London Interbank Offered Rate (LIBOR). Floating-rate notes have therefore been positively, though imperfectly, correlated with inflation. Many commodity-related assets can also help cushion a portfolio against the impact of inflation because their total returns usually rise in an inflationary environment. However, some commodity-based investments are influenced by factors other than commodity prices. Oil stocks, for example, can fluctuate based on company-specific issues and therefore oil stock prices and oil prices are not always aligned.

Effect of Inflation on Investments

It is inflation that is reducing your purchasing power, then this is the question that would also arise on your mind. How will inflation affect my investment portfolio? The effects of inflation definitely cannot be under-valued but there are quite a lot of other considerations that can impact your earnings than mere inflation.

Let us have a look at the stock market: If the majority of your investments are in the form of shares and securities, a rising inflation need not give you months of sleepless nights. The reason behind this is simple. The companies' earnings and profits will also rise at the same pace or even faster than inflation.

For example, the value of a stock belonging to XYZ Company is Rs 500 per share. Three months later the value of the same share is Rs 800. You get flat 40% hike on your investment value altogether. So rising prices of commodities need not strike your nerve on what will happen to the investment. This is if you have invested most part of your money into shares, securities or derivatives.

But if the economy is continuously performing on a sluggish note and despite the gloomy scenario, prices of goods and services keep rising resulting in growing inflation, then there is something concrete to really worry about.

Company's books of accounts are overstated while inflation is the real thief: Let us have a look at the impact of inflation from a slightly different angle. With growing inflation, stocks of companies tend to remain overstated.

Suppose a company offers you a return on investment to the tune of 10% per annum. In other words, the investment value is Rs 1,000 and by the end of the year, you are offered a sum of Rs 1,100. Do you think this Rs 100 is the tangible value of your investment? No, definitely it is not. The company's real returns are not 10%.

Growing inflation, as it is already discussed, reduces the purchasing power of real-time tangible goods.

If the rate of inflation for that particular year stood at 4%, then your real rate of return or rather the tangible rate of returns is calculated as 10% minus 4% which is 6%. In short, you have only received 6% from the company as the tangible rate of returns on your investment.

The real-time tangible rate of return is the actual value of your investment portfolio. However, most of the investors fail to understand this underlying concept. Most of the investors simply get carried away by the nominal rate of returns a company offers on their investment. They forget about the inflation factor altogether.

Henceforth, when a company oers a fabulous rate of returns on investment, it might apparently look as if the company is moving on a progressing note. But it is inflation that lies behind the growth. Growing inflation can also prove havoc to the returns or earnings a company offers its investors, overall. However, if companies use clever techniques to value inventory, investors can be spared of their dear investment.

Inflation Investment Bonds

To help investors safeguard their capital money and to help investors get rates of return in such a way that they are not wiped out by growing inflation, Indian mutual fund companies oer investments with inflation protection schemes.

In other words, no matter how inflation strikes the economy hard, you are assured of getting your principal money back along with the stipulated rates of return, the company has initially offered you.

Inflation-indexed securities are more appealing for the fixed income group comprising of pensioners, senior citizens, and retirees. The rate of returns might be a little nominal, but you are assured of getting ample protection for your funds against inflation. In other words, the effects of inflation are made marginal, in this case.

If you want to get yourself protected from the evil consequences of inflation, it is better you start your savings in your early 20s.

You start saving money every single month and the interest rate gets compounded and early savings help you build your investment portfolio in a big way. By the time, you are in your early 30s you need a substantial sum of money to have your wedding done or to build your dream home.

Investment Income

Investment income is money that someone earns from an increase in the value of investments. It includes dividends paid on stocks, capital gains derived from property sales and interest earned on a savings or money market account.

Whether self-employed or working for a company, most people earn the majority of their money through income received for doing work. Many of these people also use investment vehicles such as a 401(k) and stocks to save for retirement.

As these investments increase in value, they produce interest income that can accumulate over time to produce investment income. The investment income later pays for significant purchases like a child's college education, real estate and retirement.

In most cases, investment income is taxable. The tax rate varies, depending on the type of investment.

Capital gains, or the profit made through the sale of property, have a tax rate up to 20 percent for long-term investments. The tax rate for interest earned on an account equals the taxpayer's marginal tax rate.

Dividends have several tax rates, ranging from 15 percent for qualified dividends to 39.6 percent for dividends paid to the highest wage earners in the country.

Investment Income Example

The stock market provides an example of investment income. If you purchase 10 shares of stock for $20 each, you have $200 invested in a company that's listed in stock market. When the value of those stocks increases to $25 per share, you earn $50 on the investment.

Investment income is not limited to stocks and bonds. Real estate also can provide investment income. For example, you can purchase a rental home for $100,000 and rent it for the next 15 years to cover the cost of the mortgage and maintenance expenses. If you later sell the property for $150,000, you earn $50,000.

Technical Analysis in Investment Management

Technical analysis is a method of evaluating securities by analyzing the statistics generated by market activity, such as past prices and volume. Technical analysts do not attempt to measure a security's intrinsic value, but instead use charts and other tools to identify patterns that can suggest future activity.

Just as there are many investment styles on the fundamental side, there are also many different types of technical traders. Some rely on chart patterns; others use technical indicators and oscillators, and most use some combination of the two. In any case, technical analysts' exclusive use of historical price and volume data is what separates them from their fundamental counterparts. Unlike fundamental analysts, technical analysts don't care whether a stock is undervalued - the only thing that matters is a security's past trading data and what information this data can provide about where the security might move in the future.

Before embarking on a journey to technical trading, we are best served to understand the five main assumptions of this approach. These are:

Art over Science

Many investment approaches require us to perform a great deal of math to generate an answer. Technical analysis does not. Looking at the samc chart, many investors will derive different answers. Therefore, reading charts evolves into an art form where each analyst can provide a unique insight.

No Need to Know

As more information becomes available, people become obsessed with knowing why events occur. In the markets, we often never know. Instead of searching for the next piece of data that magically unlocks the puzzles, technicians focus on the past and interpolate how it will affect the future.

History Repeats

A study of history shows that set patterns repeat themselves over long periods. By relying on the past to predict the future, we can take advantage of these patterns.

Self-fulfilling Prophecy

Enough people seeing the same pattern will take actions that force the prediction to occur. While this is positive if you are on the right side of the trade, it presents a major weakness when everyone attempts to exit at the same time.

Momentum Reverses

When a trade becomes very crowded with everyone assuming the same position, unexpected surprises can drive prices. If the exit becomes crowded, what first looked promising quickly becomes a nightmare.

In many markets, technical analysis serves as a solid series of guiding posts. By examining trends, we increase the likelihood that markets remain in our favor and trades remain profitable.

Consumption and Saving

The consumption function is a relationship between current disposable income and current consumption. It is intended as a simple description of household behavior that captures the idea of consumption smoothing. We typically suppose the consumption function is upward-sloping but has a slope less than one. So as disposable income increases, consumption also increases but not as much. More specifically, we frequently assume that consumption is related to disposable income through the following relationship:

Consumption = autonomous consumption + marginal propensity to consume × disposable income.

A consumption function of this form implies that individuals divide additional income between consumption and saving.

- We assume autonomous consumption is positive. Households consume something even if their income is zero. If a household has accumulated a lot of wealth in the past or if a household expects its future income to be larger, autonomous consumption will be larger. It captures both the past and the future.
- We assume that the marginal propensity to consume is positive. The marginal propensity to consume captures the present; it tells us how changes in current income lead to changes in current consumption. Consumption increases as current income increases, and the larger the marginal propensity to consume, the more sensitive current spending is to current disposable income. The smaller the marginal propensity to consume, the stronger is the consumption-smoothing effect.

- We also assume that the marginal propensity to consume is less than one. This says that not all additional income is consumed. When a household receives more income, it consumes some and saves some. Figure below "The Consumption Function" shows this relationship.

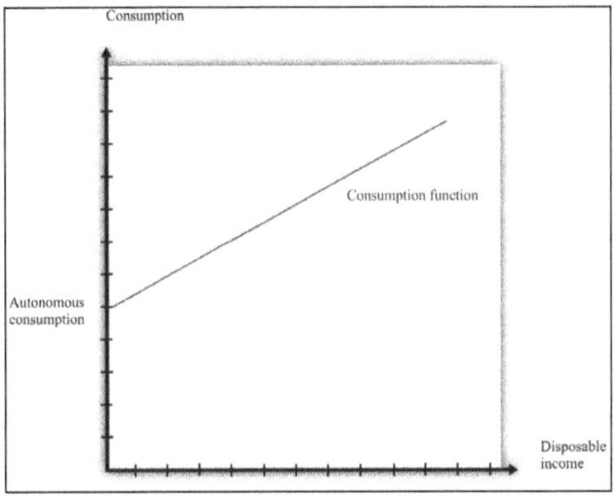

Figure: The Consumption Function.

More Formally

In symbols, we write the consumption function as a relationship between consumption (C) and disposable income (Y^d):

$$C = a + bY^d$$

where a and b are constants. Here a represents autonomous consumption and b is the marginal propensity to consume. We assume three things about a and b:

- $a > 0$
- $b > 0$
- $b < 1$

The first assumption means that even if disposable income is zero ($Y^d = 0$), consumption will still be positive. The second assumption means that the marginal propensity to consume is positive. By the third assumption, the marginal propensity to consume is less that one. With $0 < b < 1$, part of an extra dollar of disposable income is spent.

What happens to the remainder of the increase in disposable income? Since consumption plus saving is equal to disposable income, the increase in disposable income not consumed is saved. More generally, this link between consumption and saving (S) means that our model of consumption implies a model of saving as well.

Using,

$$Y^d = C + S$$

And

$$C = a + bY^d$$

we can solve for S:

$$S = Y^d - C = -a + (1-b)Y^d.$$

So $-a$ is the level of autonomous saving and $(1 - b)$ is the marginal propensity to save.

We can also graph the savings function. The savings function has a negative intercept because when income is zero, the household will dissave. The savings function has a positive slope because the marginal propensity to save is positive.

Economists also often look at the average propensity to consume (APC), which measures how much income goes to consumption on average. It is calculated as follows:

$$APC = C / Y^d.$$

When disposable income increases, consumption also increases but by a smaller amount. This means that when disposable income increases, people consume a smaller fraction of their income: the average propensity to consume decreases. Using our notation, we are saying that using $C = a + bY^d$.

so we can write,

$$APC = a / Y^d + b.$$

An increase in disposable income reduces the first term, which also reduces the APC.

References

- Investment-management: investopedia.com, Retrieved 2 March, 2019
- Basic-investment-objectives, managing-wealth: investopedia.com, Retrieved 13 January, 2019
- Investment-objectives: investmentbank.com, Retrieved 19 May, 2019
- Determinants-of-investment, macroeconomics-principles: lardbucket.org, Retrieved 9 April, 2019
- Types-investments, investors: finra.org, Retrieved 17 July, 2019
- Investing-basics, different-types-of-investments: thebalance.com, Retrieved 7 June, 2019
- Traditional-investments-stocks-and-bonds, investing, personal-finance: dummies.com, Retrieved 11 February, 2019
- Types-alternative-investments-guide: wallstreetmojo.com, Retrieved 20 August, 2019
- Investment-outsourcing-definition: capital.com, Retrieved 1 May, 2019
- Investment-control-definition: capital.com, Retrieved 21 January, 2019

- Investment-demand, international-finance-theory-and-policy: saylordotorg.github.io, Retrieved 10 March, 2019
- What-is-Investment-Demand-Curve: chegg.com, Retrieved 30 August, 2019
- Investment-demand-types-meaning-and-determinants, economics: yourarticlelibrary.com, Retrieved 14 June, 2019
- Understanding-inflation: pimco.com, Retrieved 19 May, 2019
- Effect-inflation-investments, business: deccanherald.com, Retrieved 17 February, 2019
- Investment-income: bankrate.com, Retrieved 27 July, 2019
- Meaning-of-technical-analysis, security-analysis-and-investment-management: wisdomjobs.com, Retrieved 6 March, 2019
- Consumption-and-saving, macroeconomics-theory-through-applications: saylordotorg.github.io, Retrieved 13 April, 2019

2

Investment Strategies

The set of behaviors, rules or procedures which have been designed to assist an investor in selecting an investment portfolio is known as investment strategy. There are various kinds of investment strategies such as liability driven, insider driven and benchmark-driven investment strategy. The topics elaborated in this chapter will help in gaining a better perspective about these investment strategies.

An investment strategy is what guides an investor's decisions based on goals, risk tolerance, and future needs for capital. Some investment strategies seek rapid growth where an investor focuses on capital appreciation, or they can follow a low-risk strategy where the focus is on wealth protection.

Understanding Investment Strategies

Many investors buy low-cost, diversified index funds, use dollar-cost averaging, and reinvest dividends. Dollar-cost averaging is an investment strategy where a fixed dollar amount of stocks or a particular investment are acquired on a regular schedule regardless of the cost or share price. The investor purchases more shares when prices are low and fewer shares when prices are high. Over time, some investments will do better than others, and the return averages out over time.

Some experienced investors select individual stocks and build a portfolio based on individual firm analysis with predictions on share price movements.

Five Investment Strategies

In 1949, Benjamin Graham identified five strategies for common stock investing in "The Intelligent Investor":

- General trading: The investor predicts and participates in the moves of the market similar to dollar-cost averaging.
- Selective trading: The investor picks stocks that they expect will do well in the market over the short term; a year, for example.
- Buying cheap and selling dear: The investor enters the market when prices low and sells a stock when the prices are high.
- Long-pull selection: The investor selects stocks that they expect to grow quicker than other sticks over a period of years.

- Bargain purchases: The investor selects stocks that are priced below their true value as measured by some techniques.

Graham emphasized that every investor must decide how they want to manage their portfolio. Experienced investors may prefer and be comfortable with a buy low and sell high strategy, whereas investors who have less time to research and follow the market might benefit more from investing in funds that track the market and adopt a long-term view.

There is no right way to manage a portfolio, but investors should behave rationally by using facts and data to back up decisions by attempting to reduce risk and maintain sufficient liquidity.

Investment Strategy and Risk

Risk is a huge component of an investment strategy. Some individuals have a high tolerance for risk while other investors are risk-averse. One overarching rule, however, is that investors should only risk what they can afford to lose. Another rule of thumb is the higher the risk, the higher the potential return, and some investments are riskier than others. There are investments that guarantee an investor will not lose money, but there will also be minimal opportunity to earn a return.

For example, U.S. Treasury bonds, bills, and bank certificates of deposit (CDs) are considered safe because they are backed by the credit of the United States. However, these investments provide a low return on investment. Once the cost of inflation and taxes have been included in the return on income equation, there may be little growth in the investment.

Types of Investment Strategies

Strategic asset allocation is a part of the asset allocation in the planning stage. The following are the approaches used to execute the strategic asset allocation:

- Passive Investment: These strategies comprise of portfolios that do not respond to any changes in expectations. Buy and hold and indexing are examples of such passive strategies.
- Active Investment: These strategies respond much more to changing expectations. They aim to benefit from the differences between the beliefs of a portfolio manager concerning the valuations and those of the marketplace. Making investments according to a particular style of investment and generating alpha are examples of such active investments.
- Hybrids: These include enhanced index, risk-controlled active and semi-active strategies, which are hybrids of active and passive strategies. Index tilting is one

example of a hybrid strategy, where the portfolio manager tries to match the risk attributes of a benchmark portfolio, but at the same time deviates from the same benchmark portfolio allocations to earn superior returns.

Liability-Driven Investment Strategy

Liability-driven investment policies and asset management decisions are those largely determined by the sum of current and future liabilities attached to the investor, be it a household or an institution. As it purports to associate constantly both sides of the balance sheet in the investment process, it has been called a "holistic" investment methodology.

In essence, the liability-driven investment strategy (LDI) is an investment strategy of a company or individual based on the cash flows needed to fund future liabilities. It is sometimes referred to as a "dedicated portfolio" strategy. It differs from a "benchmark-driven" strategy, which is based on achieving better returns than an external index such as the S&P 500 or a combination of indices that invest in the same types of asset classes. LDI is designed for situations where future liabilities can be predicted with some degree of accuracy. For individuals, the classic example would be the stream of withdrawals from a retirement portfolio that a retiree will make to pay living expenses from the date of retirement to the date of death. For companies, the classic example would be a pension fund that must make future payouts to pensioners over their expected lifetimes.

LDI for Individuals

A retiree following an LDI strategy begins by estimating the income needed each year in the future. Social security payments and any other income is subtracted from the income needed to determine how much will have to be withdrawn each year from the money in the retirement portfolio to meet the income need. These withdrawals become the liabilities that the investment strategy targets. The portfolio must be invested so as to provide the cash flows that match the withdrawals each year, after factoring in adjustments for inflation, irregular spending (such as an ocean cruise every other year), and so on. Individual bonds provide the ability to match the cash flows needed, which is why the term "cash flow matching" is sometimes used to describe this strategy. Because the bonds are dedicated to providing the cash flows, the term "dedicated portfolio" or "asset dedication" is sometimes used to describe the strategy.

LDI for Pension Funds

A pension fund following an LDI strategy focuses on the pension-fund assets in the context of the promises made to employees and pensioners (liabilities). This is in contrast to an approach which focuses purely on the asset side of the pension fund balance sheet. There is no single accepted definition or approach to LDI and different managers apply different approaches. Typical LDI strategies involve hedging, in whole or in part, the fund's exposure to changes in interest rates and inflation. These risks can eat into a pension scheme's ability to keep their promises to members. Historically, bonds were used as a partial hedge for these interest rate risks but the recent growth in LDI has focused on using swaps and other derivatives. Various approaches will pursue a "glide path" which over time seeks to reduce interest rate and other risks while achieving a return that matches or exceeds the growth in projected pension plan liabilities. These various approaches offer significant additional flexibility and capital efficiency compared to bonds, but also raise issues of added complexity, especially when the rebalancing of an LDI portfolio following changes in interest rates is considered.

LDI investment strategies have come to prominence in the UK as a result of changes in the regulatory and accounting framework. IAS 19 (one of the International Financial Reporting Standards) requires that UK companies post the funding position of a pension fund on the corporate sponsor's balance sheet. In the US the introduction of FAS 158 (Financial Accounting Standards Board) has created a similar requirement.

Insider Investment Strategy

The insider investment strategy is an investment strategy that follows the buying and selling decisions of insiders. The primary insiders have information advantage and the proven theory is that they as a group over time will do better than the average investor on the Stock Exchange. However, in the world there are only a few investment funds that follow the insider trades, both of them were established in 2011. In America Catalyst Capital Advisors LLC manages Catalyst Insider Buying Fund. This fund is a large-cap, long-only equity fund that only invests in companies where corporate insiders are buying their own company's stock on the open market. In Europe Dovre Forvaltning UAB manages Dovre Inside Nordic fund. This fund is a Nordic equity fund, which strategy is to follow the primary insiders in listed companies and/or shareholders with assumed close relationship to company, board and management.

A Lorie-Niederhoffer study indicates that proper and prompt analysis of data on insider trading can be profitable.

Glass examines 14 different calendar months and selects the eight securities with the greatest excess of buyers to sellers among insiders within a month. He finds that the average return on these securities is 10 percent above the return on the stock market as a whole in the 7 months following the individual months of intensive buying.

In 2014 Dovre Forvaltning shared there analysis on insiders influence in the Nordic region. The company analyzed these different yearly portfolios (both for Purchases and Sales):

- Had an insider Purchases in the past 1/3/6 months.
- Had only insider Purchases in the past 1/3/6 months.
- Last insider transaction in the past 1/3/6 months was an insider Purchase.
- Had an insider Sales in the past 1/3/6 months.
- Had only insider Sales in the past 1/3/6 months.
- Last insider transaction in the past 1/3/6 months was an insider Sale.

Only transactions above 80.000 SEK were included (33% of all insider trades were excluded because they were too small). If there were no Purchases/Sales in 1,3,6 months after a company's inclusion, it was excluded from the portfolio. All stocks are equally weighted. The analysis showed that:

- Highest outperformance is in Small Caps insider Purchase portfolios. Smaller in Mid Caps Purchase portfolios. And smallest in Large Caps insider Purchase portfolios.
- 'Insider effect' fades away with longer holding horizon.
- Sell signals are stronger than Buy signals.
- Sell signals are the strongest when more than 50% of holdings are sold.
- Buy signals are the strongest when signal transaction value is <80.000 SEK.

Long/Short Equity

Equity long/short strategy is a strategy through which a fund manager buys undervalued stocks which are expected to outperform, and short sells overvalued stocks which are expected to underperform. This type of portfolio is sometimes called "market neutral", although strictly speaking a market neutral portfolio is achieved only if the long exposure balances the short exposure so as to eliminate systemic market risk. Some market neutral funds even go one step further to eradicate industry risk by making pair-wise bets within each sector, but such an objective can only be achieved if strict risk controls are kept constantly in place. Market neutral portfolios are perceived to be a lower risk type of hedge fund. In reality, however, most equity long/short funds tend to range between a slightly net short position to 100% net long, depending on whether the manager is bullish or bearish on the market, although recently some have widened those ranges.

The beauty of an equity long/short strategy is that it can fully take advantage of the fund managers' stock picking capabilities. Note that the end-result of the fund managers' stock research is the identification of winning stocks i.e. the buy candidates. On the flip side, those stocks which fail this test are identified as the losing stocks and could become the short candidates. In other words, alpha[1] can potentially be generated from both the long and the short sides, as opposed to a traditional long-only fund where alpha is generated from the buy side only.

In order to profit from a long/short strategy, the short picks need not necessarily drop or the long picks need not necessarily rise – it will be profitable as long as the long picks outperform the short picks so that a positive spread can be pocketed. Of course, if everything goes against the fund manager and those stocks which constitute his long positions underperform, while those stocks which he shorts outperform, it will be a double whammy.

Some equity long/short managers may employ leverage to gear their stock bets if they have a very strong conviction in their stock selections. The logic behind this is that a long/short fund can buy more good stocks without taking as much risk as a fund which merely buys and does not short. With the added dimension of downside risk management through the shorts, one can be bolder in pursuing stocks with strong appreciation potential. This could potentially increase the fund's return while minimising broad market risk, but stock-specific risk will increase in this case.

The ability to short individual stocks is often limited in less developed markets and among smaller stocks, either due to low liquidity, regulatory restrictions or lack of suitable instruments. Paradoxically, these are often the areas with the least market efficiency and hence the biggest opportunity to generate alpha. In that case, how can we "neutralise" our long positions or exploit the pricing anomalies on the short side? Fund managers may hedge overall market exposure through selling the broad market indices in the futures market or buying put options. If these are not available either, then proxies such as ADR/GDRs (American Depositary Receipts and Global Depositary Receipts) trading in other markets, OTC (over-the-counter) derivatives or exchange traded unit trusts could be valuable tools. However, you must be careful to distinguish between aggressive, speculative hedge funds that make highly leveraged directional bets using derivatives and those that use derivatives primarily to hedge downside risks. Bear in mind that while the maximum you can lose on a long position is your invested capital, there is no ceiling on how much you can lose on a short position as there is no limit as to how high a stock can go. That is why risk control is so important in hedge fund management.

Equity long/short strategy is most valuable when there is a big divergence of performance across stocks (of course that hinges on the fund manager's ability to identify those winners and losers), or when broad market volatility is high. In the first case, such a strategy could produce superior returns even if the average market performance is flat (i.e. with rising stocks offsetting declining ones). In the latter case, a long/short approach should be able to provide much smoother returns than the general market. In this sense, it can serve to enhance returns and/or reduce volatility to produce a better risk-adjusted return.

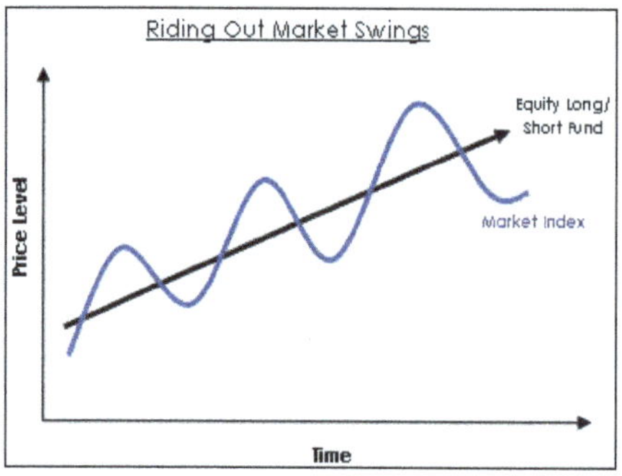

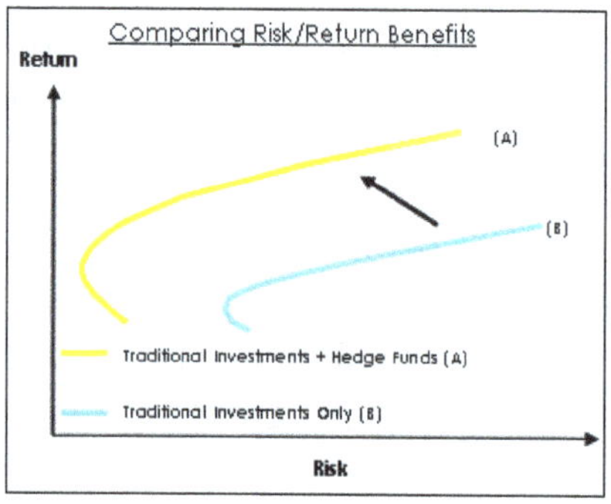

The above information is shown for illustrative purposes only. It is not intended and should not be interpreted as the performance of an actual investment.

An equity long/short strategy can also help cushion the downside during a bear market. But of course, everything comes with a price as this strategy typically underperforms the traditional long-only approach during a bull market. Given its low correlation with traditional asset classes, this type of fund is classified under "alternative investment" in the investment universe. Investors should consider buying such hedge funds to enhance the risk/return profile of their existing portfolios, i.e. to get "more dollar bang for each risk buck". Allocation can be adjusted between equities, bonds, cash and hedge funds to arrive at your desired level of risk, while maximising your potential return. Depending on your objectives and risk tolerance, in general we recommend an allocation between 5-15% to hedge funds.

As opposed to a long-only fund whose return is derived more from broad market movement than manager skills, an equity long/short fund relies largely on the manager's stock picking capabilities. Therefore, in choosing which equity long/short fund to buy, investors should pay attention to the fund manager's research resources, investment process, risk control, experience and consistency of performance. This can help discern real expertise from pure luck. If you have a chance, try to check upon the fund manager's performance attribution reports to unveil his strengths and weaknesses (i.e. where he has added or lost value). An analysis of his stock rankings would definitely help too.

For example, at JF Asset Management we constantly run performance analyses of the stocks our fund managers rank in each market. We have a ranking system of 1 to 5, with 1 being those stocks which we like most and 5 being those we most dislike. We then look at the aggregate performance of those stocks of the same rank to see if they outperform or underperform over time as expected. The following chart for the Hong Kong stock market confirms that JF Asset Management has been able to identify both the winning and the losing stocks in a consistent manner. This is exactly the type of managers that one should look for.

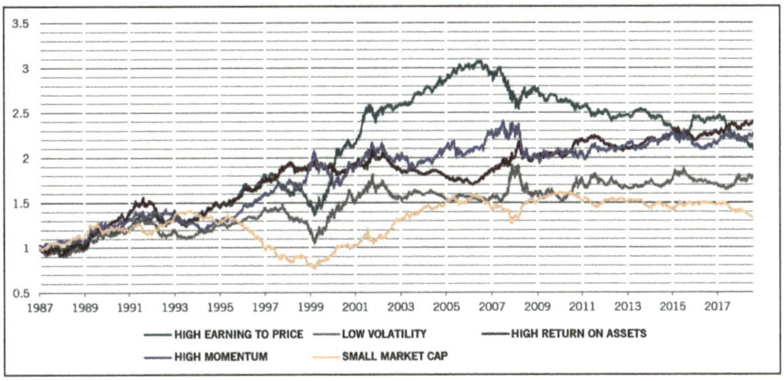

Long-Short Equity Strategy

A long-short strategy is built as follows:

- Define Universe: Identify a universe of stocks in which we will take positions. The universe can be defined based on dollar-volume, market capitalization, price and impact cost.
- Bucketing stock: From the universe of stocks, we will bucket stocks based on the sector such technology, pharmaceuticals, automobiles, financial services, and FMCG.
- Define parameter to long or short security: This is the key step in the workflow. Here, for each bucket defined in step 2, we will rank stocks in the bucket based on previous quarter earnings. Stocks with good earnings growth will be ranked higher and stocks with negative earnings will be ranked lower. Then, we will go long on 5 stocks with higher rank and go short on 5 stocks with lower rank. Note: A combination of parameters such as PE ratio, P/BV, moving averages and RSI should be used here with different weights on each parameter to create a profitable strategy.
- Capital allocation: We allocate an equal amount of capital to each stock shortlisted from step 3. Equal weight approach helps to avoid a concentration to a particular stock in the portfolio.

Risk Management

As with all strategy, this strategy also comes with risk. The risk lies in deviation of the performance of the stocks selected in the portfolio from the expectation. In the above example, if the securities on the long side see a fall in price and the securities on the short side see a rise in price, then the portfolio will suffer losses.

A prudent risk management is required such as squaring of the stocks on hitting stop loss and keeping profit cap at individual stock level. Apart from this, the portfolio must be reconstructed with fresh stocks at regular intervals and portfolio must hold a large number of stocks. This will help to limit concentration to a stock.

Industry Trends

As per latest industry trends, more hedge fund are biased towards the long side to capitalize on rising equity markets. More details about this trend can be found in the article on Bloomberg: Long-Short Hedge Funds Are Ditching the Shorts to Focus on Longs.

Performance

Historical performance of the long-short strategies of a hedge fund can be found at EurekaHedge. The Eurekahedge Long Short Equities Hedge Fund Index is an equally weighted index of 1102 constituent hedge funds. The index shows a return of 7.55% in 2017 YTD (as at Aug 2017) and returns of 3.75% in 2016.

Fees

Hedge fund charge roughly 2% as annual management fees and 20% of profit as performance fees. These fees are on the higher side compared to mutual funds and ETFs which have around 1% to 3% as the expense ratio.

Benchmark-Driven Investment Strategy

Benchmark-driven investment strategy is an investment strategy where the target return is usually linked to an index or combination of indices of the sector or any other like S&P 500.

With the Benchmarks approach the investor chooses an index of the market (benchmark). The goal of the fund manager is to try to beat the index performance-wise:

- The strategic asset allocation is usually delegated to the benchmark chosen.
- The asset managers stay concentrated to tactical asset allocation and fund (security) selection.
- No volatility control over time.
- Without volatility constraints over a long period the investor is expected to get higher returns.

Strategic Sustainable Investing

Strategic sustainable investing (SSI) is an investment strategy that recognizes and rewards leading companies that are moving society towards sustainability. SSI relies on a consensus-based scientific definition of sustainability, and the assumption that '*Backcasting from Principles of Sustainability*', whereby a vision of a sustainable future is set as the reference point for developing strategic actions, is the preferred approach to strategically move a company towards sustainability. It was developed by researchers at the Blekinge Institute of Technology in Sweden.

The Strategic Sustainable Investment System

SSI outlines that the financial investment will offer a competitive risk-adjusted return, while providing investment capital to companies that are actively attempting to become more sustainable. It implies lower exposure to sustainability-related risks and it considers financial metrics together with environmental, social, and governance (ESG) aspects, as well as strategy analyses to educate investment decision-making.

Characteristics of SSI:

- Lower sustainability risk exposure.
- A definition of sustainability based on scientific consensus.
- Primarily driven by movement towards sustainability.
- Considers financial, ESG, and strategy analysis.

SSI operates by prioritizing investment capital allocation to companies that are taking the lead in shifting away from unsustainable behaviour towards new ways of doing business. This capital allocation will provide an incentive for companies to move forward in a sustainable direction. This movement is reported in corporate social responsibility (CSR) and other extra-financial reports, but is also recorded in traditional areas of a firm's financial balance sheets.

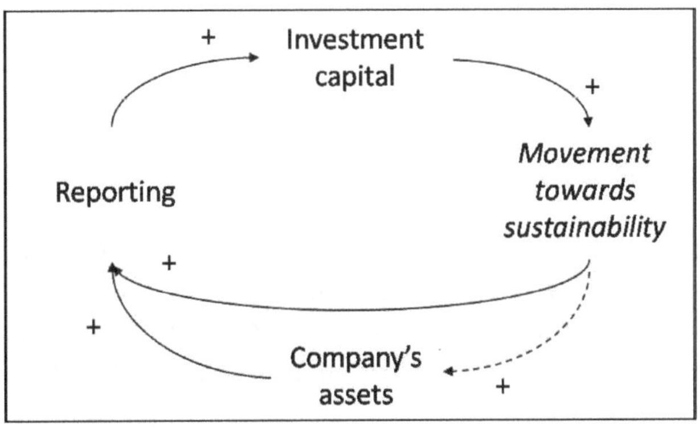

Causal loop diagram illustrating the strategic sustainable investment.

By incorporating sustainability investment and returns into traditional financial reporting, a clearer picture of the bottom-line impact of a company's actions towards sustainability is made available. In this positive reinforcing loop, greater investor returns and increased movement towards sustainability are generated with every cycle.

Institutional investors, such as mutual and pension funds, take a longer-term position on investments and are thus ideally suited to incorporate SSI strategies.

SSI Analysis Tool

In order to evolve current SRI and traditional investment practices into Strategic Sustainable Investment, two gaps must be considered:

- The recognition of companies with true leading strategies for a sustainable future.
- A robust and well defined link must be made between movement towards sustainability and higher investment returns.

The SSI analysis tool addresses the first gap by measuring a company's strategy for addressing sustainability. It allows investors to recognize which companies are leading the transition in a new direction, and which are most likely to be strong performers in tomorrow's market.

This tool is divided in two main parts: the emerging sustainability issue (ESI) chart and the strategy analysis component:

ESI Chart

	Assessment Categories		
Sustainability Issues	**Urgency**	**Severity**	**Systematic Contribution**
{Issue}			Local
{Issue}			Local Global
{Issue}			Global
{Issue}			Global

ESI Chart Sample.

The Sectoral Emerging Sustainability Issue (ESI) chart is used to identify which aspects of a determined market sector will become a socio-environmental problem. In the common sense, an issue is called 'emergent' when it gets media exposure. Instead, the Tool relies on scientific Principles of sustainability to identify what is emergent.

It exposes which Sustainability Issues present high risks for companies within that sector in the short-term; as well as which Issues will be emerging in the medium and long-terms. Due to differences within a sector, the Sectoral ESI Chart should be made as specific as needed, being flexible to account for various geographical locations and sub-sector subtleties.

The process of composing an ESI chart follows:

Once a sector is selected for an ESI analysis, a list of relevant sustainability issues is assembled. This baseline analysis will result in a list of issues outlining the subject sector's strengths and concerns that impact society and the environment. Next, prioritization colours are assigned to each sustainability issue: red for very high priority; orange for high priority; yellow for medium priority, and green for low priority according to its assessment in each of three categories: urgency, severity, and systematic contribution.

Urgency assesses the time frame pressing each Issue. The *severity* assesses the seriousness of the Issue, in terms of its potential consequences for the environment, society, and companies within that sector. The *systematic contribution* is used to gauge the sector's contribution to the overall Issue.

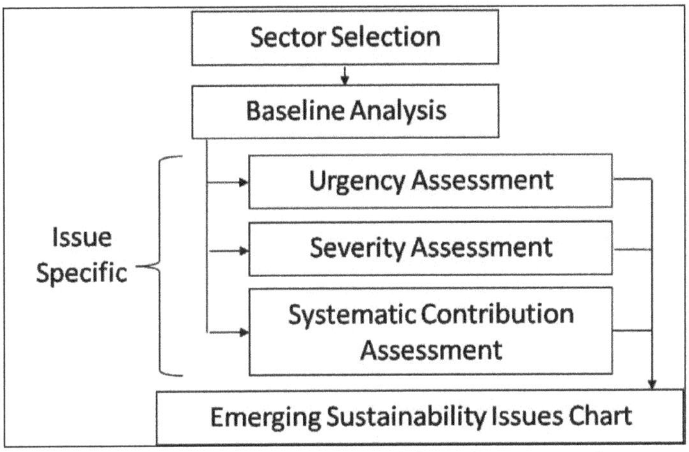

To fill out the Chart, Researchers follow this process flow.

Strategy Analysis Component

Strategic Plan

The Strategic Plan element assesses the subject company's planned goals in relation to the emerging sustainability issue (ESI). The qualitative description includes, but is not limited to, information regarding: public commitments planned operational and business initiatives, political action/lobbying, and third party partnerships (with NGOs, consultative firms etc.). There is also a comment on the subject company's core business in relation to the ESI; as this will assist in determining the subject company's exposure to the emerging risk.

Strategic Actions

The strategic actions element looks at assessing the subject company's recent actions taken in relation to the emerging sustainability issue (ESI), thus determining whether the subject company is 'walking the talk' in comparison to the vision and goals outlined.

The subject company's actions are seen through the lens of strategic sustainable development, and thus three questions are emphasized as a mental guideline:

a. Does this action provide a competitive return on investment (ROI)?

b. Is this action taking the subject company in the right direction?

c. Is this action a versatile platform?

Strategy Analysis Graph

The strategy analysis graph shows the subject company's planned path for dealing with the ESI, tangible progress made, and if existent, government regulations. The trajectory of the subject company's planned path reveals the extent of their future risk exposure. This graph is placed in the center of the strategy analysis page.

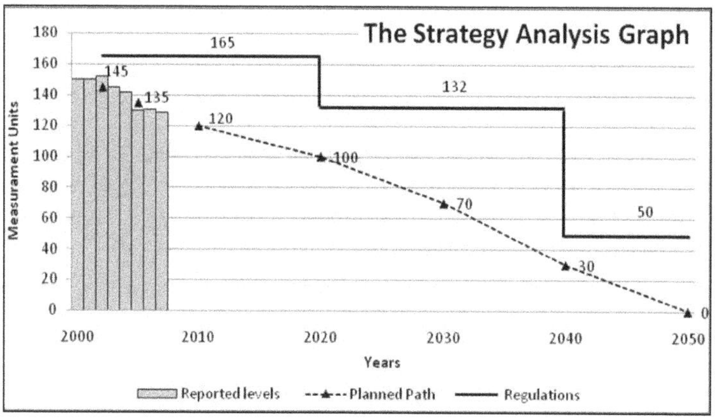

Sample of strategy analysis graph.

Assurance Assessment

The assurance assessment provides an overall impression of the validity of the information gathered. This assessment may be applied if the data is verified by an external third party, or if discrepancy is evident between different sources of information used on the report.

Fixed-Income Relative-Value Investing

Fixed-Income Relative-Value Investing (FI-RV) is a hedge fund investment strategy made popular by the failed hedge fund Long-Term Capital Management. FI-RV Investors most commonly exploit interest-rate anomalies in the large, liquid markets of North America, Europe and the Pacific Rim. The financial instruments traded include government bonds, interest rate swaps and futures contracts.

Investment Strategy

Most FI-RV Investors focus on large, long-term mispricings in the global fixed-income markets, capturing relative-value anomalies via multi-product trades. Trades of interest include:

- Yield Curve: Trade LIBOR yield curve using combinations of futures and swaps of varying maturities.
- Bond vs Bond: Identify and trade bonds that are mispriced compared to other very similar bonds.
- LIBOR vs Bond: Take advantage of anomalies in the spread between Bond and Libor Curves.

Frequently, these anomalies occur when market participants are forced to make non-economic decisions due to accounting regulations, book clean-up, public furor or exuberance over a certain product, or sheer panic. The FI-RV Investor aims to capitalize on these and other inefficiencies. When a mispricing is identified between products, FI-RV Investors have the freedom to wait until the anomaly corrects. In contrast, other market participants, such as bank proprietary desks, are often limited by balance sheet considerations and accounting standards which influence the size and timing of their trades.

However, the irony of Long-Term Capital Management's failure is that they were correct on all of their trades and hedges. They just did not have the excess collateral to meet the margin calls after the Russian financial crisis hit in 1998. In an Opalesque TV interview, fund manager Bob Treue, who started a hedge fund specifically to capitalize on the opportunities left over by LTCM's failure, says that excess collateral is the key to the survival of a fixed-income relative-value strategy, and that this is the primary reason LTCM failed. He also says that LTCM's failure has had an enormous impact on the public perception of the fixed-income relative-value space, possibly an irreversible impact, with investors fearing the strategy is too risky.

Relative Value

Classic Arbitrage

In times when there are dramatic flows into or out of a specific asset, there can be disparate pricings on products that are, for all economic purposes, identical. The FI-RV Investor can capture these inefficiencies by combining bonds, swaps, options, currencies and/or futures into products that replicate another product in every sense.

One example of this occurred in late 1998. The Euro had been defined as .6242 Deutsche Marks, 1.332 French francs, .08784 British pounds, 151.8 Italian Lira, .2198 Dutch Guilder, 3.431 Belgian Franc, 6.885 Spanish Peseta, .1976 Danish Krone, .00855 Irish Punt, 1.44 Greek Drachma and 1.393 Portuguese Escudo. On December 31, 1998, the Euro would officially become a currency and these exchange rates would become irrevocable and trading DeutscheMarks for Euros would be like exchanging nickels for dimes. Yet, leading up to this conversion, the demand for Euros was so incredibly high that one could buy all of the constituent currencies of the Euro for 98.25% of the value of the Euro and then sell the Euro itself for its full value. This was caused when corporates, governments and banks had decided that after January 1, 1999, the majority of their electronic billing and transfers would be done in Euros. So naturally, these entities (who aren't interested in buying 11 currencies in hopes of exchanging them later) went out and started buying Euros in anticipation of European Monetary Union European Monetary Union. The flows from this were dominant and pushed the value of the now favored Euro out of line with its parts.

Yield Curve Anomalies

At various times, yield curves will be hit by a wave of purchases or sales in a specific area of the curve. This will cause that area to form a 'trough' or 'hump' to it. By exploiting this odd shape through receiving the high rates around 'hump' and paying the low rates within the trough, The FI-RV Investor hopes to profit by waiting until the yield curve normalizes.

An example of this type of distortion occurred in late 1994 and early 1995 when Alan Greenspan raised the US Fed Funds rate from 3.00% in May 1994 to 5.25% in February 1995. Prior to these hikes, Orange County had initiated highly leveraged bets on short maturity interest rate derivative products in the hopes that interest rates would decline. As short maturity rates moved higher as a result of continued action on the part of the US central bank, market participants, including Orange County, were forced to exit out of their short end positions. The leveraged nature of Orange County's positions and its imminent bankruptcy forced them to continue to dump risk at a time when the financial markets were unwilling to receive it.

In addition to loss management and panic, a second powerful force drove traders out of the short end of the curve. At the time, Orange County was ridiculed by the press for their imprudence with the public's money. In fear that year end accounting would reveal that they held similar positions to the 'toxic waste' which poisoned Orange County, traders stampeded out of short end positions.

Credit Spreads

The FI-RV also seeks to take advantage of periodic mispricings between LIBOR (London Inter-Bank Offered Rate, essentially AAA and AA rated credit) and government credit. Since all of the major futures exchanges list both LIBOR (or the respective national equivalent) based contracts and government bond contracts, a fund such as The FI-RV Investor can take advantage of opportunities in this area of relative value as well. Frequently, as the credit concerns of either banks, governments or corporations comes into question, the spreads between these issuers moves quite substantially.

In the fall/winter of 1998, Long Term Capital Management's Long term capital management takeover prompted rumors in the market that unwinds of their positions would be forthcoming. Hedge Funds would be forced to liquidate their long German Asset spreads (long German government credit against short bank credit in Deutschemarks) and their short Sterling Asset Spreads (short English government credit and long bank credit in British Pounds). At the time, the British Government had paused in its debt issuance and was running a small budget surplus, while the Germans had just elected a left leaning government and had large pension liabilities as well as a deficit in excess of 2% of GDP for 1998. Based on these fundamentals, the credit spread between government bonds and banks should have been larger in Britain than in Germany, but the crucial question was 'How much larger should the spread be.' The credit spreads for 5 yr. bonds started 1998 around 40 basis points in Britain and near 15 basis points in Germany. As news of problems in the Hedge Fund industry and potential credit unwinds began to permeate the market, the British spread exploded out to 140 basis points in October of '98 while the German spread managed only a meager move to 20 basis points. Although the British spreads deserved to be wider, they did not merit a 120 basis point premium over German Spreads. By November 1998, the premium had already contracted to 80 basis points.

Global Macro

Market imbalances can cause fundamental, as well as relative, mispricings. These anomalies are more difficult to capitalize on since you must make assumptions as to where inflation, GDP, trade balance, etc. will be in the future. In addition, the fundamentals themselves are not tradable; you must employ market instruments as a proxy. While acknowledging the limiting nature of these assumptions, The FI-RV Investor will trade certain products that are mispriced from a fundamental prospective. For example, the 10 yr. bond contract in Japan had a yield of 0.70% as of early November 1998. This seemed inconsistent with long term expectations of the fundamentals. The Japanese Government was set to run the largest deficit in the history of the world (in absolute terms) and the Bank of Japan had said that they were going to target monetary growth rather than inflation. These policies would seem to create an enormous amount of new bond issuance and some future inflation due to the monetary growth. The variables which pushed yields to this low level could not last forever. The Japanese had been hurt in every investment they had made over the previous few years (Tokyo real estate prices were down 75% from their highs, the Nikkei had gone from 40,000 in January 1990 to 14,000 in November 1998 and the Yen had gone from 82 in April 1995 to 123 in November 1998, stopping at 145 along the way) and as a result, the Japanese had bought up bonds. The JGBs (Japanese Government Bonds) had given them nothing but gains and assurance of capital. It was no longer an issue of return on capital, but rather return of capital. With yields at this low level though, the market seemed to have made the assumption that a strong or even neutral economy would never return to Japan. By the spring of 1999, yields had risen to the 1.5-2.0% range from the 0.70% of early November 1998.

Volatility

Occasionally, The FI-RV Investor will trade volatility. In the hedge fund unwind panic of October 1998, equity volatility on the S&P soared to around 40%. This unusual premium proved excessive and as of November 1998, these volatilities had returned to the high 20s. Also, sometimes volatility products will be used as a tool to implement the previously mentioned arbitrage strategies.

Investment Management Strategies

The term investment strategy refers to an investors plan to guide their investment decisions. According to Investopedia "Investment strategies can differ greatly from a rapid growth strategy where an investor focuses on capital appreciation to a safety strategy where the focus is on wealth protection. The most important part of an investment strategy is that it aligns with the individual's goals and is closely followed by the investor".

Investment strategies are an important part of any investor's crucial portfolio where an individual is planning to meet his financial goals. Precisely there are two types of investment management styles:

- Active management strategy.
- Passive management strategy.

We shall explore the theme of active management strategy of money management; its significance and its various characteristics:

Active management is nothing but an attempt to outperform the market by a certain benchmark or a particular index. In active management strategy, the fund manager's decisions are influenced by prevailing market trends, company specific fundamentals, economic and political events. Precisely, it is the art of market timing and stock picking. The fund manager builds and oversees a mix of portfolio that seeks to outperform certain benchmarks, after charging a certain fees. Some of the commonly adopted benchmarks by Indian equity mutual fund managers are S&P BSE 200, Nifty 500, Nifty 50, S&P BSE 500, etc. For example, a large cap stock fund manager would look to beat the performance of the S&P 200 Index. The believers of active management do not abide by efficient market hypothesis and intend to profit from certain mispriced stocks.

Advantages

The possibility of higher than the index returns is one of the biggest draws towards active management. The expert analysis of the fund manager helps him make proactive judgments based on their experience and knowledge. Managers can also take defensive measures if they foresee a downturn in the markets.

Disadvantages

Higher fees and operating expenses may pinch the investors; especially when the performance is subpar. The risk of managers making unwise choices; hampering the returns are equally challenging in this style. The fund manager may have a certain approach or a style which may be in or out of favor with the market. Investment strategies employed by active managers include:

- Top down approach.
- Bottom up approach.
- Value investing.
- Growth investing.

No strategy: Investors who don't have a strategy have been called Sheep. Arbitrary choices modeled on throwing darts at a page (referencing earlier decades when stock prices were listed daily in the newspapers) have been called Blind Folded Monkeys Throwing Darts. This famous test had debatable outcomes.

Active vs Passive: Passive strategies like buy and hold and passive indexing are often used to minimize transaction costs. Passive investors don't believe it is possible to time the market. Active strategies such as momentum trading are an attempt to outperform benchmark indexes. Active investors believe they have the better than average skills.

Momentum Trading: One strategy is to select investments based on their recent past performance. There is evidence both for and against this strategy.

Buy and Hold: This strategy involves buying company shares or funds and holding them for a long period. It is a long term investment strategy, based on the concept that in the long run equity markets give a good rate of return despite periods of volatility or decline. This viewpoint also holds that market timing, that one can enter the market on the lows and sell on the highs, does not work for small investors, so it is better to simply buy and hold.

Long Short Strategy: A long short strategy consists of selecting a universe of equities and ranking them according to a combined alpha factor. Given the rankings we long the top percentile and short the bottom percentile of securities once every re-balancing period.

Indexing: Indexing is where an investor buys a small proportion of all the shares in a market index such as the S&P 500, or more likely, an index mutual fund or an exchange-traded fund (ETF). This can be either a passive strategy if held for long periods, or an active strategy if the index is used to enter and exit the market quickly.

Pairs Trading: Pairs trade is a trading strategy that consists of identifying similar pairs of stocks and taking a linear combination of their price so that the result is a stationary time-series. We can then compute Altman Z-score for the stationary signal and trade on the spread assuming mean reversion: short the top asset and long the bottom asset.

Value vs Growth: Value investing strategy looks at the intrinsic value of a company and value investors seek stocks of companies that they believed are undervalued. Growth investment strategy looks at the growth potential of a company and when a company that has expected earning growth that is higher than companies in the same industry or the market as a whole, it will attract the growth investors who are seeking to maximize their capital gain.

Dividend growth investing: This strategy involves investing in company shares according to the future dividends forecast to be paid. Companies that pay consistent and predictable dividends tend to have less volatile share prices. Well-established dividend-paying companies will aim to increase their dividend payment each year, and those who make an increase for 25 consecutive years are referred to as a dividend aristocrat. Investors who reinvest the dividends are able to benefit from compounding of their investment over the longer term, whether directly invested or through a Dividend Reinvestment Plan (DRIP).

Dollar cost averaging: The dollar cost averaging strategy is aimed at reducing the risk of incurring substantial losses resulted when the entire principal sum is invested just before the market falls.

Contrarian investment: A contrarian investment strategy consists of selecting good companies in time of down market and buying a lot of shares of that company in order to make a long-term profit. In time of economic decline, there are many opportunities to buy good shares at reasonable prices. But, what makes a company good for shareholders? A good company is one that focuses on the long term value, the quality of what it offers or the share price. This company must have a durable competitive advantage, which means that it has a market position or branding which either prevents easy access by competitors or controls a scarce raw material source. Some examples of companies that response to these criteria are in the field of insurance, soft drinks, shoes, chocolates, home building, furniture and many more. We can see that there is nothing "fancy" or special about these fields of investment: they are commonly used by each and every one of us. Many variables must be taken into consideration when making the final decision for the choice of the company. Some of them are:

- The company must be in a growing industry.
- The company cannot be vulnerable to competition.
- The company must have its earnings on an upward trend.
- The company must have a consistent returns on invested capital.
- The company must be flexible to adjust prices for inflation.

Smaller companies: Historically medium-sized companies have outperformed large cap companies on the Stock market. Smaller companies again have had even higher returns. The very best returns by market cap size historically are from micro-cap companies. Investors using this strategy buy companies based on their small market cap size on the stock exchange. One of the greatest investors Warren Buffett made money in small companies early in his career combining it with value investing. He bought small companies with low P/E ratios and high assets to market cap.

Indexing

Indexing is a passive investment strategy where you construct a portfolio to track the performance of a market index. This is commonly done with the S&P 500 Index, where investors try to mimic the performance of the index.

Indexing also refers to metrics used to gauge the performance of economic activity. For example, the Consumer Price Index (CPI) is used to estimate the purchasing power of the US dollar. The CPI is also used to measure the rate of inflation.

The S&P 500 Index and the Dow Jones Industrial Average (DJIA) are used to track the performance of the US equity market. The NASDAQ Composite Index tracks the performance of large companies in order to predict major economic trends.

Uses of Indexing

There are two main uses of indexing in financial markets. They include:

1. As a Gauge for linking values:

The Consumer Price Index (CPI) provides a basis for calculating the cost of living adjustment (COLA), designed to reflect the current cost of living based on changes in prices of consumer goods and services. Pension plans also rely on the CPI to adjust retirement benefits.

The CPI tracks the changes in the prices of consumer goods and services in a specific location. Apart from calculating the annual COLA and retirement benefit payouts, the CPI is also used to adjust salaries and interest rates.

2. As Indicators of economic trends:

Indexes or indices can also be used as indicators of economic trends. For example, an index that tracks the performance of large, publicly-traded companies may give indications of future economic growth. Examples of such economic indices include the Index of Leading Economic Indicators – LEI, the Purchasing Managers' Index – PMI, the Labor Market Index – LMI, and the GDP deflator index. Indexes can provide an overview of current economic trends, as well as clues to possible future trends.

For example, if the LEI reading is increasingly positive for three or four months in a row during a time when the economy has been in recession, this is typically interpreted as signaling an impending economic trend change to a period of strong growth. The LEI figures are released on the third Thursday of each month.

Indexes in the Investment Market

Two of the world's best-known investment indices are the Standard & Poors 500 (S&P 500) and the Dow Jones Industrial Average (DJIA). These indices are:

S&P 500

The S&P 500 comprises about 70% of all the stocks traded in the United States, and it is one of the most popular benchmarks for measuring the performance of the stock market. It is based on the market capitalization of 500 publicly-traded companies.

Unlike many other indices, the S&P 500 uses a market capitalization-weighted methodology and is comprised of a very diverse list of stocks. The index's components are determined by a committee that evaluates stocks for listing based on their liquidity, public float, sector classification, market capitalization, financial viability, and other factors.

Dow Jones Industrial Average (DJIA)

The Dow Jones Industrial Average (DJIA) measures the stocks of 30 of the largest publicly traded companies in the US. The companies must be listed either on the NYSE or NASDAQ. The DJIA uses a price-weighted methodology, such that high-priced stocks are given greater weight than low-priced stocks. Originally, the stocks that made up the DJIA index were all large industrial firms – hence the name. However, this is no longer the case, as many non-industrial firms have become more significant bellwhethers of the overall equity market.

If one of the listed publicly-traded companies experiences financial difficulties or its performance declines, the composition of the index will change.

Index Investing

Index investing refers to a strategy used to generate returns that are similar to a specific market index. Investors achieve this goal by replicating specific indices such as a fixed income or equity index. One means of index investing is to purchase shares of exchange-traded funds that track an underlying benchmark index.

Index investing is a passive form of investing, which usually results in relatively lower management fees and expense ratios. This is due to the fact that the holdings in an index investing portfolio do not change frequently. Therefore, the fund or portfolio does not incur heavy transaction costs.

Active Investing vs. Passive Investing

In active investing, portfolio managers use their skills to try to outperform the overall market average. They typically seek to identify stocks with high, long-term growth potential. Active investing usually means higher management fees and transaction costs, as the portfolio's holdings are likely to change much more frequently than is the case with a passive investing strategy. An active approach can be affected by the uncertainties in the market and the biases of the manager.

The holdings of actively managed portfolios may be more diverse than index-based portfolios. The portfolio manager may invest in domestic stocks, international stocks, and in other asset classes besides equities. For example, part of the holdings of an actively managed portfolio may consist of bonds, commodities, or foreign currency.

In contrast, index-based equity portfolios will be invested solely in domestic equities. The portfolio's holdings will mirror, as closely as possible, the holdings of the chosen underlying benchmark index. Portfolio holdings will only change when the composition of the underlying index changes.

Indexing can refer to either economic indexes or market indexes designed to reflect the performance of the overall market. Economists, market analysts, and investors all pay attention to the performance of major indices to help them predict future economic trends and market price movements.

Importance of Defining your Investment Strategy

Investment strategies is the game plan to your portfolio. Use the one that's right for you and significantly increase your chances of success.

People extensively plan for their workday, a vacation, college financing, golf matches, buying a car, but they often forget about the most plan-required task of them all: investing. Investing your money without an investment strategy is like a football team going into a game without a playbook, although they are not required, they significantly improve your chances of winning. Creating an investment strategy is a seamless, number two step, after learning the ins and out's of stock quotes and how to buy them.

Having an investment strategy is like having an instruction booklet guiding you through the investment process. It will help you discard many potential investments that may perform poorly overtime or that are not right for the investment goals you are looking to achieve.

When creating an investment strategy, it is important to quantitatively figure out what you are seeking to accomplish. Stating that you simply want to make money or become wealthy is not helpful. A better objective would be to say "I want to achieve an 8%

average annual return on my investment contributions over the next 10 years in order to amass $200,000 that will be used to purchase a cottage home." The more specific the objective, the better. And it doesn't stop there. An investment strategy is useless without a proper understanding of it. There are many different strategies that apply to different investment objectives, the key is pairing the right strategy with the right objective.

Types of Investment Strategies

1. Value Investing

   An investment strategy made popular by Warren Buffet, the principle behind value investing is simple: buy stocks that are cheaper than they should be. Finding stocks that are under-priced takes a lot of research on the fundamentals of the underlying companies. And once you've found them, it often takes a long time for their price to rise. This buy and hold technique requires a patient investor but should the right call be made, handsome payoffs could be earned. All investors should understand at least the basics of value investing.

2. Income Investing

   A great way to build wealth over time, income investing involves buying securities that generally pay out returns on a steady schedule. Bonds are the best known type of fixed income security, but the category also includes dividend paying stocks, exchange-traded funds (ETFs), mutual funds, and real estate investment trusts (REITs). Fixed income investments provide a reliable income stream with minimal risk and depending on the risk the investor is looking to take, should comprise at least a small portion of every investment strategy.

3. Growth Investing

   An investment strategy that focuses on capital appreciation. Growth investors look for companies that exhibit signs of above-average growth, through revenues and profits, even if the share price appears expensive in terms of metrics such as price-to-earnings or price-to-book ratios. What Warren Buffet did for value investing, Peter Lynch did for growth investing. A relatively riskier strategy, growth investing involves investing in smaller companies that have high potential for growth, blue chips and emerging markets.

4. Small Cap Investing

   An investment strategy fit for those looking to take on a little more risk in their portfolio. As the name suggests, small cap investinginvolves purchasing stock of small companies with smaller market capitalization (usually between $300 million and $2 billion). Small Cap stocks are appealing to investors due to their ability to go unnoticed. Large-cap stocks will often have inflated prices since everyone's paying attention to them. Small cap stocks tend to have less attention on them because: a) Investors stay away from their riskiness and b) Institutional investors (like mutual funds) have restrictions when it comes to investing in small cap companies. Small cap investing should only be used by more experienced stock investors as they are more volatile and therefore difficult to trade.

5. Socially Responsible Investing

   A portfolio built of environmentally and socially friendly companies while staying competitive alongside other kinds of securities in a typical market environment. In today's modern world, investors and the general public expect companies to maintain some social conscience, and they're putting their money where their mouth is. SRI is one path to seeking returns that poses a significant collateral benefit for everyone.

Choosing Right Investment Strategy

Setting up your investment strategy is like buying a new car, before you look at the different models, you need to figure out what style suits you best. And just like cars, there are many styles to choose from when creating an investment strategy. When choosing the right investing strategy, there are questions that need to be answered first. What is your investment horizon? What returns are you seeking to achieve? What amount of risk are you able to tolerant? What are the funds in this investment to be used for? Answering these questions will ultimately also help in building your portfolio.

Determining what will be your breakdown between cash, fixed-income securities and stocks is a good start towards creating your investment strategy. The breakdown of your asset allocation ultimately depends on your risk tolerance. A conservative investor may prefer to hold 80% of his portfolio in fixed-income and 20% in stocks. The reverse would be true for an aggressive investor, while a balanced investor will follow a 50-50 split.

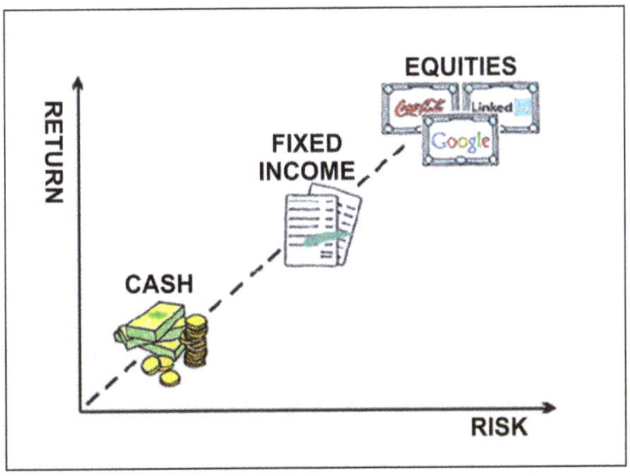

In terms of specific investment strategies within your asset allocation, if you are a high risk investor with a long investment horizon, you may want to include small cap and growth investing in your portfolio. If you have a moderate risk tolerance and shorter investment horizon, you may be more suitable for value and income investing. If you have a low risk tolerance and short investment horizon, you may want to focus solely on income investing. For those looking for companies that aim to do no harm, you can add socially responsible assets to your portfolio with relative ease. It is also important to adapt to the investment strategy you are most comfortable with. Someone with a knack for choosing growth stocks may make that strategy the priority in their portfolio.

Common Investment Strategies of Fund Managers

The criteria that mutual fund managers use to select their assets vary widely according to the individual manager. So when choosing a fund, you should look closely at the manager's investment style to make sure it fits your risk-reward profile.

"Investment style is incredibly important because of the way that investing works," says Chris Geczy, director of The Wharton School's wealth management program at the University of Pennsylvania.

"Both risk and return are connected to style. According to current practice portfolio theory, you can optimize a blend of styles for diversification, balancing reward and risk."

Here's a look at six common investment strategies among fund managers, including:

- Top-down investing,
- Bottom-up investing,
- Fundamental analysis,
- Technical analysis,
- Contrarian investing,
- Dividend investing.

Top-down or Bottom-up Investing

Top-down investing strategies involve choosing assets based on a big theme.

For example, if a fund manager anticipates that the economy will grow sharply, he or she might buy stocks across the board. Or the manager might just buy stocks in particular economic sectors, such as industrial and high technology, which tend to outperform when the economy is strong.

If the manager expects the economy to slump, it may spur him or her to sell stocks or purchase shares in defensive industries such as health care and consumer staples.

Bottom-up managers choose stocks based on the strength of an individual company, regardless of what's happening in the economy as a whole or the sector in which that company lies.

"The great advantage of top-down is that you're looking at the forest rather than the trees," says Mick Heyman, an independent financial adviser in San Diego. That makes screening for stocks or other investments easier.

And, "When you're right, you're really right," says Tim Ghriskey, co-founder of Solaris Asset Management in Bedford Hills, New York.

Of course, managers might be wrong on their big idea. And even if they're right, that doesn't guarantee they'll choose the right investments.

"A good example is gold," says James Holtzman, a shareholder at Legend Financial Advisors in Pittsburgh. "That would make sense for a top-down investor. But what if you're looking at a gold-mining stock and the company is being run into the ground? The particular stock could be ready to collapse, even though investing in gold makes sense."

A bottom-up manager benefits from thorough research on an individual company, but a market plunge often pulls even the strongest investments down.

Fundamental or Technical Analysis

Fundamental analysis involves evaluating all the factors that affect an investment's performance. For a stock, it would mean looking at all of the company's financial information, and it may also entail meeting with company executives, employees, suppliers, customers and competitors. "You want to analyze management, really understand what's driving the company and where growth is coming from," Heyman says.

Technical analysis involves choosing assets based on prior trading patterns. You're looking at the trends of an investment's price.

Most managers emphasize fundamental analysis, because they want to understand what will drive growth. Investors expect the stock to rise if a company is growing profits, for example.

But fundamentals don't always carry the day. "You can have a period of time where the market moves on technicals," Holtzman says.

Heyman sees power in technical analysis, because he believes an asset's price at any single moment reflects all the information available about it.

The best managers use both fundamentals and technicals, he says. "If a stock has good fundamentals, it should be stable to rising. If it's not rising, the market is telling you you're wrong or you should be focusing on something else."

Contrarian Investing

Contrarian managers choose assets that are out of favor. They determine the market's consensus about a company or sector and then bet against it.

The contrarian style is generally aligned with a value-investing strategy, which means buying assets that are undervalued by some statistical measure, says Wharton's Geczy.

"In the long run, value has beaten growth in assets around the world, though during certain periods that's not true," he says. "The contrarian style generally rewards investors, but you have to choose the right assets at the right time."

The risk, of course, is that the consensus is right, which results in wrong bets and losses for a contrarian manager.

Dividend Investing

As the name suggests, dividend funds buy stocks with a strong record of earnings and dividends. Because of the stock market volatility of recent years, many investors like the idea of a fund that offers them a regular payout.

"Even if the price goes down, at least you're getting some income," says Russ Kinnel, director of mutual fund research at Morningstar. "It's a nice way to supplement income if you're retired."

However, the recent popularity of dividend stocks causes some market pundits to wonder if they're currently overvalued. Also, beware of funds with extremely high yields. That could be a sign that companies are taking outsized risk and are headed for declines.

Most experts advise diversifying among investment styles. "In the end, a balanced way of looking at things tends to create fewer errors.

References

- Investmentstrategy: investopedia.com, Retrieved 2 March, 2019
- Portfolio-management-process, investment-decisions: efinancemanagement.com, Retrieved 12 May, 2019
- Two-edged-Sword: eurekahedge.com, Retrieved 11 July, 2019
- Alan Gregory, John Matatko and Ian Tonks (1997). "Detecting Information From Directors Trades: Signal definition and variable size effects". Journal of Business Finance & Accounting. 24 (3): 309–342. doi:10.1111/1468-5957.00107
- Long-short-equity-strategy: quantinsti.com, Retrieved 20 February, 2019
- Investment-management-strategies: amc.ppfas.com, Retrieved 13 April, 2019

- Holmberg, J and Robèrt, K-H "Backcasting from non-overlapping sustainability principles – a framework for strategic planning", International .Journal of Sustainable Development and World Ecology, 7:1–18. 2000
- Indexing, trading-investing: corporatefinanceinstitute.com, Retrieved 3 June, 2019
- Investment-strategies: wallstreetsurvivor.com, Retrieved 23 August, 2019
- Common-investment-strategies-of-fund-managers, investing: bankrate.com, Retrieved 7 April, 2019

Portfolio Management

The science of allocating assets for institutions and individuals, making decisions about investment mix and policy, balancing risk against performance and matching investments to objectives is known as portfolio management. This chapter discusses in detail the theories and methodologies related to management of portfolio as well as the strategies which are involved in it.

Portfolio management is the art and science of making decisions about investment mix and policy, matching investments to objectives, asset allocation for individuals and institutions, and balancing risk against performance. Portfolio management is all about determining strengths, weaknesses, opportunities and threats in the choice of debt vs. equity, domestic vs. international, growth vs. safety, and many other trade-offs encountered in the attempt to maximize return at a given appetite for risk.

Although it is common to use the terms "portfolio management" and "financial planning" as synonyms, these staples of the financial services industry are not the same. Portfolio management is the act of creating and maintaining an investment account, while financial planning is the process of developing financial goals and creating a plan of action to achieve them. Professional licensed portfolio managers are responsible for portfolio management on behalf of others, while individuals may choose to self-direct their own investments and build their own portfolio. Portfolio management's ultimate goal is to maximize the investments' expected return given an appropriate level of risk exposure.

Portfolio management, in general, can by either passive or active in nature. Passive management is a set-it-and-forget-it long-term strategy that often involves simply tracking a broad market index (or group of indexes), commonly referred to as indexing or index investing.

Active management instead involves a single manager, co-managers or a team of managers who attempt to beat the market return by actively managing a fund's portfolio through investment decisions based on research and decisions on individual holdings. Closed-end funds are generally actively managed.

The Key Elements of Portfolio Management

Asset Allocation: The key to effective portfolio management is the long-term mix of assets. Asset allocation is based on the understanding that different types of assets do not move in concert, and some are more volatile than others. Asset allocation seeks to optimize the risk/return profile of an investor by investing in a mix of assets that have low correlation to each other. Investors with a more aggressive profile can weight their portfolio toward more volatile investments. Investors with a more conservative profile can weight their portfolio toward more stable investments. Indexed portfolios may employ modern portfolio theory (MPT) to aid inbuilding an optimized portfolio, while active managers may use any number of quantitative and/or qualitative models.

Diversification: The only certainty in investing is it is impossible to consistently predict the winners and losers, so the prudent approach is to create a basket of investments that provide broad exposure within an asset class. Diversification is the spreading of risk and reward within an asset class. Because it is difficult to know which particular subset of an asset class or sector is likely to outperform another, diversification seeks to capture the returns of all of the sectors over time but with less volatility at any one time. Proper diversification takes place across different classes of securities, sectors of the economy and geographical regions.

Rebalancing is a method used to return a portfolio to its original target allocation at annual intervals. It is important for retaining the asset mix that best reflects an investor's risk/return profile. Otherwise, the movements of the markets could expose the portfolio to greater risk or reduced return opportunities. For example, a portfolio that starts out with a 70% equity and 30% fixed-income allocation could, through an extended market rally, shift to an 80/20 allocation that exposes the portfolio to more risk than the investor can tolerate. Rebalancing almost always entails the sale of high-priced/low-value securities and the redeployment of the proceeds into low-priced/high-value or out-of-favor securities. The annual iteration of rebalancing enables investors to capture gains and expand the opportunity for growth in high potential sectors while keeping the portfolio aligned with the investor's risk/return profile.

Active Portfolio Management

Investors who implement an active management approach use fund managers or brokers to buy and sell stocks in an attempt to outperform a specific index, such as the Standard & Poor's 500 Index or the Russell 1000 Index.

An actively managed investment fund has an individual portfolio manager, co-managers, or a team of managers actively making investment decisions for the fund. The success of an actively managed fund depends on combining in-depth research, market forecasting, and the experience and expertise of the portfolio manager or management team.

Portfolio managers engaged in active investing pay close attention to market trends, shifts in the economy, changes to the political landscape, and factors that may affect specific companies. This data is used to time the purchase or sale of investments in an effort to take advantage of irregularities. Active managers claim that these processes will boost the potential for returns higher than those achieved by simply mimicking the stocks or other securities listed on a particular index.

Since the objective of a portfolio manager in an actively managed fund is to beat the market, he or she must take on additional market risk to obtain the returns necessary to achieve this end. Indexing eliminates this, as there is no risk of human error in terms of stock selection. Index funds are also traded less frequently, which means that they incur lower expense ratios and are more tax-efficient than actively managed funds.

Active management traditionally charges high fees, and recent research has cast doubts on managers' ability to consistently outperform the market.

Passive Portfolio Management

Passive management, also referred to as index fund management, involves the creation of a portfolio intended to track the returns of a particular market index or benchmark as closely as possible. Managers select stocks and other securities listed on an index and apply the same weighting. The purpose of passive portfolio management is to generate a return that is the same as the chosen index instead of outperforming it.

A passive strategy does not have a management team making investment decisions and can be structured as an exchange-traded fund (ETF), a mutual fund, or a unit investment trust. Index funds are branded as passively managed because each has a portfolio manager replicating the index, rather than trading securities based on his or her knowledge of the risk and reward characteristics of various securities. Because this investment strategy is not proactive, the management fees assessed on passive portfolios or funds are often far lower than active management strategies.

Index mutual funds are easy to understand and offer a relatively safe approach to investing in broad segments of the market.

Typical Portfolio Management Investments and Services

Portfolio management involves managing an individual's investments in many forms, including the following:

- Bonds,
- Stocks,
- Shares,

- Cash,
- Mutual Funds,
- Exchanged-Traded Funds,
- Closed Funds.

Expert portfolio management services entails determining marketplace strengths, weaknesses, opportunities and threats when it comes to the following:

- Debt versus equity – There is always risk when investing and that risk comes down to the marketplace being either:
    - Not in your favor – The marketplace is unpredictable and when this sometimes yields financial loss.
    - In your favor – When the economy is doing well or your particular investments are in stock/businesses thriving, which yields return on investments.
- Domestic versus international – Domestic and international markets vary greatly and have different investment strategies as the global economy fluctuates from the U.S. economy. The economy is increasingly global, which is why asset allocation and diversification can be important.
- Growth versus safety – Riskier investments can mean faster growth, but it's also sometimes to have a conservative portfolio for stability reasons.

Portfolio Management is not 'One-Size-Fits-All'

Every individual has a unique investment portfolio and requires a customized investment plan. This means that the best investment plan for one person is completely different for someone else. For example, there is a different strategy or investment plan for each individual based on their income, budget, age and risk ability.

There are also many considerations per individual and household, which is why portfolio managers need to provide customized investment solutions to clients based on each client's unique needs and requirements. For example, someone who is in his or her 20s will have a completely different investment portfolio plan than someone who is planning to retire in ten years as variables such as time, inflation and risk need to be measured differently for each person's situation.

Fundamentals of Portfolio Management

There is a delicate balance of key elements when it comes to expert portfolio management.

Asset Allocation

A long-term mix of assets desired for an effective financial portfolio. Asset allocation is based on the concept that different types of assets have different marketplace performance. Asset allocations seeks to optimize the risk versus return profile of an investor by investing in a mix of assets that have low correlation to each other.

- Investors with a more aggressive profile can weight their portfolio toward more volatile investments.
- Investors with a more conservative profile can weight their portfolio toward more stable investments.

Diversification

The spreading of risk and reward within an asset class. A certainty in investing is that it's impossible to consistently predict the winners and losers, which is why it's imperative to have a mix, or diversified, portfolio.

- Diversification seeks to capture the returns of all the sectors over time, but with less volatility at any one time.
- Diversification takes place across different classes of securities, sectors of the economy and geographical regions.

Rebalancing

Rebalancing is used to return a portfolio to its original target allocation at annual intervals. It's important for retaining the asset mix that best reflects an investor's risk/return profile. If rebalancing isn't done, the movements of the markets could expose the portfolio to greater risk or reduced return opportunities.

- Portfolio rebalancing typically happens annually and enables investors to capture gains and expand their opportunity for growth in high potential sectors while keeping a portfolio aligned with the desired risk/return profile.

Active Portfolio Management Strategy

Active Portfolio Management Strategy refers to a portfolio management strategy that involves making precise investments for outperforming an investment benchmark index. The portfolio manager that follows the active management strategy exploits the market inefficiencies by buying undervalued securities or by short selling overvalued securities. Any of these procedures can be used alone or in combination.

Active portfolio managers may create less volatility (or risk) than the benchmark index depending on the targets of the specific hedge fund or mutual fund or investment portfolio. The risk reduction is considered as goal of creating an investment return larger than the benchmark. They use large number of factors and strategies for constructing their portfolio.

Strategies for Constructing the Portfolio

- Quantitative measures like price/earnings ratio (P/E ratios) and PEG ratios,
- Sector investments that are expected to deliver long-term macroeconomic trends,
- Buying stocks of companies that are disliked temporarily,
- Selling at a discount of their intrinsic value,
- Merger arbitrage,
- Short positions,
- Option writing,
- Asset allocation.

Active Portfolio Management Strategy Performance

The performance of an actively-managed investment portfolio relies on the proficiency of the portfolio manager and research staff. There are many mutual funds that are supposed to be actively managed and they stay invested irrespective of market conditions along with only negligible adjustments in allocation over time. In conditions of prolonged market declines, the managers may use hedging strategies. The performance characteristics are different with two groups of active managers.

Benefits of Active Management

- The active portfolio management strategy allows the portfolio managers to select a variety of investments rather than investing in the market as a whole.

There may be different kinds of motivations for the investors to follow active management strategy.

- In order to generate profits, the investors consider that some market segments are less efficient than others.
- Portfolio Manager may manage the volatility or risks of market by investing in less-risky and high-quality companies instead of investing in market as a whole.
- Investors may take additional risk for achieving higher-than-market returns.
- Those investments which are not vastly correlated to the market function as portfolio diversifier and decrease the portfolio volatility as a whole.
- Investors may follow a strategy for avoiding certain industries in comparison to the market as a whole.
- Investors that follow actively-managed fund are more aligned for achieving their specific investment goals.

Drawbacks of Active Management

- There are chances of bad investment choices to be made by fund manager.
- Fund Manager may follow an unsafe theory for the management of the portfolio.
- The costs related to the active management are higher in comparison to passive management in case of lack of frequent trading.
- Fund managers should actively evaluate the fund's prospectus before investing in an actively-managed mutual fund because most of the actively-managed large and mid-cap stock funds fail to beat or outperform their passively managed counterparts.
- Higher transaction costs results due to frequent trading with active fund management strategies that reduces the fund's return.
- The short-term capital gains due to frequent trading have an unfavourable income tax impact.

Passive Portfolio Management Strategy

Passive portfolio management strategy refers to the financial investment strategy where an investor makes an investment as per the fixed strategy that doesn't involve any forecasting. It stresses on minimizing the investing fees and avoiding the unpleasant results of failing to correctly predict the future.

Passive portfolio management strategy employs the most popular method of imitating the performance of a superficially specified index. It is done by retail investors by buying one or more 'index funds'. An investment portfolio tracks an index and achieves low turnover, very low management fees and good diversification.

The low management fees enable the investor to receive higher returns in comparison to similar fund investments with higher management fees or transaction costs. Passive management is widely used in the equity market and involves tracking of stock market index by index funds. However, it is getting more common in other types of investment including hedge funds, bonds and commodities. There is vast number of market indexes all over the world and different index funds (in thousands) track several of them.

Implementation of Passive Portfolio Management Strategy

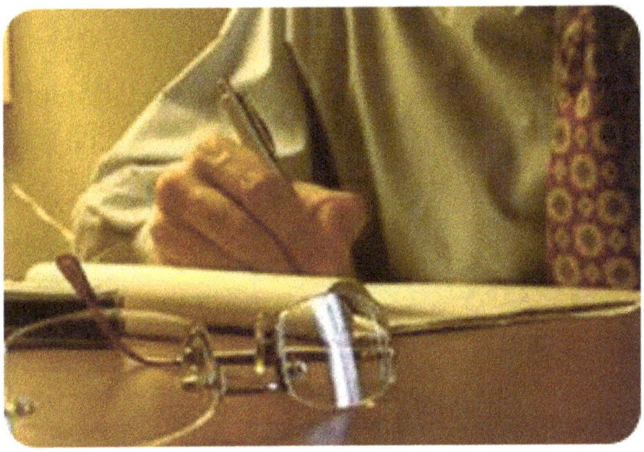

An index fund can be implemented by buying securities in the similar proportion as present in the stock market index. Sampling can also be done to implement passive portfolio management strategy.

The sampling involves purchasing each type of stocks from various sectors in the index but do not include some quantity of stocks of every individual stock. Some of the sampling techniques are very advanced and sophisticated that involves purchasing of specific shares that have high probability of good performance.

Those investment managers who run the investment funds and closely follow the index in their managed portfolios; are called as closet trackers. These investment managers offer little value as managers and charge fees for active management. These managers do not actively manage the fund but secretively follows the index.

Index funds refer to the collective investment schemes that utilize passive investment strategies for tracking the performance of a stock market index. Exchange-traded funds track commodity indices and a specific market. These are managed by passive investment strategies rather than active management.

Advantages of Passive Portfolio Management Strategy

Passive portfolio management strategy provides various advantages:

- Low cost: Passive investment strategy incurs low costs as compared to active investment counterparts. It provides meaningful and specific incremental advantage. On other hand, an active manager is required to add enough value for beating the cost disadvantage.
- Reduced uncertainty of decision errors: By making investments, investors are exposed to market risks and passive investment strategy reduces the uncertainty of decision errors. In case of active management, the pressure of achieving the returns that beats the market, may lead to the extra risk for making the wrong investments.
- Style consistency: Indexing enables the investors to control their overall allocation by selecting the appropriate indexes.
- Tax efficiency: Indexing is considered as more tax efficient especially in cases of larger-cap indexes that involve less trading and which are fairly stable.

Portfolio Volatility

Volatility is a formal measure of a stock's risks. The higher the volatility of a stock, the greater its up and down swings. The volatility of a portfolio of stocks, on the other hand, is a measure of how wildly the total value of all the stocks in that portfolio appreciates or declines. Understanding the concept of portfolio volatility can be the difference between a safe growth path for your money and many sleepless nights.

Stock Risk

Say you're comparing stocks A and B, both of which have advanced an average of half a percent per month over the last two years. Does that mean both carry the same level of risk? Absolutely not. Stock A might have always advanced between 0.3 and 0.7 percent every month, never registering a monthly loss, for an average of half a percent return per month. B, on the other hand, might have advanced by more than 30 percent per month on several occasions, while losing more than 35 percent of its value several times as well, yet it might also register a half percent monthly return on average. The true measure of risk is how much returns tend to deviate from the average return.

Standard Deviation

Statisticians calculate something called standard deviation to measure how stable a variable has been over time. Financial experts use standard deviation of a stock's past return as a measure of its risk. The formula for standard deviation is relatively detailed, and calculating the standard deviation of a stock's monthly return over several years is a laborious process. However, plugging the monthly returns into a spreadsheet application makes the calculation a breeze. When looking at standard deviation of a stock's past returns, keep in mind that the higher the figure, the more spread out the returns. This means the stock had many months of very good and very bad returns and is a high risk, high return investment.

Correlation

If you have $5,000 worth of stock A and $5,000 of B, in your portfolio and they return 4 and 6 percent, respectively, this portfolio of stocks will have returned 5 percent, which is the average of 4 and 6 percent. However, if the standard deviation, of the stocks are 4 and 6 percent, you cannot average the stock's standard deviations to find the portfolio's standard deviation. Before you can combine the standard deviations of the stocks in your portfolio to arrive at the portfolio's standard deviation, you have to understand whether these stocks tend to move up and down together -- or in financial lingo, how correlated the stocks are. If both stocks are issued by oil firms, they will tend to go up and down together as oil prices fluctuate. Such stocks have a high correlation.

Portfolio Risk

The main idea behind investing in a portfolio of stocks is to reduce risk. However, it is not only the number of shares in your portfolio but also their correlation to each other that determines the portfolio's total risk. High correlation results in high total risk, because the stocks in your portfolio will have a higher chance of declining all at once. Shares of firms in unrelated fields have low correlation. A portfolio of such stocks has lower total risk, which makes intuitive sense. After all, the stocks of oil drillers, automakers and food manufacturers are rarely hit all at once, save for a huge economic downturn in the country. With the use of a spreadsheet, you can also calculate the correlation between stocks in your portfolio and the resulting total risk.

Expected Portfolio Return

The expected return is the profit or loss an investor anticipates on an investment that has known or anticipated rates of return (RoR). It is calculated by multiplying potential outcomes by the chances of them occurring and then totaling these results. For example, if an investment has a 50% chance of gaining 20% and a 50% chance of losing 10%, the expected return is 5% (50% x 20% + 50% x -10% = 5%).

Expected Return Works

The expected return is a tool used to determine whether an investment has a positive or negative average net outcome. The sum is calculated as the expected value (EV) of an investment given its potential returns in different scenarios, as illustrated by the following formula:

$$\text{Expected Return} = \text{SUM}(\text{Return}_i \times \text{Probability}_i)$$

where: "i" indicates each known return and its respective probability in the series.

The expected return is usually based on historical data and is therefore not guaranteed. This figure is merely a long-term weighted average of historical returns. In the example above, for instance, the 5% expected return may never be realized in the future, as the investment is inherently subject to systematic and unsystematic risks. Systematic risk the danger to a market sector or the entire market whereas unsystematic risk applies to a specific company or industry.

Limitations of Expected Return

It is quite dangerous to make investment decisions based on expected returns alone. Before making any buying decisions, investors should always review the risk characteristics of investment opportunities to determine if the investments align with their portfolio goals.

For example, assume two hypothetical investments exist. Their annual performance results for the last five years are:

- Investment A: 12%, 2%, 25%, -9%, and 10%.
- Investment B: 7%, 6%, 9%, 12%, and 6%.

Both of these investments have expected returns of exactly 8%. However, when analyzing the risk of each, as defined by the standard deviation, Analyst use standard deviation to reveal historical volatility in investments. Investment A is approximately five times riskier than Investment B. That is, Investment A has a standard deviation of 12.6% and Investment B has a standard deviation of 2.6%.

In addition to expected returns, wise investors should also consider the likelihood of a return to better assess risk. After all, one can find instances where certain lotteries offer a positive expected return, despite the very low chances of realizing that return.

- Pros:
  - Gages the performance of an asset.
  - Weighs different scenarios.

- Cons:
  - Doesn't take risk into account.
  - Based largely on historic data.

Real World Example of Expected Return

The expected return doesn't just apply to a single security or asset. It can also be expanded to analyze a portfolio containing many investments. If the expected return for each investment is known, the portfolio's overall expected return is a weighted average of the expected returns of its components.

For example, let's assume we have an investor interested in the tech sector. His portfolio contains the following stocks:

- Alphabet Inc. (GOOG): $500,000 invested and an expected return of 15%.
- Apple Inc. (AAPL): $200,000 invested and an expected return of 6%.
- Amazon.com Inc. (AMZN): $300,000 invested and an expected return of 9%.

With a total portfolio value of $1 million the weights of Alphabet, Apple, and Amazon in the portfolio are 50%, 20%, and 30%, respectively.

Thus, the expected return of the total portfolio is 11.4%:

(50% x 15% = 7.5%) + (20% x 6% = 1.2%) + (30% x 9% = 2.7%).

(7.5% + 1.2% + 2.7% = 11.4%).

Step by Step Portfolio Planning Process

There are few things more important and more daunting than creating a long-term investment strategy that can enable an individual to invest with confidence and with clarity about his or her future. Constructing an investment portfolio requires a deliberate and precise portfolio-planning process that follows five essential steps.

Assess Current Financial Situation and Goals

Planning for the future requires having a clear understanding of an investor's current situation in relation to where they want to be. That requires a thorough assessment of current assets, liabilities, cash flow and investments in light of the investor's most important goals. Goals need to be clearly defined and quantified so that the assessment can identify any gaps between the current investment strategy and the stated goals.

This step needs to include a frank discussion about the investor's values, beliefs and priorities, all of which set the course for developing an investment strategy.

Establish Investment Objectives

Establishing investment objectives centers on identifying the investor's risk-returnprofile. Determining how much risk that an investor is willing and able to assume, and how much volatility that the investor can withstand, is key to formulating a portfolio strategy that can deliver the required returns with an acceptable level of risk. Once an acceptable risk-return profile is developed, benchmarks can be established for tracking the portfolio's performance. Tracking the portfolio's performance against benchmarks allows smaller adjustments to be made along the way.

Determine Asset Allocation

Using the risk-return profile, an investor can develop an asset allocation strategy. Selecting from various asset classes and investment options, the investor can allocate assets in a way that achieves optimum diversification while targeting the expected returns. The investor can also assign percentages to various asset classes, including stocks, bonds, cash and alternative investments, based on an acceptable range of volatility for the portfolio. The asset allocation strategy is based on a snapshot of the investor's current situation and goals, and is usually adjusted as life changes occur. For example, the closer an investor gets to his or her retirement target date, the more the allocation may change to reflect less tolerance for volatility and risk.

Select Investment Options

Individual investments are selected based on the parameters of the asset allocation strategy. The specific investment type selected depends in large part on the investor's preference for active or passive management. An actively managed portfolio might include individual stocks and bonds if there are sufficient assets to achieve optimum diversification, which is typically over $1 million in assets. Smaller portfolios can achieve the proper diversification through professionally managed funds, such as mutual funds or with exchange-traded funds. An investor might construct a passively managed portfolio with index funds selected from the various asset classes and economic sectors.

Monitor, Measure and Rebalance

After implementing a portfolio plan, the management process begins. This includes monitoring the investments and measuring the portfolio's performance relative to the benchmarks. It is necessary to report investment performance at regular intervals, typically quarterly, and to review the portfolio plan annually. Once a year, the investor's situation and goals get a review to determine if there have been any significant changes. The portfolio review then determines if the allocation is still on target to track the investor's risk-reward profile. If it is not, then the portfolio can be rebalanced, selling investments that have reached their targets, and buying investments that offer greater upside potential.

When investing for lifelong goals, the portfolio planning process never stops. As investors move through their life stages, changes may occur, such as job changes, births, divorce, deaths or shrinking time horizons, which may require adjustments to their goals, risk-reward profiles or asset allocations. As changes occur, or as market or economic conditions dictate, the portfolio planning process begins anew, following each of the five steps to ensure that the right investment strategy is in place.

Business Portfolio Management

When baking a cake, many good cooks follow a recipe with precise measurements, cooking times, and list of ingredients. Simply collecting good raw components does not guarantee success. We need to follow proven processes to achieve the best possible results. That's the idea behind business portfolio management.

Business portfolio management is a process that enables organizations to manage multiple projects or individual projects for optimal results. The business portfolio management process works by identifying an organization's best project managers and using best management practices, strategic priorities, and valuable lessons learned in a project management office. Business portfolio management allows the organization to evaluate and balance conflicting demands for project resources. By aligning with organizational strategies and prioritizing the work, business portfolio management helps manage risk and provides cost-effective allocation of resources to the most deserving projects.

- The functions and goals of business process management.
- The difference between business portfolio management and project management.
- How business portfolio management compares to project management.
- How organizational culture affects business portfolio management.

Functions and Goals

Business portfolio management provides an opportunity for an organization to:

- Prioritize which projects should be done first and receive adequate funding.
- Assure that scopes of work and work breakdown structures are clearly written.

- Track that timelines and budgets remain on schedule.
- Validate that all milestones and deliverables are completed on time and within budget to meet their sponsors' quality requirements.

That is much easier said than done. It's also why so many companies are turning to business portfolio management to meet these goals and objectives. It is tough enough to assure one or two projects are completed on time. Now imagine how difficult that problem becomes when dozens of projects must be managed well, including those with crucial new product or operations deadlines, very large budgets, or long timelines that span multiple years. Business portfolio management can manage high priority projects or all of the projects at their designated organizational level. More often than not, it also provides other support as a center of excellence for project management.

Typical goals for business portfolio management include:

- Establishing a communications project management policy.
- Providing project management training from basic through advanced levels.
- Mentoring project managers and team members.

Portfolio Management Strategies

Portfolio Management Strategies refer to the approaches that are applied for the efficient portfolio management in order to generate the highest possible returns at lowest possible risks. There are two basic approaches for portfolio management including Active Portfolio Management Strategy and Passive Portfolio Management Strategy.

Active Portfolio Management Strategy

The Active portfolio management relies on the fact that particular style of analysis or management can generate returns that can beat the market. It involves higher than average costs and it stresses on taking advantage of market inefficiencies. It is implemented by the advices of analysts and managers who analyze and evaluate market for the presence of inefficiencies.

The active management approach of the portfolio management involves the following styles of the stock selection.

Top-down Approach: In this approach, managers observe the market as a whole and decide about the industries and sectors that are expected to perform well in the ongoing economic cycle. After the decision is made on the sectors, the specific stocks are selected on the basis of companies that are expected to perform well in that particular sector.

Bottom-up: In this approach, the market conditions and expected trends are ignored and the evaluations of the companies are based on the strength of their product pipeline, financial statements, or any other criteria. It stresses the fact that strong companies perform well irrespective of the prevailing market or economic conditions.

Passive Portfolio Management Strategy

Passive asset management relies on the fact that markets are efficient and it is not possible to beat the market returns regularly over time and best returns are obtained from the low cost investments kept for the long term.

The passive management approach of the portfolio management involves the following styles of the stock selection.

- Efficient market theory: This theory relies on the fact that the information that affects the markets is immediately available and processed by all investors. Thus, such information is always considered in evaluation of the market prices. The portfolio managers who follows this theory, firmly believes that market averages cannot be beaten consistently.
- Indexing: According to this theory, the index funds are used for taking the advantages of efficient market theory and for creating a portfolio that impersonate a specific index. The index funds can offer benefits over the actively managed funds because they have lower than average expense ratios and transaction costs.

Apart from Active and Passive Portfolio Management Strategies, there are three more kinds of portfolios including Patient Portfolio, Aggressive Portfolio and Conservative Portfolio.

- Patient Portfolio: This type of portfolio involves making investments in well-known stocks. The investors buy and hold stocks for longer periods. In this portfolio, the majority of the stocks represent companies that have classic growth and those expected to generate higher earnings on a regular basis irrespective of financial conditions.
- Aggressive Portfolio: This type of portfolio involves making investments in "expensive stocks" that provide good returns and big rewards along with carrying big risks. This portfolio is a collection of stocks of companies of different sizes that are rapidly growing and expected to generate rapid annual earnings growth over the next few years.
- Conservative Portfolio: This type of portfolio involves the collection of stocks after carefully observing the market returns, earnings growth and consistent dividend history.

Active Management

Active management is the use of a human element, such as a single manager, co-managers or a team of managers, to actively manage a fund's portfolio. Active managers rely on analytical research, forecasts, and their own judgment and experience in making investment decisions on what securities to buy, hold and sell. The opposite of active management is passive management, better known as "indexing."

Investors who believe in active management do not follow the efficient market hypothesis. They believe it is possible to profit from the stock market through any number of strategies that aim to identify mispriced securities. Investment companies and fund sponsors believe it's possible to outperform the market and employ professional investment managers to manage one or more of the company's mutual funds. David Einhorn, founder and president of Greenlight Capital, is an example of a well-known active fund manager.

Objective of Active Management

Active management seeks to produce better returns than those of passively managed index funds. For example, a large cap stock fund manager attempts to beat the performance of the Standard & Poor's 500 index. Unfortunately, for a large majority of active managers, this has been difficult to achieve. This phenomenon is simply a reflection of how hard it is, no matter how talented the manager, to beat the market. Actively managed funds typically have higher fees than passively managed funds.

Advantages of Active Management

A fund manager's expertise, experience, skill and judgment is being utilized when investing in an actively managed fund. For example, a fund manager may have extensive experience in the automotive industry, so as a result, the fund may be able to beat benchmark returns by investing in a select group of car-related stocks that the manager believes are undervalued. Active fund managers have flexibility. There is typically freedom in the stock selection process as performance is not tracked to an index. Actively managed funds allow for benefits in tax management. The ability to buy and sell when deemed necessary makes it possible to offset losing investments with wining investments.

Active Management and Risk

By not being compelled to follow specific benchmarks, active fund managers can manage risk more proficiently. For example, a global banking exchange-traded fund (ETF) may be required to hold a specific number of British banks; the fund is likely to have significantly decreased in value following the shock Brexit result in 2016. Alternatively, an actively managed global banking fund has the ability to reduce or terminate exposure to British banks due to heightened levels of risk. Active managers can also mitigate risk by using various hedging strategies such as short selling and using derivatives to protect portfolios.

Active Management and Performance

Controversy surrounds the performance of active managers. Whether investors will enjoy superior results through an actively managed fund as opposed to a mechanically traded ETF depends on the person managing the fund and the time period. Over the 10 years ended in 2017, active managers who invest in large-cap value stocks were most likely to beat the index, outperforming by 1.13% on average per year. A study showed that 84% of active managers in this category outperformed their benchmark index gross-of-fees. Over the short term of three years, active managers underperformed the index by an average of 0.36%, and over five years, they trailed it by 0.22%.

Another study showed that for the 30 years ended in 2016, actively managed funds returned 3.7% on average annually, compared to 10% for returns for passively managed funds.

Steps to Ensure Smart Investment

Security Analysis

Security analysis is the first step of the process of portfolio management. If we want to cook a delicious recipe then what all we need is perfect ingredients. If you have all the ingredients to make your dish lip-smacking then it's cooking time. If not then you need to ensure all the ingredients. In the same way, to construct a right portfolio, you need perfect securities. Here perfection is about the matchability with your risk aspects and returns expectation. In this step, all the securities from your portfolio are analyzed. As well as at the same time the potential securities which can be good buying opportunities available in the market are also considered. Keeping your financial goal on the line, portfolio managers shortlist the best securities for your portfolio.

Portfolio Analysis

Portfolio analysis is the second step in portfolio management. Have you ever seen your kid playing Meccano or block building game? Whats his process of thinking. Basically, after collecting the blocks or nuts, the permutation, and combination possible shapes starts. In the same way, the after collecting the best possible securities, the process of shaping portfolio starts. With the number of potential securities, a number of portfolios created. These portfolios are also known as feasible portfolios. These feasible portfolios are further analyzed to pick the exact match of your requirements.

Portfolio Selection

Portfolio selection is the third and most important step of the portfolio management process. Feasible portfolios are the permutation and combinations of the securities. It's a rough layout from which optimum selection needs to be done. In a simpler way, when you go to service car, the possible problems and regular servicing requirements are explained to you at the beginning. However, many times the estimated cost and your exact bill seem different. Basically, It's a permutation and combination of possible requirements for repairing. But while repairing the exact tools and exact spares are used which ultimately reduces your costs than estimated sometime. In the same way the from the number of portfolios the optimum and exact portfolio is selected in the selection process. The portfolio is selected on the basis of your investment capabilities and return expectation. Portfolio manager selects the portfolio which will create wealth for you without hampering your risk appetite.

Portfolio Revision

After selecting the portfolio, the portfolio manager and his team of analysts, keep an eye on the portfolio. This also a key step in the process of portfolio management. It's like maintaining your car, after purchasing it. Once, you have created a portfolio, monitoring it closely to ensure profits it's also important. In this step, the portfolio manager ensures the close monitoring as well as take the informed decision as and when required.

Portfolio Evaluation

To achieve a specific financial goal, consistent evaluation of the performance is necessary. The risk-return ratio is consistently evaluated in this step. This is the last step of the portfolio management process. Here, the portfolio manager ensures the tracking of the strategies implemented.

The process itself suggests the idea behind PMS. It's made for making you free from all the hassles related to your stock market investment. The service helps you in each stage of your investing life. The process starts with selecting the constituents and continues until the achievement of the long-term financial goal. This personalized service is offered by many investment advisors and brokers India who offer PMS.

Leveraged Portfolio

A portfolio that contains securities purchased with borrowed money. The portfolio is risky since securities may end with a loss making the investor liable to repay borrowed capital. In the event the securities make a gain, the investor has made a profit for themselves without having to use their own money.

Leverage results from using borrowed capital as a funding source when investing to expand the firm's asset base and generate returns on risk capital. Leverage is an investment strategy of using borrowed money—specifically, the use of various financial instruments or borrowed capital—to increase the potential return of an investment. Leverage can also refer to the amount of debt a firm uses to finance assets. When one refers to a company, property or investment as "highly leveraged," it means that item has more debt than equity.

Working of Leverage

Leverage is the use of debt (borrowed capital) in order to undertake an investment or project. The result is to multiply the potential returns from a project. At the same time, leverage will also multiply the potential downside risk in case the investment does not pan out.

The concept of leverage is used by both investors and companies. Investors use leverage to significantly increase the returns that can be provided on an investment. They lever their investments by using various instruments that include options, futures and margin accounts. Companies can use leverage to finance their assets. In other words, instead of issuing stock to raise capital, companies can use debt financing to invest in business operations in an attempt to increase shareholder value.

Investors who are not comfortable using leverage directly have a variety of ways to access leverage indirectly. They can invest in companies that use leverage in the normal course of their business to finance or expand operations—without increasing their outlay.

The Difference between Leverage and Margin

Although interconnected—since both involve borrowing—leverage and margin are not the same. Leverage refers to taking on debt, while margin is debt or borrowed money a firm uses to invest in other financial instruments. A margin account allows you to borrow money from a broker for a fixed interest rate to purchase securities, options or futures contracts in the anticipation of receiving substantially high returns.

You can use margin to create leverage.

Example of Leverage

A company formed with an investment of $5 million from investors, the equity in the company is $5 million; this is the money the company can use to operate. If the company uses debt financing by borrowing $20 million, it now has $25 million to invest in business operations and more opportunity to increase value for shareholders. An automaker, for example, could borrow money to build a new factory. The new factory would enable the automaker to increase the number of cars it produces and increase profits.

Leverage Formulas

Through balance sheet analysis, investors can study the debt and equity on the books of various firms and can invest in companies that put leverage to work on behalf of their businesses. Statistics such as return on equity, debt to equity and return on capital employed help investors determine how companies deploy capital and how much of that capital companies have borrowed. To properly evaluate these statistics, it is important to keep in mind that leverage comes in several varieties, including operating, financial, and combined leverage.

Fundamental analysis uses the degree of operating leverage. One can calculate the degree of operating leverage by dividing the percentage change of a company's earnings per share by its percentage change in its earnings before interest and taxes over a period. Similarly, one could calculate the degree of operating leverage by dividing a company's EBIT by its EBIT less its interest expense. A higher degree of operating leverage shows a higher level of volatility in a company's EPS.

DuPont analysis uses the "equity multiplier" to measure financial leverage. One can calculate the equity multiplier by dividing a firm's total assets by its total equity. Once figured, one multiplies the financial leverage with the total asset turnover and the profit margin to produce the return on equity. For example, if a publicly traded company has total assets valued at $500 million and shareholder equity valued at $250 million, then the equity multiplier is 2.0 ($500 million/$250 million). This shows the company has financed half its total assets by equity. Hence, larger equity multipliers suggest more financial leverage.

If reading spreadsheets and conducting fundamental analysis is not your cup of tea, you can purchase mutual funds or exchange-traded funds that use leverage. By using these vehicles, you can delegate the research and investment decisions to experts.

The Disadvantages of Leverage

Leverage is a multi-faceted, complex tool. The theory sounds great, and in reality, the use of leverage can be profitable, but the reverse is also true. Leverage magnifies both gains and losses. If an investor uses leverage to make an investment and the investment moves against the investor, his or her loss is much greater than it would've been if he or she had not leveraged the investment.

In the business world, a company can use leverage to generate shareholder wealth, but if it fails to do so, the interest expense and credit risk of default destroy shareholder value.

Optimal Portfolio

Portfolio in which the risk-reward combination is such that it yields the maximum returns (provides the highest utility) possible under the current and anticipated circumstances.

The optimal portfolio concept falls under the portfolio theory.

The theory assumes that investors fanatically try to minimize risk while striving for the highest return possible.

The theory states that investors will act rationally, always making decisions aimed at maximizing their return for their acceptable level of risk.

The optimal portfolio was used in 1952 by Harry Markowitz, and it shows us that it is possible for different portfolios to have varying levels of risk and return.

Each investor must decide how much risk they can handle and then allocate or diversify their portfolio according to this decision.

The chart below illustrates how the optimal portfolio works.

The optimal-risk portfolio is usually determined to be somewhere in the middle of the curve because as you go higher up the curve, you take on proportionately more risk for a lower incremental return.

On the other end, low risk/low return portfolios are pointless because you can achieve a similar return by investing in risk-free assets, like government securities.

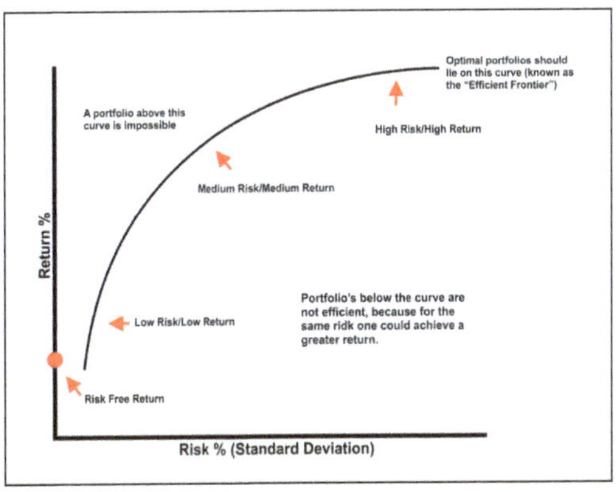

You can choose how much volatility you are willing to bear in your portfolio by picking any other point that falls on the efficient frontier. This will give you the maximum return for the amount of risk you wish to accept.

Optimizing your portfolio is not something you can calculate in your head.

There are computer programs that are dedicated to determining optimal portfolios by estimating hundreds (and sometimes thousands) of different expected returns for each given amount of risk.

Portfolio Diversification

Portfolio diversification is the process of investing your money in different asset classes and securities in order to minimize the overall risk of the portfolio.

Just imagine what would happen if you invested all your money in a single security. Everything would be great as long as the stock's performance is good. But in case the market takes a sudden U-turn, you could stand to lose your entire investment in a single blow.

It is something like what happens when all the kids in the hide and seek game hide in the same spot. When the seeker comes looking, everyone gets caught and the game is over.

The Purpose of Portfolio Diversification

The fundamental purpose of portfolio diversification is to minimize the risk on your investments; specifically unsystematic risk.

Unsystematic risk—also known as specific risk—is risk that is related to a specific company or market segment. By diversifying your portfolio, this is the risk you hope to cut. This way, all your investments would not be uniformly affected in the same way by market events.

Diversify your Portfolio

Here are a few interesting ways that you can diversify your portfolio to reduce the risk and increase your wealth.

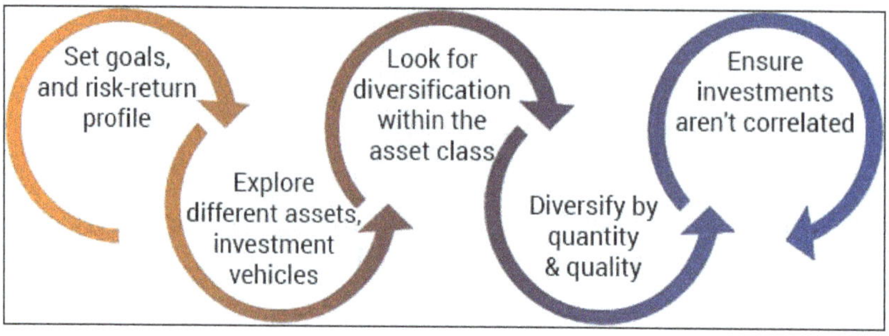

Spread Out your Investments

Investing in equities is good but that doesn't mean you should put all your wealth in a single stock or a single sector. The same applies to your investments in other options like Fixed Deposits, Mutual Funds or gold too.

For instance, you might invest in six stocks. But if the whole market suddenly takes a tumble, you could have a problem. This problem is compounded if the stocks belonged to the same sector like manufacturing. This is because any news item or information that affects the performance of one manufacturing stock could as well affect the other stocks in some way or other.

So, even if you choose the same asset, you can diversify by investing in different sectors and industries. There are so many different industries and sectors to explore with exciting opportunities like pharmaceuticals, Information Technology (IT), consumer goods, mining, aeronautics, energy and so on.

Explore other Investment Avenues

You could also add other investment options and assets to your portfolio. Mutual funds, bonds, real estate and pension plans are other investments you can consider. Also, make sure that the securities vary in risk and follow different market trends.

It has been generally observed that the bond and equity markets have contrasting movements. So, by investing in both these avenues, you can offset any negative results in one market by positive movements in the other. This way, you can ensure that you are not in a lose-lose situation.

Limits of Diversification

Many investors are curious about the ideal number of stocks, mutual funds and other investments they should have in the portfolio for ideal diversification. Clearly, it is better to own 7 stocks or MFs than to own just one or two. But where should you draw the line?

In reality, there is no fixed number. This is because, after a certain point, adding more stocks or MFs to your portfolio may not make any major difference. In fact, over-diversification could result in lower returns due to lost opportunities. In this regard, most experts say that anywhere between 15-20 stocks spread across multiple industries and sectors is appropriate. You can extend this rule to MFs and other investments too.

Diversification doesn't mean that you don't face any losses. After the entire process, it is still possible to lose some money when you invest. After all, it is not possible to eliminate risk completely. However, diversification helps you to lower the risk of losses in the market to the minimum possible.

Try to find a good balance between risk and return so that you can earn good returns without worrying constantly about your portfolio.

Primary Components of a Diversified Portfolio

Domestic Stocks

Stocks represent the most aggressive portion of your portfolio and provide the opportunity for higher growth over the long term. However, this greater potential for growth carries a greater risk, particularly in the short term. Because stocks are generally more volatile than other types of assets, your investment in a stock could be worth less if and when you decide to sell it.

Bonds

Most bonds provide regular interest income and are generally considered to be less volatile than stocks. They can also act as a cushion against the unpredictable ups and downs of the stock market, as they often behave differently than stocks. Investors who are more focused on safety than growth often favor US Treasury or other high-quality bonds, while reducing their exposure to stocks. These investors may have to accept lower long-term returns, as many bonds—especially high-quality issues—generally don't offer returns as high as stocks over the long term. However, note that some fixed income investments, like high-yield bonds and certain international bonds, can offer much higher yields, albeit with more risk.

Short-term Investments

These include money market funds and short-term CDs (certificates of deposit). Money market funds are conservative investments that offer stability and easy access to your money, ideal for those looking to preserve principal. In exchange for that level of safety, money market funds usually provide lower returns than bond funds or individual bonds. While money market funds are considered safer and more conservative, however, they are not insured or guaranteed by the Federal Deposit Insurance Corporation (FDIC) the way many CDs are. When you invest in CDs though, you may sacrifice the liquidity generally offered by money market funds.

You could lose money by investing in a money market fund. Although the fund seeks to preserve the value of your investment at $1.00 per share, it cannot guarantee it will do so. The Fund may impose a fee upon the sale of your shares or may temporarily suspend your ability to sell shares if the Fund's liquidity falls below required minimums because of market conditions or other factors. An investment in the fund is not insured or guaranteed by the Federal Deposit Insurance Corporation or any other government agency. Fidelity Investments and its affiliates, the fund's sponsor, have no legal obligation to provide financial support to the fund, and you should not expect that the sponsor will provide financial support to the fund at any time.

International Stocks

Stocks issued by non-US companies often perform differently than their US counterparts, providing exposure to opportunities not offered by US securities. If you're searching for investments that offer both higher potential returns and higher risk, you may want to consider adding some foreign stocks to your portfolio.

Additional Components of a Diversified Portfolio

Sector Funds

Although these invest in stocks, sector funds, as their name suggests, focus on a particular segment of the economy. They can be valuable tools for investors seeking opportunities in different phases of the economic cycle.

Commodity-focused Funds

While only the most experienced investors should invest in commodities, adding equity funds that focus on commodity-intensive industries to your portfolio—such as oil and gas, mining, and natural resources—can provide a good hedge against inflation.

Real Estate Funds

Real estate funds, including real estate investment trusts (REITs), can also play a role in diversifying your portfolio and providing some protection against the risk of inflation.

Asset Allocation Funds

For investors who don't have the time or the expertise to build a diversified portfolio, asset allocation funds can serve as an effective single-fund strategy. Fidelity manages a number of different types of these funds, including funds that are managed to a specific target date, funds that are managed to maintain a specific asset allocation, funds that are managed to generate income, and funds that are managed in anticipation of specific outcomes, such as inflation.

Reducing the Impact of Market Volatility

The primary goal of diversification isn't to maximize returns. Its primary goal is to limit the impact of volatility on a portfolio. To better understand this concept, look at the charts below, which depict hypothetical portfolios with different asset allocations. The average annual return for each portfolio from 1926 through 2015, including reinvested dividends and other earnings, is noted, as are the best and worst 20-year returns.

The most aggressive portfolio shown comprises 60% domestic stocks, 25% international stocks, and 15% bonds: it had an average annual return of 9.65%. Its best 12-month return was 136%, while its worst 12-month return would have lost nearly 61%. That's probably too much volatility for most investors to endure.

Changing the asset allocation slightly, however, tightened the range of those swings without giving up too much in the way of long-term performance. For instance, a portfolio with an allocation of 49% domestic stocks, 21% international stocks, 25% bonds, and 5% short-term investments would have generated average annual returns of almost 9% over the same period, albeit with a narrower range of extremes on the high and low end. As you can see when looking at the other asset allocations, adding more fixed income investments to a portfolio will slightly reduce one's expectations for long-term returns, but may significantly reduce the impact of market volatility. This is a trade-off many investors feel is worthwhile, particularly as they get older and more risk-averse.

The impact of asset allocation on long-term performance and short-term volatility.

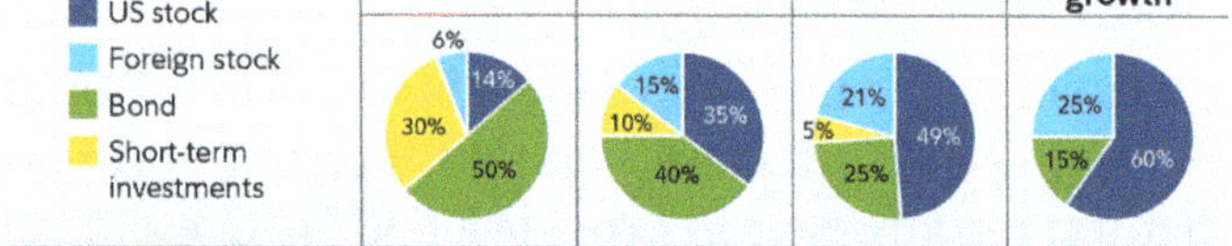

	Conservative	Balanced	Growth	Aggressive growth
Annual return %				
Average annual return	5.96%	7.96%	8.97%	9.65%
Best 12-month return	31.06%	76.57%	109.55%	136.07%
Worst 12-month return	-17.67%	-40.64%	-52.92%	-60.78%
Best 20-year return (annualized)	10.98%	13.83%	15.34%	16.49%
Worst 20-year return (annualized)	2.92%	3.43%	3.10%	2.66%

Asset mix performance figures are based on the weighted average of annual return figures for certain benchmarks for each asset class represented. Historical returns and volatility of the stock, bond, and short-term asset classes are based on the historical performance data of various indexes from 1926 through the most recent year-end data available from Morningstar. Domestic stocks represented by S&P 500 1926 – 1986, Dow Jones U.S. Total Market 1987– most recent year end; foreign stock represented by S&P 500 1926 – 1969, MSCI EAFE 1970 – 2000, MSCI ACWI Ex USA 2001 – most recent year end; bonds represented by U.S. intermediate-term bonds 1926 – 1975, Barclays U.S. Aggregate Bond 1976 – most recent year end; short term represented by 30-day U.S. Treasury bills 1926 – most recent year end. It is not possible to invest directly in an index. Although past performance does not guarantee future results, it may be useful in comparing alternative investment strategies over the long term. Performance returns for actual investments will generally be reduced by fees and expenses not reflected in these investments' hypothetical illustrations. Indexes are unmanaged.Generally, among asset classes, stocks are more volatile than bonds or short-term instruments and can decline significantly in response to adverse issuer, political, regulatory, market, or economic developments. Although the bond market is also volatile, lower-quality debt securities, including leveraged loans, generally offer higher yields compared with investment-grade securities, but also involve greater risk of default or price changes. Foreign markets can be more volatile than U.S. markets due to increased risks of adverse issuer, political, market, or economic developments, all of which are magnified in emerging markets.

Factoring Time into your Diversification Strategy

People are accustomed to thinking about their savings in terms of goals: retirement, college, a down payment, or a vacation. But as you build and manage your asset allocation—regardless of which goal you're pursuing—there are 2 important things to consider. The first is the number of years until you expect to need the money—also known as your time horizon. The second is your attitude toward risk—also known as your risk tolerance.

For instance, think about a goal that's 25 years away, like retirement. Because your time horizon is fairly long, you may be willing to take on additional risk in pursuit of long-term growth, under the assumption that you'll usually have time to regain lost ground in the event of a short-term market decline. In that case, a higher exposure to domestic and international stocks may be appropriate.

But here's where your risk tolerance becomes a factor. Regardless of your time horizon, you should only take on a level of risk with which you're comfortable. So even if you're saving for a long-term goal, if you're more risk-averse you may want to consider a more balanced portfolio with some fixed income investments. And regardless of your time horizon and risk tolerance, even if you're pursuing the most aggressive asset allocation models, you may want to consider including a fixed income component to help reduce the overall volatility of your portfolio.

The other thing to remember about your time horizon is that it's constantly changing. So, let's say your retirement is now 10 years away instead of 25 years—you may want to reallocate your assets to help reduce your exposure to higher-risk investments in favor of more conservative ones, like bond or money market funds. This can help mitigate the impact of extreme market swings on your portfolio, which is important when you expect to need the money relatively soon.

Once you've entered retirement, a large portion of your portfolio should be in more stable, lower-risk investments that can potentially generate income. But even in retirement, diversification is key to helping you manage risk. At this point in your life, your biggest risk is outliving your assets. So just as you should never be 100% invested in stocks, it's probably a good idea to never be 100% allocated in short-term investments if your time horizon is greater than one year. After all, even in retirement you will need a certain exposure to growth-oriented investments to combat inflation and help ensure your assets last for what could be a decades-long retirement.

Regardless of your goal, your time horizon, or your risk tolerance, a diversified portfolio is the foundation of any smart investment strategy.

Types of Portfolio Diversification

Across Asset Class

You might want to diversify your investments in different asset classes like equity (mutual funds, stocks), Real estate, Debt products, commodities like gold, silver and finally Cash. Its important to do this kind of diversification if you are not an expert in one asset class and can not handle it fully.

Within Asset Class

When you invest your money in one asset class but in different kind of instrument or company, you are diversifying it across various instruments of same types. A very simple example is opening Fixed Deposits in various banks. If you had to open a 10 lacs FD, the chances are you will choose 4 banks and put 2.5 lacs in each rather than doing it for 10 lacs in just one bank. In the same way some one investing in 5 different equity mutual funds. While the underlying asset class is exactly same (equities), but still some kind of diversification is there (different fund managers handling it).

Geography Wise

Then you can diversify location wise or geography wise. You can invest in real estate in India, US, UK You can also invest in real estate across different cities India. You can buy stocks in US stock markets and other countries too. The idea is to take advantage of currencies fluctuations too, but this is only for experts who understand that.

Across Capitalization

When you invest in mutual funds, you can choose to invest in small cap funds, large cap funds, extra large cap funds, small companies, big companies, etc. Note that the risk and return potential will be different and anyways you will invest in different companies.

Across Time

Your investments can be across time also, like long term investments, short term investments, medium term investments, You can have a 5 yrs deposit, 2 yrs deposit and 6 months deposit as well Imagine if you have done 5 yrs deposits only – which can affect your liquidity

Across Style

There can be diversification across styles – You can invest in products giving you fixed income, or which are just for growth purpose. You can invest in some thing which has value investing principles or more of speculative idea's.

Importance of Diversification in Investing

The benefit of diversification in your investments is to minimize the risk of a bad event taking out your entire portfolio. When you keep a high percentage of your portfolio in a single type of investment, you risk losing it if that investment sours.

There's also the "opportunity cost of not being diversified," Nauman says. "If you're not diversified, you may miss out on growth opportunities in a different asset class that you are not exposed to."

When you're invested in the winning team, however, diversification can feel like a punishment. It's hard to keep money in a lagging – or worse: a declining – investment when your other investments are doing so much better. But it's important to remember that today's top-performer may become tomorrow's fallen star.

"During a bull market, it can be easy to forget that the market delights in surprises," Dabit says. "The best safeguard against market cycles, while still benefiting from the upside, is through committing to a well-diversified portfolio and long-term focus."

Diversification is important regardless of your time horizon and goal. Any time you're investing in the stock market, you should aim for a diversified portfolio.

As your goals or timeframe change, "the levers to shift should be on how aggressive that diversified portfolio is built," Dabit says. Investments allocated to a long-term goal can lean more heavily on stocks, for instance, than those geared toward near-term goals. But even if you're 80% stocks, you should diversify those stock holdings across sectors, regions and size.

Diversify your Portfolio

Contrary to sometime-popular belief, diversification is not a number's game. He who owns the most investments doesn't necessarily win the crown. The trick to diversifying your portfolio is owning investments that play different roles on your team.

Think about diversification as building a baseball team. A team of only right fielders – even if you had 100 of them – won't do you much good in a game. To have a well-rounded team, you need outfielders and infielders, pitchers and a catcher. Likewise with your portfolio.

Each investment in your portfolio should serve a different function. For instance, for stock diversification you may have an S&P 500 index fund for exposure to U.S. large-cap stocks and another focused on small-cap stocks. You'd want domestic companies and international, and representatives from all 11 market sectors.

Your bond portfolio should be similarly diversified across "both short and long term bonds, corporates and sovereign debt, and high and lower quality bonds, to help reduce the inherent risks associated with fixed income products," Nauman says.

For optimal diversification of risk in a portfolio, Ed Egilinsky, managing director and head of Alternative Investments at Direxion in New York City, says to consider alternative investments such as commodities. Alternatives don't have a "high degree of correlation to traditional investments" like stocks and bonds.

When stocks and bonds are stuck moving up and down, alternatives can move diagonally. They're a bit like taking the escalator instead of the elevator to your goals. With alternative investments in your portfolio, you're less likely to get trapped between floors.

Tell if you're Diversified

An easy way to determine if your portfolio is diversified is by looking at your current performance. Diversified investments won't move in the same direction at the same time. If some of your investments are up while others are down, you've got diversification. Think of diversification as a Christmas tree: Red and green together means you'll fair better in all weather.

Disadvantages of Diversification in Investing

Reduces Quality

There are only so many quality companies and even less that are priced at levels that provide a margin of safety. The more stocks you put into your portfolio the less concentrated your portfolio will be in the best opportunities.

Too Complicated

Many investors include so many assets in their portfolio they don't really understand what's in them. Diversification in investing is important, but keep your portfolio simple enough that you can stay on top of your investments.

Indexing

If you have too many assets in your portfolio it essentially becomes an index fund. If you want an index fund, buy an index fund; don't waste transaction fees on purchasing numerous assets that morph into an index fund.

The more stocks you own the more correlated your portfolio will be to market returns. While passive management or indexing might work in bull markets it does not work well in flat or bear markets. Most indices are skewed toward stocks that have already risen and underweight stocks that have fallen, and may be at bargain prices.

Market Risk

Before you buy an index fund be sure you understand the mathematics of how portfolio volatility lowers your portfolio performance. Few investors ever achieve even close to "average" returns because of volatility caused by market risk.

Below Average Returns

Indexing and over diversification are disadvantages of diversification because quality suffers when you own inferior investments along with good investments. Below average returns result from transaction fees or high mutual fund fees. In addition to portfolio volatility lowering returns, many investors let their emotions cause them to buy high and sell low.

Bad Investment Vehicles

Most investors who over diversify use investment vehicles such as index funds, or even worse, actively traded mutual funds. Actively managed mutual funds trade in and out of stocks and have a tendency to focus on short term trading instead of value. Studies show these funds underperform market indices in the long run.

Lack of Focus or Attention to your Portfolio

If someone else is managing your portfolio you probably don't pay as much attention to it, or you wait until it's too late (i.e. after your quarterly statement arrives).

Proper Diversification

Allocate your money based on valuation and not some wall street manufactured formula. That may mean holding more cash when bargains are not available. Over diversification is common in ETFs and mutual funds. When purchasing stocks stick to the highest quality companies priced at valuations that put the odds of success heavily in your favor.

You can avoid the disadvantages of diversification in investing by managing your own portfolio. Diversification is one of the most important concepts in investment portfolio management, but proper diversification is the key. While building your portfolio keep in mind the disadvantages of diversification in investing to help you achieve optimal diversification.

References

- Portfoliomanagement: investopedia.com, Retrieved 2 February, 2019
- Portfolio-management, investments: seniorfinanceadvisor.com, Retrieved 12 August, 2019
- Active-portfolio-management-strategy: portfoliomanagement.in, Retrieved 1 April, 2019
- Passive-portfolio-management-strategy: portfoliomanagement.in, Retrieved 11 January, 2019
- Portfolio-volatility: thenest.com, Retrieved 15 June, 2019
- Expectedreturn: investopedia.com, Retrieved 18 May, 2019
- Portfolio-planning-process-step-step, company-insights: investopedia.com, Retrieved 8 April, 2019
- Business-portfolio-management-definition-example: study.com, Retrieved 28 February, 2019
- Portfolio-management-strategies: portfoliomanagement.in, Retrieved 9 January, 2019
- Activemanagement: investopedia.com, Retrieved 19 August, 2019
- Portfolio-management-process-steps-ensure-smart-investment: niveza.in, Retrieved 26 April, 2019
- Leveraged-portfolio: investorwords.com, Retrieved 6 January, 2019
- Leverage: investopedia.com, Retrieved 21 March, 2019
- Optimal-portfolio: investorwords.com, Retrieved 30 May, 2019
- The-optimal-portfolio: greekshares.com, Retrieved 25 June, 2019
- What-is-portfolio-diversification, introduction-to-investing: edelweiss.in, Retrieved 5 February, 2019
- Diversification, mutual-funds, investment-products: fidelity.com, Retrieved 15 March, 2019
- Portfolio-diversification-strategies: jagoinvestor.com, Retrieved 19 July, 2019
- Why-diversification-is-important-in-investing, investing: usnews.com, Retrieved 7 March, 2019
- Disadvantages-of-diversification-in-investing: arborinvestmentplanner.com, Retrieved 12 July, 2019

4

Asset and Asset Allocation

Any resource which is owned by the business, and which is expected to generate cash flow in the future is known as an asset. Assets are usually classified on the basis of their convertibility, usage and physical existence. The chapter closely examines these key concepts of assets and their allocation to provide an extensive understanding of the subject.

Assets

An asset is a resource with economic value that an individual, corporation or country owns or controls with the expectation that it will provide a future benefit. Assets are reported on a company's balance sheet and are bought or created to increase a firm's value or benefit the firm's operations.

An asset can be thought of as something that, in the future, can generate cash flow, reduce expenses, or improve sales, regardless of whether it's manufacturing equipment or a patent.

An asset represents an economic resource for a company or represents access that other individuals or firms do not have. A right or other access is legally enforceable, which means economic resources can be used at a company's discretion, and its use can be precluded or limited by an owner.

For an asset to be present, a company must possess a right to it as of the date of the financial statements. An economic resource is something that is scarce and has the ability to produce economic benefit by generating cash inflows or decreasing cash outflows.

Assets can be broadly categorized into short-term (or current) assets, fixed assets, financial investments, and intangible assets.

Examples of Assets

Current Assets

Current assets are short-term economic resources that are expected to be converted into cash within one year. Current assets include cash and cash equivalents, accounts receivable, inventory, and various prepaid expenses.

While cash is easy to value, accountants periodically reassess the recoverability of inventory and accounts receivable. If there is evidence that accounts receivable might be uncollectible, it'll become impaired. Or if inventory becomes obsolete, companies may write off these assets.

Fixed Assets

Fixed assets are long-term resources, such as plants, equipment, and buildings. An adjustment for the aging of fixed assets is made based on periodic charges called depreciation, which may or may not reflect the loss of earning powers for a fixed asset.

Generally accepted accounting principles (GAAP) allow depreciation under two broad methods. The straight-line method assumes that a fixed asset loses its value in proportion to its useful life, while the accelerated method assumes that the asset loses its value faster in its first years of use.

Financial Assets

Financial assets represent investments in the assets and securities of other institutions. Financial assets include stocks, sovereign and corporate bonds, preferred equity, and other hybrid securities. Financial assets are valued depending on how the investment is categorized and the motive behind it.

Intangible Assets

Intangible assets are economic resources that have no physical presence. They include patents, trademarks, copyrights, and goodwill. Accounting for intangible assets differs depending on the type of asset, and they can be either amortized or tested for impairment each year.

Balance Sheet

The balance sheet is one of the three fundamental financial statements and is key to both financial modeling and accounting. The balance sheet displays the company's total assets, and how these assets are financed, through either debt or equity. It can also be referred to as a statement of net worth, or a statement of financial position. The balance sheet is based on the fundamental equation: Assets = Liabilities + Equity.

As such, the balance sheet is divided into two sides. The left side of the balance sheet outlines all a company's assets. On the right side, the balance sheet outlines the companies liabilities and shareholders' equity. On either side, the main line items are generally classified by liquidity. More liquid accounts like Inventory, Cash, and Trades Payables are placed before illiquid accounts such as Plant, Property, and Equipment (PP&E) and Long-Term Debt. The assets and liabilities are also separated into two categories: current asset/liabilities and non-current (long-term) assets/liabilities.

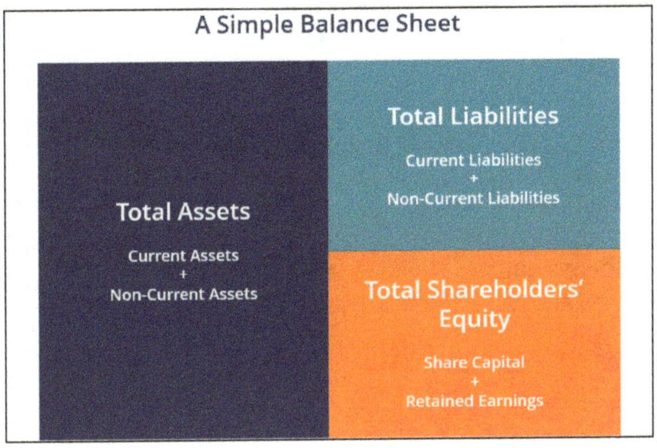

Balance Sheet Example

It starts with current assets, then non-current assets and total assets. Below that is liabilities and stockholders' equity which includes current liabilities, non-current liabilities, and finally shareholders' equity.

CONSOLIDATED BALANCE SHEETS
(in millions, except per share data)

	December 31,	
	2016	2017
ASSETS		
Current assets:	$ 19,334	$ 20,522
Cash and cash equivalents	6,647	10,464
Marketable securities	11,461	16,047
Inventories	8,339	13,164
Accounts receivable, net and other	45,781	60,197
Total current assets	29,114	48,866
Property and equipment, net	3,784	13,350
Goodwill	4,723	8,897
Other assets	83,402	$ 131,310
Total assets		
LIABILITIES AND STOCKHOLDERS' EOCITY		
Current liabilities:	$ 25,309	$ 34,616
Accounts payable	13,739	18,170
Accrued expenses and other	4,768	5,097
Unearned revenue	43,816	57,883
Total current liabilities	7,694	24,743
Long-term debt	12,607	20,975
Other long-term liabilities		
Commitments and contingencies		
Stockholders' equity:		
Preferred stock $0.01 par value:		

Authorized shares – 500	–	–
Issued and outstanding shares-none - -		
Common stock $0.01 par value:		
Authorized shares - 5,000		
Issued shares - 500 and 507		
Outstanding shares - 477 and 484	5	5
Treasury stock, at cost	(1,837)	(1,837)
Additional paid-in capital	17,186	21,389
Accumulated other comprehensive loss	(985)	(484)
Retained earnings	4,916	8.636
Total stockholders' equity	19,285	27.709
Total liabilities and stockholders' equity	$ 83,402	$ 131.310

Structure of Balance Sheet

Balance sheets, like all financial statements, will have minor differences between organizations and industries. However, there are several "buckets" and line items that are almost always included in common balance sheets. We briefly go through commonly found line items under Current Assets, Long-Term Assets, Current Liabilities, Long-Term Liabilities, and Equity.

Current Assets

Cash and Equivalents

The most liquid of all assets, cash, appears on the first line of the balance sheet. Cash Equivalents are also lumped under this line item and include assets that have short-term maturities under three months or assets that the company can liquidate on short notice, such as marketable securities. Companies will generally disclose what equivalents it includes in the footnotes to the balance sheet.

Accounts Receivable

This account includes the balance of all sales revenue still on credit, net of any allowances for doubtful accounts (which generates a bad debt expense). As companies recover accounts receivables, this account decreases and cash increases by the same amount.

Inventory

Inventory includes amounts for raw materials, work-in-progress goods, and finished goods. The company uses this account when it reports sales of goods, generally under cost of goods sold in the income statement.

Non-Current Assets

Plant, Property and Equipment (PP&E)

Property, Plant, and Equipment (also known as PP&E) capture the company's tangible fixed assets. This line item is noted net of depreciation. Some companies will class out their PP&E by the different types of assets, such as Land, Building, and various types of Equipment. All PP&E is depreciable except for Land.

Intangible Assets

This line item will include all of the companies intangible fixed assets, which may or may not be identifiable. Identifiable intangible assets include patents, licenses, and secret formulas. Unidentifiable intangible assets include brand and goodwill.

Current Liabilities

Accounts Payable

Accounts Payables, or AP, is the amount a company owes suppliers for items or services purchased on credit. As the company pays off their AP, it decreases along with an equal amount decrease to the cash account.

Current Debt/Notes Payable

Includes non-AP obligations that are due within one year time or within one operating cycle for the company (whichever is longest). Notes payable may also have a long-term version, which includes notes with a maturity of more than one year.

Current Portion of Long-Term Debt

This account may or may not be lumped together with the above account, Current Debt. While they may seem similar, the current portion of long-term debt is specifically the portion due within this year of a piece of debt that has a maturity of more than one year. For example, if a company takes on a bank loan to be paid off in 5-years, this account will include the portion of that loan due in the next year.

Non-Current Liabilities

Bonds Payable

This account includes the amortized amount of any bonds the company has issued.

Long-Term Debt

This account includes the total amount of long-term debt (Excluding the current portion, if that account is present under current liabilities). This account is derived from the debt schedule, which outlines all the companies outstanding debt, the interest expense and the principal repayment for every period.

Shareholders' Equity

Share Capital

This is the value of funds that shareholders have invested in the company. When a company is first formed, shareholders will typically put in cash. For example, an investor starts a company and seeds it with $10M. Cash (an asset) rises by $10M, and Share Capital (an equity account) rises by $10M, balancing out the balance sheet.

Retained Earnings

This is the total amount of net income the company decides to keep. Every period, a company may pay out dividends from its net income. Any amount remaining (or exceeding) is added to (deducted from) retained earnings.

Uses of Balance Sheet in Financial Modeling

This statement is a great way to analyze a company's financial position. An analyst can generally use the balance sheet to calculate a lot of financial ratios that can determine how well a company is performing, how liquid or solvent a company is, and how efficient it is.

Changes in balance sheet accounts are also used to calculate cash flow in the cash flow statement. For example, a positive change in plant, property, and equipment is equal to capital expenditure minus depreciation expense. If depreciation expense is known, capital expenditure can be calculated and included as a cash outflow under cash flow from investing in the cash flow statement.

Financial Model	Historical Result				Forecast Period				
	2014	2015	2016	2017	2018	2019	2020	2021	2022
Balance Sheet									
Assets									
Cash	81,210	83,715	111,069	139,550	159,474	182,573	190,511	224,399	261,248
Accounts Receivable	5,904	6,567	7,117	7,539	8,179	8,997	9,896	10,758	11,650
Inventory	9,601	9,825	10,531	11,342	15,267	19,343	24,191	26,894	29,772
Current Assets	96,715	100,107	128,717	150,430	182,920	210,913	224,599	262,051	302,670
Property & Equipment	42,350	40,145	38602	37,521	45,017	51,013	55,811	59,649	62,719
Goodwill									
Total Assets	139,065	140,252	167,319	195,951	227,937	261,927	280,410	321,700	365,389
Liabilities									

Short Term Debt									
Accounts Payable	4,800	4,912	5,265	5,671	7,061	7,952	8,951	9,951	11,016
Current Liabilities	4,800	4,912	5,265	5,671	7,061	7,952	8,951	9,951	11,016
Long Term Debt	50,000	30,000	30,000	30,000	30,000	30,000	10,000	10,000	10,000
Total Liabilities	54,800	34,912	35,265	35,671	37,061	37,952	18,951	19,951	21,016
Shareholder's Equity									
Equity Capital	70,000	70,000	70,000	70,000	70,000	70,000	70,000	70,000	70,000
Retained Earnings	14,265	35,340	62,053	90,280	120,876	153,974	191,459	231,749	274,373
Shareholder's Equity	84,265	105,340	132,053	160,280	190,876	223,974	261,459	301,749	344,373
Total Liabilities & Shareholder's Equity	139,065	140,252	167,319	195,951	227,937	261,927	280,410	231,700	365,389
Check	0.0000	0.0000	0.0000	0.0000	0.0000	0.0000	0.0000	0.0000	0.0000

Importance of the Balance Sheet

The balance sheet is a very important financial statement for many reasons. It can be looked at on its own, and in conjunction with other statements like the income statement and cash flow statement to get a full picture of a company's health.

Important Takeaways Include:

1. Liquidity: Comparing a company's current assets to its current liabilities provides a picture of liquidity. Current assets should be greater than current liabilities so the company can cover its short-term obligations. The Current Ratio and Quick Ratio are examples of liquidity financial metrics.

2. Leverage: Looking at how a company is financed indicates how much leverage it has, which in turn indicates how much financial risk the company is taking. Comparing debt to equity and debt to total capital are common ways of assessing leverage on the balance sheet.

3. Efficiency: By using the income statement in connection with the balance sheet it's possible to assess how efficiently a company uses its assets. For example, dividing revenue into fixed assets produces the Asset Turnover Ratio to indicate how efficiently the company turns assets into revenue. Additionally, the working capital cycle shows how well a company manages its cash in the short term.

4. Rates of Return: The balance sheet can be used to evaluate how well a company generates returns. For example, dividing net income into shareholders' equity produces Return on Equity (ROE), and dividing net income into total assets produces Return on Assets (ROA), and dividing net income into debt plus equity results in Return on Invested Capital (ROIC).

Types of Assets

Common types of assets include: current, non-current, physical, intangible, operating, and non-operating. Correctly identifying and classifying the types of assets is critical to the survival of a company, specifically its solvency and associated risks.

The International Financial Reporting Standards (IFRS) Framework defines an asset as follows: "An asset is a resource controlled by the enterprise as a result of past events and from which future economic benefits are expected to flow to the enterprise."

Examples of assets include:

- Cash and cash equivalents,
- Inventory,
- Investments,
- PPE (Property, Plant, and Equipment),
- Land,
- Buildings,
- Vehicles,
- Furniture,
- Patents,
- Stock,
- Equipment.

Properties of an Asset

There are three key properties of an asset:

- Ownership: Assets represent ownership that can be eventually turned into cash and cash equivalents.

- Economic Value: Assets have economic value and can be exchanged or sold.
- Resource: Assets are resources that can be used to generate future economic benefits.

Classification of Assets

Assets are generally classified in three ways:

- Convertibility: Classifying assets based on how easy it is to convert them into cash.
- Physical Existence: Classifying assets based on their physical existence.
- Usage: Classifying assets based on their business operation usage.

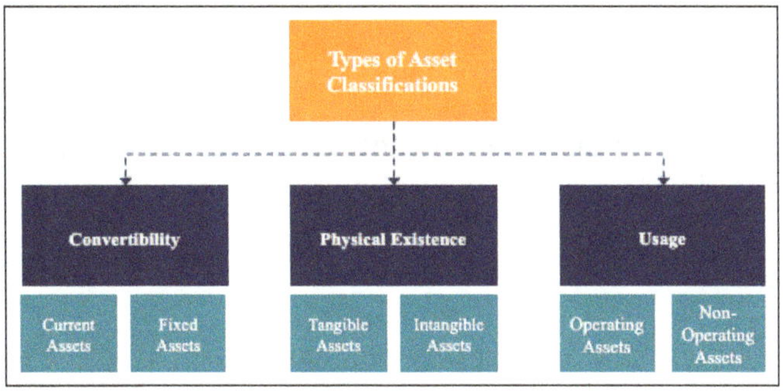

Classification of Assets: Convertibility

If assets are classified based on their convertibility into cash, assets are classified as either current assets or fixed assets.

Current Assets

Current assets are assets that can be easily converted into cash and cash equivalents (typically within a year). Current assets are also termed liquid assets and examples of such are:

- Cash,
- Cash equivalents,
- Short-term deposits,
- Stock,
- Marketable securities,
- Office supplies.

Fixed or Non-Current Assets

Non-current assets are assets that cannot be easily and readily converted into cash and cash equivalents. Non-current assets are also termed fixed assets, long-term assets, or hard assets. Examples of non-current or fixed assets include:

- Land,
- Building,
- Machinery,
- Equipment,
- Patents,
- Trademarks.

Classification of Assets: Physical Existence

If assets are classified based on their physical existence, assets are classified as either tangible assets or intangible assets.

Tangible Assets

Tangible assets are assets that have a physical existence (we can touch, feel, and see). Examples of tangible assets include:

- Land,
- Building,
- Machinery,
- Equipment,
- Cash,
- Office supplies,
- Stock,
- Marketable securities.

Intangible Assets

Intangible assets are assets that do not have a physical existence. Examples of intangible assets include:

- Goodwill,
- Patents,

- Brand,
- Copyrights,
- Trademarks,
- Trade secrets,
- Permits,
- Corporate intellectual property.

Classification of Assets: Usage

If assets are classified based on their operational usage, assets are classified as either operating assets or non-operating assets.

Operating Assets

Operating assets are assets that are required in the daily operation of a business. In other words, operating assets are used to generate revenue. Examples of operating assets include:

- Cash,
- Stock,
- Building,
- Machinery,
- Equipment,
- Patents,
- Copyrights,
- Goodwill.

Non-Operating Assets

Non-operating assets are assets that are not required for daily business operations but can still generate revenue. Examples of non-operating assets include:

- Short-term investments.
- Marketable securities.
- Vacant land.
- Interest income from a fixed deposit.

Importance of Asset Classification

Classifying assets is important to a business. For example, understanding which assets are current assets and which are fixed assets is important in understanding the net working capital of a company. In the scenario of a company in a high-risk industry, understanding which assets are tangible and intangible will help it determine its solvency and risk. Determining which assets are operating assets and which assets are non-operating assets is important to understanding the contribution of revenue from each asset. Therefore, knowing how to classify assets is integral to business success.

Stranded Asset

Stranded assets are "assets that have suffered from unanticipated or premature write-downs, devaluations or conversion to liabilities". Stranded assets can be caused by a variety of factors and are a phenomenon inherent in the 'creative destruction' of economic growth, transformation and innovation, as such they pose risks to individuals and firms and may have systemic implications. Coal and other hydrocarbon resources may have the potential to become stranded as the world engages in a fossil fuel phase out.

The term is important to financial risk management in order to avoid economic loss after an asset has been converted to a liability. Accountants have measures to deal with the impairment of assets (e.g. IAS 16) which seek to ensure that an entity's assets are not carried at more than their recoverable amount. In this context, stranded assets are also defined as an asset that has become obsolete or non-performing, but must be recorded on the balance sheet as a loss of profit.

Toxic Asset

Toxic assets are financial assets that are now worth considerably less than they used to be, will likely continue falling in value, and for which the market has frozen, i.e. there is no longer a functioning market for them.

The holder of a toxic asset finds that it is no longer possible to sell it at a satisfactory price.

Toxic assets featured as major problems among many banks and financial institutions during the 2007/8 global financial crisis, including securitizations of subprime mortgages where the creators of the securities did not take into account the true rate of mortgage default, and how contagious this would become across securities.

Markets for several toxic assets froze during the last financial crisis. The problem started in 2007 and gradually got worse, so that by mid-2008 the world was facing a devastating financial meltdown.

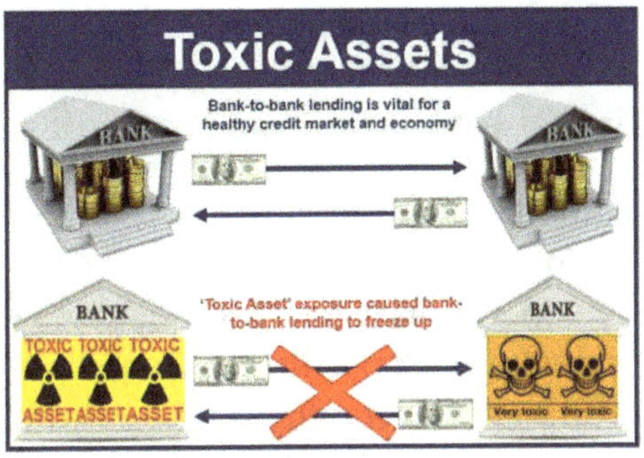

Toxic assets pushed the global economy to the edge of an abyss.

Assets with a AAA rating were suddenly no better than junks bonds – within a matter of months their value plummeted.

Holders Fear Selling Toxic Assets

The freezing of toxic asset markets occurred because of several factors. The assets' values were extremely sensitive to economic conditions, and growing uncertainty and pessimism in these conditions made it hard to estimate their value.

Financial institutions did not want to sell the assets at super knock-down prices – if they did, they would be forced to considerably reduce their stated assets, which would make them (on paper) insolvent.

Example of a Toxic Asset

Imagine Fred Smith purchases a house with a $500,000 mortgage loan through XYZ Bank, which charges a 5% interest rate. XYZ now has a mortgage-backed security – this is an asset.

ABC Bank buys the asset from XYZ and receives the 5% interest paid by Mr. Smith. As long as Mr. Smith keeps up with his installments, it is a good asset.

If Mr. Smith defaults on the loan, the owner of the mortgage-backed security (ABC Bank) will stop receiving the payments. The bank will take possession of the house and sell it. However, if house prices have declined, it will only recover a fraction of the money.

Nobody is going to want to buy that asset, because it is a money-looser. It has become a toxic asset.

Hidden Asset

Hidden assets are those which are purposefully secreted from disclosure to another. The issue of hidden assets commonly arises in tax and divorce matters, among others. For example, in dividing assets and payments between spouses seeking a divorce, a court often requires a financial disclosure statement to be filed by the parties. One of the parties may seek to misrepresent their financial status by hiding assets through various means, such as filing false documents and conveying assets to third parties.

The discovery of such hidden assets is often difficult and expensive. There are court procedures that may be employed to obtain discovery of such assets. The party seeking the information must seek cooperation from the other side; wait for results from interrogatories, subpoenas, and requests to produce. Often, a private investigator is hired. Sometimes, it is only by setting aside or modifying the existing judgment of divorce that can the aggrieved party receive some relief. Therefore, parties may include a "disclosure clause" in the divorce judgment saying all property has been disclosed by both parties. Language may be included that if a party does not reveal an asset, it may be subject to further discovery and future division as part of the marital property. In such cases, the property settlement involving known assets is final; however, if newly discovered evidence shows the parties undervalued or overvalued the marital estate, the aggrieved party has a basis to re-open the judgment or start a new lawsuit.

Capital Asset

Capital assets are significant pieces of property such as homes, cars, investment properties, stocks, bonds, and even collectibles or art. For businesses, a capital asset is a tangible asset with a useful life longer than a year that is not intended for sale in the regular course of the business's operation. For example, if one company buys a computer to use in its office, the computer is a capital asset. If another company buys the same computer to sell, it is considered inventory.

Businesses and Capital Assets

A capital asset is generally owned for its role in contributing to the business's ability to generate profit. Furthermore, it is expected that the benefits gained from the asset will extend beyond a time span of one year. On a business's balance sheet, capital assets are represented by the property, plant, and equipment (PP&E) figure.

Examples of PP&E include land, buildings, and machinery. These assets may be liquidated in worst-case scenarios, such as if a company is restructuring or declares bankruptcy. In other cases, a business disposes of capital assets if the business is growing and needs something better. For example, a business may sell one property and buy a larger one in a better location.

Businesses may dispose of capital assets by selling them, trading them, abandoning them, or losing them in foreclosures. In some cases, condemnation also counts as a disposition. In most cases, if the business owned the asset for longer than a year, it incurs a capital gain or loss on the sale. However, in some instances, the IRS treats the gain like regular income.

Capital assets can also be damaged or become obsolete. When an asset is impaired, its fair value decreases, which will lead to an adjustment of book value on the balance sheet. A loss will also be recognized on the income statement. If the carrying amount exceeds the recoverable amount, an impairment expense amounting to the difference is recognized in the period. If the carrying amount is less than the recoverable amount, no impairment is recognized.

Individuals and Capital Assets

Any significant tangible asset owned by an individual is a capital asset. If an individual sells a stock, a piece of art, an investment property, or another capital asset and earns money on the sale, he realizes a capital gain. The IRS requires individuals to report capital gains on which a capital gains tax is levied.

Even an individual's primary home is considered a capital asset. However, the IRS gives couples filing jointly a $500,000 tax exclusion and individuals filing as single a $250,000 exclusion on capitals gains earned through the sale of their primary residences. However, an individual cannot claim a loss from the sale of his primary residence. If an individual sells a capital asset and loses money, he can claim the loss against his gains.

For example, if an individual buys a $100,000 stock and sells it for $200,000, he reports a $100,000 capital gain, but if he buys a $100,000 home and sells it years later for $200,000, he does not have to report the gain due to the $250,000 exemption. Although both the home and the stock are capital assets, the IRS treats them differently.

Recording Capital Assets

The cost for capital assets may include transportation costs, installation costs, and insurance costs related to the purchased asset. If a firm purchased machinery for $500,000 and incurred transportation expenses of $10,000 and installation costs of $7,500, the cost of the machinery will be recognized at $517,500.

When a business purchases capital assets, the Internal Revenue Service (IRS) considers the purchase a capital expense. In most cases, businesses can deduct expenses incurred during a tax year from their revenue collected during the same tax year, and report the difference as their business income. However, most capital expenses cannot be claimed in the year of purchase, but instead must be capitalized as an asset and written off to expense incrementally over a number of years.

Using depreciation, a business expenses a portion of the asset's value over each year of its useful life, instead of allocating the entire expense to the year in which the asset is purchased. The purpose of depreciating an asset over time is to align the cost of the asset to the same year as the revenue generated by the asset, in line with the matching principle of U.S. generally accepted accounting principles (GAAP). This means that each year that the equipment or machinery is put to use, the cost associated with using up the asset is recorded. In effect, capital assets lose value as they age. The rate at which a company chooses to depreciate its assets may result in a book value that differs from the current market value of the assets.

Asset Classes

An asset class is a collection of securities, manifesting comparable traits and goes through similar market fluctuations. Securities in one asset class are almost always bound by similar legalities. Experts put different investment tools in various asset classes to help investors diversify their portfolio easily. Risk factors, taxation, return rates, liquidity, tenures and market volatility differ according to asset classes. Hence, investors often rely on asset category diversification to earn maximum returns with minimal costs.

Types of Asset Classes

There can be numerous criteria to classify asset classes. You may classify them based on purpose i.e. whether it is a consumption asset like oil and natural gas or whether it is an investment asset like stocks and bonds. You may also categorize them on the basis of location or the markets like domestic securities, foreign or international investments, or emerging markets and developed markets.

However, for now, let us dive into the popular asset classes and explore their distinct characteristics and unique selling propositions.

Fixed Income

As the most popular among Indians, fixed income asset class is one of the most trusted and oldest forms of investments. Fixed deposits and public provident funds (PPF) are two examples of this. But is this an investment though? You are just letting the bank borrow from you under conditions of capital protection, returns in the form of pre-agreed returns and liquidity.

With zero risks attached to fixed income asset classes, you will not lose the money you invest. And you earn steady returns as promised at the time of investing. You may get 7%-8% returns on Fixed Income schemes, but they are not inflation-beating returns. Subject to STCG or LTCG as per the tenure, fixed income schemes only offer security and not wealth-growth.

Equity

Equity asset class is a fascinating one and has been gaining popularity in the recent years. Investing in equity means to buy into a business – when you buy shares of a firm, you have a percentage of ownership. The only hitch is that it comes with a certain amount of risk. Any business takes time to grow and it is subject to market fluctuations, which can impact the share price.

Among equity investments, Equity Linked Savings Scheme (ELSS) is the only tax-saving (under section 80-C) and wealth-building scheme with the shortest lock-in term of 3 years. But equity investments (including ELSS) work well when you invest for the long term as they have historically delivered 16%-18% returns and rising above inflation. Choose an AMC with a proven record, if you are planning to invest in equities.

Real Estate

Real estate asset class, as the name implies, focuses on plots, apartments, commercial buildings, industrial areas, villas etc. The millennium has witnessed a growing interest in real estate investments, This is not just in urban areas, but in semi-urban and rural regions too. However, property market can be rather unpredictable and there are numerous factors like city planning, socio-political scenes, and project movement that decide the returns. This is one asset class that is not always structured or monitored.

Commodities

Commodities can be anything ranging from goods, properties or products that can be traded for different purposes. Gold, silver, bronze, food crops, petroleum etc. are some examples of commodities under the asset class, and the market undercurrents vary for each. The price can rise or fall as per the demand. Merchandises are not meant for long-term investments unless it is gold or silver. Just buy when the prices are down and sell when the prices go up.

Cash and Cash Equivalents

These are also known as money market instruments. It is not confined to currency, but also idle money in savings account or any other liquid schemes. Nothing gives more transactional freedom than cash. Many people are reluctant to invest money except in savings account because they don't have faith in any investment schemes or to use it without any restrictions at any time. But it cannot beat inflation and the returns too are negligible (not more than 4%). People often store away cash to evade tax as they are untraceable.

Derivatives

A derivative refers to a financial security whose value depends on the underlying asset or group of assets. Standalone, the derivative has n value of its own and its price is based on the fluctuations in the price of the underlying asset. It is a kind of contract between two or more parties who have a right/obligation to perform according to the conditions of the contract. Commonly used underlying assets are equity shares, bonds, debt, foreign exchange, commodities, market indices and interest rates.

Alternative Investments

An alternative investment relates to an unconventional asset and is not one of the traditional asset classes like equity, debt, and cash. These are mostly held by institutional investors or high net worth individuals owing to their complex structure and limited regulations. These attempt to generate exceptionally huge returns but are highly illiquid and risky at the same time. Some of the alternative investments found in the capital markets are hedge funds, bitcoins, artworks and structured products.

Diversification and Asset Classes

A basic understanding of the various asset classes which are available for investment helps to build a lucrative and well-balanced portfolio. A diversified portfolio refers to the grouping of different asset classes in such a manner so that the overall risk is reduced and portfolio's performance is not affected by the inferior performance of any single asset class. Diversification helps to reduce the non-systematic or firm-related risk of your investment portfolio by allocating your finances across different asset classes.

It happens when the asset classes in the portfolio are uncorrelated or are negatively correlated. Correlation between two asset classes shows the direction in which both of them at any point in time. A negative correlation means that when the price of one asset class falls, the price of other asset class rises. Such kind of behavior is observed between equity and fixed income; especially during a market slump. The main idea behind diversification is to keep the portfolio returns in line with your expectations and minimize overall losses as much as possible. It educates you about not putting all your investment in one asset class instead distribute them among multiple asset classes.

The percentage of funds which should go into each asset class deals with the problem of asset allocation. It means how are you going to distribute a fixed some among all the asset classes in your portfolio keeping your target rate of return and risk appetite in mind. Risk appetite is about the quantum of fall in the portfolio value that you will be able to digest at a given point in time. Based on it, you decide the asset allocation of your portfolio.

Asset Tracking

Asset tracking, sometimes referred to as asset management, is the method you use to track your physical assets, whether you scan barcode labels attached to them or you use GPS or RFID tags that broadcast their location. Asset tracking is just as important as managing your inventory, because you need to know the location, status, maintenance schedule, and other important information about your organization's physical assets. Indeed, asset tracking is important to your organization's bottom line and compliance, as you are responsible for locating and replacing lost or missing physical assets, as well as those that have come to the end of their lifecycle.

Methods of Asset Tracking

While asset tracking can be time consuming and expensive, there are methods of asset tracking that can save your organization time and money. The goal of any asset tracking system, therefore, is to maximize asset control efficiency and minimize equipment loss. Through the use of mobile computers, barcode labels, handheld barcode scanners, and asset management software, you can track your assets in real time, resulting in more efficient production planning and reduced downtime. The proper management software also enables organizations to schedule necessary maintenance or service, or even preventive maintenance. Complete asset tracking solutions include barcode technology, enabling organizations to scan their fixed assets to track them accurately and efficiently.

Barcodes are the standard for data collection and asset tracking, giving each asset a unique identifier so that they may be individually recognized and tracked. Barcodes include information that is critical to business, such as project name, asset category, and more. Barcode scanners read each barcode, allowing organizations to count assets more quickly and accurately without the risk of introducing human error.

Benefits of Asset Tracking

The benefits of asset tracking are numerous, and nearly all contribute to a healthier bottom line for the organizations that properly implement effective asset management processes. We highlight some of the most beneficial advantages of employing asset tracking here:

- Improve efficiency and trim costs.
- Adjust company records as equipment is reassigned between departments, and use the updated information when calculating taxes and costs for each department.

- Quickly and easily locate assets at any time, and in real time.
- Conduct asset tracking using fewer resources, with the aid of an asset tracking system.
- Lower administrative costs, since administrators do not need to track or locate assets manually.
- Track and reduce asset loss and utilize assets more effectively.
- Grow your company and scale your asset tracking as necessary.
- Improve customer service through improved asset tracking and management practices.
- Ensure accountability and accuracy with asset loss and management.
- Immediately know where your assets have been allocated.
- Proper asset tracking is required for regulatory compliance in certain industries.
- Increase the efficiency and organization of your company's physical space by identifying which items are accessed together and creating a better structure of your physical system.
- Get real-time reports on the position of each asset and increase the accuracy of your asset management.

Asset Recovery

Asset recovery, also known as investment or resource recovery, is the process of maximizing the value of unused or end-of-life assets through effective reuse or divestment. While sometimes referred to in the context of a company undergoing liquidation, Asset recovery also can describe the process of liquidating excess inventory, refurbished items, and equipment returned at the end of a lease.

Asset recovery can also refer to the task of recovery of assets that have been wrongfully taken either stolen, fraudulently misappropriated or otherwise disposed of to remove them from their rightful owner.

Asset recovery has three main elements—identification, redeployment, and divestment. Specialized asset recovery software may assist any of these steps.

Identification

Because unproductive assets cost money, it is important to classify them as such by investment recovery personnel. Later, a decision can be made whether to redeploy or divest. Surplus assets could be in any form, including fixed equipment, mobile equipment, buildings, or land. Idle or surplus assets can be either capital assets or non-capital surplus.

Redeployment

Redeploying an idle asset to another part of an organization is often the most productive use for the asset. Asset redeployment also saves the organization money by eliminating the need to purchase a new asset at current market rates. For effective reuse, another part of the company needs to require an asset of that kind. It must also be practical to transfer and deploy the asset at the new location.

One form of internal redeployment is cannibalization of usable spare parts from one asset to another. For example, a taxicab company has two non-running cabs with different non-working parts in each. By taking a working part from one non-running cab and placing it in the other, the company has reduced its number of non-running cabs by 50%.

Disposition

Disposition of surplus or idle assets is the process of either selling, scrapping, recycling, donating, or disposing an asset. The process involves removing the asset from an organization's books. When this is done effectively, the organization obtains capital that can be placed back into the business. In addition, a good asset sale produces revenue and boosts profits. Donations also build goodwill and deliver tax benefits. The type of disposition method employed will depend on the type of asset, its fair value, and market demand.

Asset Protection

Asset protection (sometimes also referred to as debtor-creditor law) is a set of legal techniques and a body of statutory and common law dealing with protecting assets of individuals and business entities from civil money judgments. The goal of asset protection planning is to insulate assets from claims of creditors without perjury or tax evasion.

Asset protection consists of methods available to protect assets from liabilities arising elsewhere. It should not be confused with limiting liability, which concerns the ability to stop or constrain liability to the asset or activity from which it arises. Assets that are shielded from creditors by law are few (common examples include some home equity, certain retirement plans and interests in LLCs and limited partnerships [and even these are not always unreachable]). Assets that are almost always unreachable are those to which one does not hold legal title. In many cases it is possible to vest legal title to personal assets in a trust, an agent or a nominee, while retaining all the control of the assets. The goal of asset protection is similar to bankruptcy, and the two practice areas go hand-in-hand. When a debtor has none to few assets, the bankruptcy route is preferable. When the debtor has significant assets, asset protection may be the solution.

The four threshold factors that are either expressly or implicitly analyzed in each asset protection case are:

- The identity of the person engaging in asset protection planning:
    - If the debtor is an individual, does he or she have a spouse, and is the spouse also liable? If the spouse is not liable, is it possible to enter into a transmutation agreement? Are the spouses engaged in activities that are equally likely to result in lawsuits or is one spouse more likely to be sued than the other?
    - If the debtor is an entity, did an individual guarantee the entity's debt? How likely is it that the creditor will be able to pierce the corporate veil or otherwise get the assets of the individual owners? Is there a statute that renders the individual personally liable for the obligations of the entity?
- The nature of the claim:
    - Are there specific claims or the asset protection is taken as a result of a desire to insulate from lawsuits?
    - If the claim has been reduced to a judgement, what assets does the judgement encumber?
    - Is the claim dischargeable?
    - What is the statute of limitations for bringing the claim?
- The identity of the creditor:
    - How aggressive is the creditor?

  - Is the creditor a government agency? Taxing authority? Some government agencies possess powers of seizure that other government agencies do not.
- The nature of the assets:
  - To what extent are the assets exempt from the claims of the creditors? For example, the degree of protection offered by the homestead exemption, the exemption of the assets in a qualified plan, i.e. assets in a plan under the Employee Retirement Income Security Act (ERISA) etc.

Whilst the aforementioned use of Trusts will be of benefit in a number of cases the question of ownership can still arise, as although legal ownership may have been transferred to the trustees, beneficial ownership may still in many cases lie with the settler of the Trust. A Private Placement Life Insurance contract (PPLI), can provide a greater degree of protection and privacy than most Trusts, and can also be integrated with an existing trust if necessary. Whilst Trusts may not be recognised in many Jurisdictions, Life insurance also has the advantage of being Multi jurisdictional.

Asset Swap

An asset swap refers to an exchange of tangible for intangible assets, in accountancy, or, in finance, to the exchange of the flow of payments from a given security (the asset) for a different set of cash flows.

Financial Accounting

In financial accounting, an asset swap is an exchange of tangible assets for intangible assets or vice versa. Since it is a swap of assets, the procedure takes place on the active side of the balance sheet and has no impact on the latter in regard to volume. As an example, a company may sell equity and receive the value in cash, thus increasing liquidity.

A company often utilizes this method when in need for money to invest (internal financing) or to pay off debts.

Finance

In finance, the term asset swap has a particular meaning. When one refers to an asset swap, one has in mind the exchange of the flow of payments from a given security (the asset) for a different set of cash flows. An example of this is where an institution swaps the cash flows on a U.S. Government Bond for LIBOR minus a spread (say 20 basis points). Such swaps usually have stub periods in order to bring the chronology of the cash flows into line with that of the underlying bond.

An asset swap enables an investor to buy a fixed rate bond and then hedge out the interest rate risk by swapping the fixed payments to floating. In doing so the investor retains the credit risk to the fixed-rate bond and earns a corresponding return. The asset swap market was born along with the swap market in the early 1990s, and continued to be most widely used by banks which use asset swaps to convert their long-term fixed rate assets to floating rate in order to match their short-term liabilities (depositor accounts). The asset swap market is over-the-counter (OTC), i.e., not traded on any exchange.

An asset swap is the swap of a fixed investment, like a bond that will yield guaranteed coupon payments, for a floating investment, i.e. an index. It has a similar structure to a plain vanilla swap, but the underlying of the swap contract is different.

There are several variations on the asset swap structure with the most widely traded being the par asset swap. Other types include the market asset swap and the cross-currency asset swap. The most common and standard one is par asset swap.

Mechanics of a Par Asset Swap

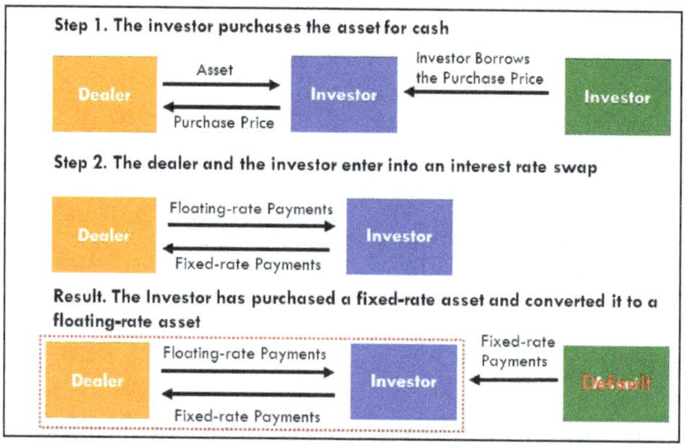

Figure: Describe the basic structure of Asset Swap.

A par asset swap is really two separate trades:

- The asset swap buyer purchases a bond from the asset swap seller in return for a full price of par. ("Full price" is also known as "dirty price", i.e. including the accrued interest in contrast to the term "clean price" which refers to quote net of accrued interest.)
- The asset swap buyer enters into a swap to pay fixed coupons to the asset swap seller equal to the fixed rate coupons received from the bond. In return the asset swap buyer receives regular payments of Libor plus (or minus) an agreed fixed spread. The maturity of this swap is the same as the maturity of the asset.

This transaction is shown in figure above. The fixed spread to Libor paid by the asset swap seller is known as the asset swap spread and is set at a break-even value so the net value of the sale of the bond plus the swap transaction is zero at inception.

Computing the Asset Swap Spread

For the purpose of the following, we assume we have constructed a market curve of Libor discount factors where z(t) is the price today of $1 to be paid at time t.

From the perspective of the asset swap seller, they sell the bond for par plus accrued interest ("dirty price"). The net up-front payment has a value 100-P where P is the full price of the bond in the market. Both parties to the swap are assumed to be AA bank credit quality and so these cash flows are priced off the Libor curve. We cancel out the principal payments of par at maturity. For simplicity we assume that all payments are annual and are made on the same dates.

As is standard for swaps, the break-even asset swap spread A is computed by setting the present value of all cash flows equal to zero.

1. From the perspective of the asset swap seller the present value is:

   100 - P + Coupon (Fixed Part) - Coupon (Floating Payment)

   The floating payment part equals $\sum \Delta i(Li + A)z(ti)$, where Δi is the accrual factor in the corresponding basis, ti is the term of time period and Li is the Libor rate set at time t i - 1. The fixed and floating sides may have different frequencies.

2. We then solve for the asset swap spread A such that the present value is zero.

On a technical note, when the asset swap is initiated between coupon dates, the asset swap buyer does not pay the accrued interest explicitly. Effectively, the full price of the bond is at par. At the next coupon period the asset swap buyer receives the full coupon on the bond and likewise pays the full coupon on the swap. However, the floating side payment, which may have a different frequency and accrual basis to fixed side, is adjusted by the corresponding accrual factor. Therefore, if we are exactly halfway between floating side coupons, the floating payment received is half of the Libor plus asset swap spread. This feature prevents the calculated asset swap spread from jumping as we move forward in time through coupon dates.

Market Asset Swap

In the market asset swap, the net upfront payment is zero. Instead the notional on the Libor side equals the price of the bond and there is an exchange of notionals at maturity.

Characteristics of Asset Allocation

One of the most widely accepted accounting definitions of asset is the one used by the International Accounting Standards Board. The following is a quotation from the

IFRS Framework: "An asset is a resource controlled by the enterprise as a result of past events and from which future economic benefits are expected to flow to the enterprise."

This means that:

- The probable present benefit involve a capacity, singly or in combination with other assets, in the case of profit oriented enterprises, to contribute directly or indirectly to future net cash flows, and, in the case of nonprofit organizations, to provide services.
- The entity can control access to the benefit.
- The transaction or event giving rise to the entity's right to, or control of, the benefit has already occurred.

Employees are not considered assets like machinery is, even though they can generate future economic benefits. This is because an entity does not have sufficient control over its employees to satisfy the Framework's definition of an asset. Resources that are expected to yield benefits only for a short time can also be considered not to be assets, for example in the USA the 12 month rule excludes items with a useful life of less than a year.

Similarly, in economics an asset is any form in which wealth can be held.

There is a growing analytical interest in assets and asset forms in other social sciences too, especially in terms of how a variety of things (e.g. personality, personal data, ecosystems, etc.) can be turned into an asset.

Accounting

In the financial accounting sense of the term, it is not necessary to be able to legally enforce the asset's benefit for qualifying a resource as being an asset, provided the entity can control its use by other means.

The accounting equation is the mathematical structure of the balance sheet. It relates assets, liabilities, and owner's equity:

Assets = Liabilities + Capital (which for a corporation equals *owner's equity*)

Liabilities = Assets – Capital

Equity = Assets – Liabilities

Assets are listed on the balance sheet. On a company's balance sheet certain divisions are required by generally accepted accounting principles (GAAP), which vary from country to country. Assets can be divided into e.g. current assets and fixed assets, often with further subdivisions such as cash, receivables and inventory.

Assets are formally controlled and managed within larger organizations via the use of asset tracking tools. These monitor the purchasing, upgrading, servicing, licensing, disposal etc., of both physical and non-physical assets.

Current Assets

Current assets are cash and other assets expected to be converted to cash or consumed either in a year or in the operating cycle (whichever is longer), without disturbing the normal operations of a business. These assets are continually turned over in the course of a business during normal business activity. There are 5 major items included into current assets:

1. Cash and cash equivalents – it is the most liquid asset, which includes currency, deposit accounts, and negotiable instruments (e.g., money orders, cheque, bank drafts).
2. Short-term investments – include securities bought and held for sale in the near future to generate income on short-term price differences (trading securities).
3. Receivables – usually reported as net of allowance for non-collectable accounts.
4. Inventory – trading these assets is a normal business of a company. The inventory value reported on the balance sheet is usually the historical cost or fair market value, whichever is lower. This is known as the "lower of cost or market" rule.
5. Prepaid expenses – these are expenses paid in cash and recorded as assets before they are used or consumed (common examples are insurance or office supplies).

Marketable securities: Securities that can be converted into cash quickly at a reasonable price.

The phrase net current assets (also called working capital) is often used and refers to the total of current assets less the total of current liabilities.

Long-term Investments

Often referred to simply as "investments". Long-term investments are to be held for many years and are not intended to be disposed of in the near future. This group usually consists of three types of investments:

1. Investments in securities such as bonds, common stock, or long-term notes.
2. Investments in fixed assets not used in operations (e.g., land held for sale).
3. Investments in special funds (e.g. sinking funds or pension funds).

Different forms of insurance may also be treated as long term investments.

Fixed Assets

Also referred to as PPE (property, plant, and equipment), these are purchased for continued and long-term use in earning profit in a business. This group includes as an asset land, buildings, machinery, furniture, tools, IT equipment, e.g., laptops, and certain wasting resources e.g., timberland and minerals. They are written off against profits over their anticipated life by charging depreciation expenses (with exception of land assets). Accumulated depreciation is shown in the face of the balance sheet or in the notes. An asset is an important factor in a balance sheet.

These are also called capital assets in management accounting.

Intangible Assets

Intangible assets lack of physical substance and usually are very hard to evaluate. They include patents, copyrights, franchises, goodwill, trademarks, trade names, etc. These assets are (according to US GAAP) amortized to expense over 5 to 40 years with the exception of goodwill.

Websites are treated differently in different countries and may fall under either tangible or intangible assets.

Tangible Assets

Tangible assets are those that have a physical substance, such as currencies, buildings, real estate, vehicles, inventories, equipment, art collections, precious metals, rare-earth metals, Industrial metals, and crops.

Depreciation is applied to tangible assets when those assets have an anticipated lifespan of more than one year. This process of depreciation is used instead of allocating the entire expense to one year.

Tangible assets such as art, furniture, stamps, gold, wine, toys and books have become recognized as an asset class in their own right and many high-net-worth individuals will seek to include these tangible assets as part of their overall asset portfolio. This has created a need for tangible asset managers.

Comparison: current assets, liquid assets and absolute liquid assets.

Current assets	Liquid assets	Absolute liquid assets
Stocks		
Prepaid expenses		
Bills receivable	Bills receivable	
Cash in hand	Cash in hand	Cash in hand
Cash at bank	Cash at bank	Cash at bank

Accrued incomes	Accrued incomes	Accrued incomes
Loans and advances (short term)	Loans and advances (short term)	Loans and advances (short term)
Trade investments (short term)	Trade investments (short term)	Trade investments (short term)

Asset Allocation

Asset allocation is an investment strategy that aims to balance risk and reward by apportioning a portfolio's assets according to an individual's goals, risk tolerance and investment horizon. The three main asset classes - equities, fixed-income, and cash and equivalents - have different levels of risk and return, so each will behave differently over time.

Importance of Asset Allocation

There is no simple formula that can find the right asset allocation for every individual. However, the consensus among most financial professionals is that asset allocation is one of the most important decisions that investors make. In other words, the selection of individual securities is secondary to the way that assets are allocated in stocks, bonds, and cash and equivalents, which will be the principal determinants of your investment results.

Investors may use different asset allocations for different objectives. Someone who is saving for a new car in the next year, for example, might invest her car savings fund in a very conservative mix of cash, certificates of deposit (CDs) and short-term bonds. Another individual saving for retirement that may be decades away typically invests the majority of his individual retirement account (IRA) in stocks, since he has a lot of time to ride out the market's short-term fluctuations. Risk tolerance plays a key factor as well. Someone not comfortable investing in stocks may put her money in a more conservative allocation despite a long time horizon.

Age-based Asset Allocation

In general, stocks are recommended for holding periods of five years or longer. Cash and money market accounts are appropriate for objectives less than a year away. Bonds fall somewhere in between. In the past, financial advisors have recommended subtracting an investor's age from 100 to determine how much should be invested in stocks. For example, a 40-year old would be 60% invested in stocks. Variations of the rule recommend subtracting age from 110 or 120 given that the average life expectancy continues to grow. As individuals approach retirement age, portfolios should generally move to a more conservative asset allocation so as to help protect assets that have already been accumulated.

Achieving Asset Allocation through Life-cycle Funds

Asset-allocation mutual funds, also known as life-cycle, or target-date, funds, are an attempt to provide investors with portfolio structures that address an investor's age, risk appetite and investment objectives with an appropriate apportionment of asset classes. However, critics of this approach point out that arriving at a standardized solution for allocating portfolio assets is problematic because individual investors require individual solutions.

The Vanguard Target Retirement 2030 Fund would be an example of a target-date fund. As of 2018, the fund has a 12-year time horizon until the shareholder expects to reach retirement. As of January 31, 2018, the fund has an allocation of 71% stocks and 29% bonds. Up until 2030, the fund will gradually shift to a more conservative 50/50 mix, reflecting the individual's need for more capital preservation and less risk. In following years, the fund moves to 67% bonds and 33% stocks.

Asset allocation involves dividing your investments among different assets, such as stocks, bonds, and cash. The asset allocation decision is a personal one. The allocation that works best for you changes at different times in your life, depending on how long you have to invest and your ability to tolerate risk.

Factors to Consider Include your:

- Time Horizon: Your time horizon is the number of months, years, or decades you need to invest to achieve your financial goal. Investors with a longer time horizon may feel comfortable taking on riskier or more volatile investments. Those with a shorter time horizon may prefer to take on less risk.
- Risk Tolerance: Risk tolerance is your ability and willingness to lose some or all of your original investment in exchange for potentially greater returns.

Diversification

The practice of spreading money among different investments to reduce risk is known as diversification. Diversification is a strategy that can be neatly summed up as "Don't put all your eggs in one basket."

One way to diversify is to allocate your investments among different kinds of assets. Historically, stocks, bonds, and cash have not moved up and down at the same time. Factors that may cause one asset class to perform poorly may improve returns for another asset class. People invest in various asset classes in the hope that if one is losing money, the others make up for those losses.

You'll also be better diversified if you spread your investments within each asset class. That means holding a number of different stocks or bonds, and investing in different industry sectors, such as consumer goods, health care, and technology. That way, if one sector is doing poorly, you may offset it with other holdings in sectors that are doing well.

Some investors find it easier to diversify by owning mutual funds. A mutual fund is a company that pools money from many investors and invests the money in stocks, bonds, and other financial products. Mutual funds make it easy for investors to own a small portion of many investments. A total stock market index fund, for example, owns stock in thousands of companies, providing a lot of diversification for one investment.

A mutual fund won't necessarily provide diversification, especially if it focuses on only one industry sector. If you invest in narrowly focused mutual funds, you may need to invest in several to be diversified. As you add more investments to your portfolio, you'll likely pay additional fees and expenses, which will lower your investment returns. So you'll need to consider these costs when deciding the best way to diversify your portfolio.

Rebalancing

Rebalancing is what investors do to bring their portfolio back to its original asset allocation mix. Rebalancing is needed because over time, some investments will grow faster than others. This may push your holdings out of alignment with your investment goals. By rebalancing, you will ensure that your portfolio does not overweight a particular asset category, and you'll return your portfolio to a comfortable level of risk.

For example, you might start with 60% of your portfolio invested in stocks, but see that rise to 80% due to market gains. To reestablish your original asset allocation mix, you'll either need to sell some of your stocks or invest in other asset categories.

There are three ways you can rebalance your portfolio:

1. You can sell investments where your holdings are over weighted and use the proceeds to buy investments for underweighted asset categories.

2. You can buy new investments for underweighted asset categories.

3. If you are continuing to add to your investments, you can alter your contributions so that more goes to underweighted asset categories until your portfolio is back into balance.

Before you rebalance your portfolio, you should consider whether the method of rebalancing you decide to use would entail transaction fees or tax consequences. Your financial professional or tax adviser can help you identify ways that you can minimize these potential costs.

Some financial experts advise rebalancing at regular intervals, such as every six or 12 months. Others recommend rebalancing when your holdings of an asset class increase or decrease more than a certain pre-set percentage. In either case, rebalancing tends to work best when done on a relatively infrequent basis.

Shifting money away from an asset class when it is doing well in favor of an asset category that is doing poorly may not be easy. But it can be a wise move. By cutting back on current "winners" and adding more current "losers," rebalancing forces you to buy low and sell high.

Asset Allocation Strategies

Asset allocation is a very important part of creating and balancing your investment portfolio. After all, it is one of the main factors that leads to your overall returns—even more than choosing individual stocks. Establishing an appropriate asset mix of stocks, bonds, cash, and real estate in your portfolio is a dynamic process. As such, the asset mix should reflect your goals at any point in time.

Strategic Asset Allocation

This method establishes and adheres to a base policy mix—a proportional combination of assets based on expected rates of return for each asset class. You also need to take your risk tolerance and investment time-frame into account. You can set your targets and then rebalance your portfolio every now and then.

A strategic asset allocation strategy may be akin to a buy-and-hold strategy and also heavily suggests diversification to cut back on risk and improve returns.

For example, if stocks have historically returned 10% per year and bonds have returned 5% per year, a mix of 50% stocks and 50% bonds would be expected to return 7.5% per year.

Constant-weighting Asset Allocation

Strategic asset allocation generally implies a buy-and-hold strategy, even as the shift in values of assets causes a drift from the initially established policy mix. For this reason, you may prefer to adopt a constant-weighting approach to asset allocation. With this approach, you continually rebalance your portfolio. For example, if one asset declines in value, you would purchase more of that asset. And if that asset value increases, you would sell it.

There are no hard-and-fast rules for timing portfolio rebalancing under strategic or constant-weighting asset allocation. But a common rule of thumb is that the portfolio should be rebalanced to its original mix when any given asset class moves more than 5% from its original value.

Tactical Asset Allocation

Over the long run, a strategic asset allocation strategy may seem relatively rigid. Therefore, you may find it necessary to occasionally engage in short-term, tactical deviations from the mix to capitalize on unusual or exceptional investment opportunities. This flexibility adds a market-timing component to the portfolio, allowing you to participate in economic conditions more favorable for one asset class than for others.

Tactical asset allocation can be described as a moderately active strategy since the overall strategic asset mix is returned to when desired short-term profits are achieved. This strategy demands some discipline, as you must first be able to recognize when short-term opportunities have run their course and then rebalance the portfolio to the long-term asset position.

Dynamic Asset Allocation

Another active asset allocation strategy is dynamic asset allocation. With this strategy, you constantly adjust the mix of assets as markets rise and fall, and as the economy strengthens and weakens. With this strategy, you sell assets that decline and purchase assets that increase.

This makes dynamic asset allocation the polar opposite of a constant-weighting strategy. For example, if the stock market shows weakness, you sell stocks in anticipation of further decreases and if the market is strong, you purchase stocks in anticipation of continued market gains.

Insured Asset Allocation

With an insured asset allocation strategy, you establish a base portfolio value under which the portfolio should not be allowed to drop. As long as the portfolio achieves a return above its base, you exercise active management, relying on analytical research, forecasts, judgment, and experience to decide which securities to buy, hold, and sell with the aim of increasing the portfolio value as much as possible.

If the portfolio should ever drop to the base value, you invest in risk-free assets, such as Treasuries (especially T-bills) so the base value becomes fixed. At this time, you would consult with your advisor to reallocate assets, perhaps even changing your investment strategy entirely.

Insured asset allocation may be suitable for risk-averse investors who desire a certain level of active portfolio management but appreciate the security of establishing a guaranteed floor below which the portfolio is not allowed to decline. For example, an investor who wishes to establish a minimum standard of living during retirement may find an insured asset allocation strategy ideally suited to his or her management goals.

Integrated Asset Allocation

With integrated asset allocation, you consider both your economic expectations and your risk in establishing an asset mix. While all of the strategies account for expectations of future market returns, not all of them account for the investor's risk tolerance. That's where integrated asset allocation comes into play.

This strategy includes aspects of all the previous ones, accounting not only for expectations but also actual changes in capital markets and your risk tolerance. Integrated asset allocation is a broader asset allocation strategy. But it cannot include both dynamic and constant-weighting allocation since an investor would not wish to implement two strategies that compete with one another.

The Bottom Line

Asset allocation can be active to varying degrees or strictly passive in nature. Whether an investor chooses a precise asset allocation strategy or a combination of different strategies depends on that investor's goals, age, market expectations, and risk tolerance.

Keep in mind, however, these are only general guidelines on how investors may use asset allocation as a part of their core strategies. Be aware that allocation approaches that involve reacting to market movements require a great deal of expertise and talent in using particular tools for timing these movements. Perfectly timing the market is next to impossible, so make sure your strategy isn't too vulnerable to unforeseeable errors.

Types of Asset Allocation Strategies

There are several types of asset allocation strategies based on investment goals, risk tolerance, time frames and diversification. The most common forms of asset allocation are: strategic, dynamic, tactical, and core-satellite.

Strategic Asset Allocation

The primary goal of a strategic asset allocation is to create an asset mix that seeks to provide the optimal balance between expected risk and return for a long-term investment horizon. Generally speaking, strategic asset allocation strategies are agnostic to economic environments, i.e., they do not change their allocation postures relative to changing market or economic conditions.

Dynamic Asset Allocation

Dynamic asset allocation is similar to strategic asset allocation in that portfolios are built by allocating to an asset mix that seeks to provide the optimal balance between expected risk and return for a long-term investment horizon. Like strategic allocation strategies, dynamic strategies largely retain exposure to their original asset classes; however, unlike strategic strategies, dynamic asset allocation portfolios will adjust their postures over time relative to changes in the economic environment.

Tactical Asset Allocation

Tactical asset allocation is a strategy in which an investor takes a more active approach that tries to position a portfolio into those assets, sectors, or individual stocks that show the most potential for perceived gains. While an original asset mix is formulated much like strategic and dynamic portfolio, tactical strategies are often traded more actively and are free to move entirely in and out of their core asset classes.

Core-satellite Asset Allocation

Core-satellite allocation strategies generally contain a 'core' strategic element making up the most significant portion of the portfolio, while applying a dynamic or tactical 'satellite' strategy that makes up a smaller part of the portfolio. In this way, core-satellite allocation strategies are a hybrid of the strategic and dynamic/tactical allocation strategies.

Some asset allocation strategies that can help the investor achieve significant returns:

- Strategic asset allocation: This technique is based on the expected return from investments. For example, if the investor expects a return of 13%, he/she has to base his/her investment in a mix of equities and debt. This strategy has to be continuously tweaked to get the desired return. Strategic asset allocation focuses on the buying and holding of investments. The advantage of this strategy is that it enables the portfolio to stay liquid.
- Constant-weight allocation: This strategy focuses on maintaining predetermined weight in equities, debts, or hybrids. In this strategy, the investor's portfolio has to be constantly rebalanced. The common rule of the constant weight allocation strategy is that the when any given asset class moves more than the predetermined weight from its original value, it should be rebalanced.
- Tactical asset allocation: The tactical asset allocation strategy is a more aggressive strategy than the constant-weight allocation strategy. In this strategy, the target allocation is broad, and it allows deviation to take advantage of the rare or unique investment opportunities offered by the market. The advantage of this strategy is that enables the investor to take advantage of the economic opportunities favoring any specific asset class, thereby offering flexibility. After benefiting from the possibilities, the investor needs to rebalance the portfolio for long-term profitability.
- Dynamic asset allocation: This asset allocation strategy requires constant adjustment of assets based on market ups and downs. The investor purchases

assets that are increasing in price and sells off those whose value is decreasing. The dynamic asset allocation strategy is the opposite of a constant-weight allocation strategy; however, this strategy involves constant changes in the portfolio leading to higher transactional charges.

- Insured asset allocation: With an insured asset allocation strategy, one decides on a base portfolio value below which the portfolio should not be allowed to fall. Active asset allocators use insured asset allocation strategies where investors or fund managers actively manage investments through analytical research, forecasts, records, and the experience of the fund managers and then decide on which securities to hold, buy, or sell. The rule of this approach is that the investment level should not drop beyond the base value. If that happens, investments are made in risk-free assets.

Asset allocation strategies can be undertaken at different levels to achieve financial goals. However, an asset allocation strategy should always factor in the investor's age, risk appetite, expected returns, and the investment horizon. Predicting the market is not always possible, but using a strategy that has some leeway for market surprises is a better way to achieve your financial goals.

References

- Asset: investopedia.com, Retrieved 2 March, 2019
- Balance-sheet, accounting: corporatefinanceinstitute.com, Retrieved 12 June, 2019
- Types-of-assets, accounting: corporatefinanceinstitute.com, Retrieved 24 May, 2019
- Toxic-assets: marketbusinessnews.com, Retrieved 6 July, 2019
- "Stranded Assets Programme". Smith School of Enterprise and the Environment. 25 March 2014. Archived from the original on 27 March 2014. Retrieved 11 April 2014
- hidden-assets: uslegal.com, Retrieved 5 March, 2019
- Capitalasset: investopedia.com, Retrieved 25 February, 2019
- Asset-classes: cleartax.in, Retrieved 15 August, 2019
- What-is-asset-tracking: camcode.com, Retrieved 3 April, 2019
- Richard T. Williamson (2008). The Real Estate Investor›s Guide to Corporations, LLCs & Asset Protection Entities. Kaplan Publishing. p. 43. ISBN 978-1-4277-9702-5
- Assetallocation: investopedia.com, Retrieved 13 January, 2019
- Asset-allocation, research-before-you-invest: investor.gov, Retrieved 23 June, 2019
- Asset-allocation-strategies-work, investing: investopedia.com, Retrieved 28 January, 2019
- Top-asset-allocation-strategies-that-work, news-personal-finance: indiainfoline.com, Retrieved 6 April, 2019

5

Bond Analysis and Management

The fixed income instrument which represents a loan made by an investor to a borrower is known as a bond. A bond can be issued by a government or a corporation. Some of the important types of bonds are investment-grade corporate bonds, high-yield bonds treasury bonds and foreign bonds. This chapter has been carefully written to provide an easy understanding of these types of bonds as well as bond valuation and bond strategies.

A bond is a debt investment in which an investor loans money to an entity (typically corporate or governmental) which borrows the funds for a defined period of time at a variable or fixed interest rate. Bond Analysis is used by companies, municipalities, states and sovereign governments to raise money and finance a variety of projects and activities. Owners of bonds are debt-holders, or creditors, of the issuer.

Basic Fundamentals

The bond market is large and diverse, larger than the stock market. Thus, it represents an important investment opportunity.

Bond Features

Public bonds are long-term, fixed payout debt assets. They are packaged in useful, easy to manage sizes for sale to you and big firms.

The issuer agrees to pay a fixed amount of cash over time to the holder of record. Also, they agree to pay a fixed amount of par at the date of when they end.

Public Debt Segments based on Term

- Short-term issues with terms of one year or less known as near cash or money market.
- Intermediate-term issues have terms from one to ten years known as notes.
- Long-term issues with terms over a year are bonds.

Intrinsic Features

The coupon of a bond states the income a bond investor receives over the life of the bond. Also, the term to maturity gives the date or the number of years before a bond ends.

Most bonds are term bond with a single end date. However, a serial bond has multiple end dates. They are small issues with different coupons and end dates.

The principal or par value of an issue is the original value of the debt. However, par value is not the same as the bond's value.

Issue Types

Unlike common stock, bonds can have many issues outstanding at the time. In addition, they have different types of collateral and be either senior, unsecured or subordinated. Muni are divided into general obligation or revenue bonds. Also, refunding issues provide funds to end another issue early.

The type of issue only has a little effect on yields. The credit worthiness signals bond quality. Whether an issuer pledged collateral or not is not key unless the issue gets near default.

Factors Affecting Maturity

Call options affect the life and value of bonds. Callable bonds have a call premium which is the amount above par value the issuer must pay the holders for ending the bond early.

Call Options

- Freely callable allows issuer to recall the bond at any time with a common grace time frame of 30 to 60 days.
- Non-callable means issuer cannot retire the bond prior to maturity.
- Deferred call means the issue cannot be called for a certain time after issue. Then, they are called freely.

A non-refunding feature stops a call and early recall of an issue from the proceeds of a lower-coupon refunding bond. A sinking fund feature says a bond must be paid off over its life.

Market Structure

The market for fixed-income debt is much larger than the listed stock market because firms tend to issue more bonds than common stock.

Many single buyers and big firms with diverse goals trade in the bond market. Big firms account for 90 to 95 percent of trading although the mix varies among the segments.

Bond ratings are a major part of the bond market because most corp and muni bonds are rated by one or more of the rating firms.Bond ratings provide the basic review for thousands of issues.

The main question is whether the issuer can service its debt in a timely manner over the life of a given issue. The rating firms have done a decent job except in the last cycle. They have a habit of overestimating the rate of default.

Issuers

Global Bond Markets

The US fixed income market is loaded with US Treasury debt. The US government issues their bonds backed by the full faith and credit of the US government. The interest income is subject to fed income tax but exempt from state and local taxes. These bonds are popular because of their high credit rating, highly liquid trait and non-call feature.

The second largest bond market in the world is Japan. It is controlled by the Japanese government and the Bank of Japan. These bonds are an attractive asset because their rating is equal to the US.

The third largest bond market in the world is the German market, although the government segment is somewhat small. The German market is led by banks because firms mainly finance through bank loans.

Government Agency Issues

The federal government in each country can issue agencies which can issue their own bonds. They are a large and growing segment in the US, a much smaller segment in Japan and Germany and don't exist in the UK.

They are not direct Treasury but carry an implied full faith and credit backing of the federal government. The most popular in the US is GNMA, issued by Dept of Housing and Human Services.

Muni Issues

Muni bonds are issued by states, counties, cities, and other political subdivisions. Interestingly, they represent about 10% of the bond market in most countries and do not exist in the UK.

GO bonds are mainly backed by the full faith and credit of the issuer and its entire taxing power. Also, revenue bonds are serviced by the income thrown off from single revenue-producing projects of the muni.

The key feature of munis is the income is exempt from fed income tax as well as from local and state taxes.

Corporate Bonds

- Mortgage Bonds has lien on real estate.

- Equipment Trust Certificates issued by railroads and airlines to buy rolling stock and planes.
- Collateralized Trust Bonds secured by financial assets.
- Collateralized Mortgage Obligations (CMOs) backed by pools of home loans.
- Asset-Backed Securities (ABS) secured by cars or credit cards.
- High-Yield Bonds junk bonds of less than stellar credit firms.

Bond Analysis and Valuation

The value of bonds can be described in terms of dollar values or the rates of return they promise under a set of factors. The value of the bond equals the present value of expected cash flows. The cash flows from the bond are the periodic interest payments and the repayment of par. However, the only factor which affects its value is the market discount rate- its required rate of return.

Relationship of Market Yield and Price

- The bond is priced at *premium* if the yield is below coupon rate.
- The bond is priced at *discount* if the yield is above the coupon rate.
- Also, a link between yield and price is convex- as yields decline the price goes up at an increasing rate, same in declining case.

Bond Yields

Bond Yield Measures

- Nominal yield coupon rate.
- Current yield current income rate.
- Yield to maturity expected rate of return held to end.
- Yield to call expected return for bond held to first call date.
- Realized yield expected rate for likely bond sold before end considering reinvestment rates.

Future Bond Prices

Dollar bond prices are worked up when dealing with realized yield and when issues are quoted on a promised yield basis, such as munis. Therefore the right market price is based on the current market YTM.

Term Structure Theories

- Expectations Hypothesis– shape of yield curve results for the interest expectations of market traders.
- Liquidity Preference– long-term assets should provide a higher return than short-term ones because you are willing to give up some yield to invest in short-term to avoid long-term ups and downs.
- Segmented Market – big firms have different maturity needs which leaves them to confine their bond picks to certain market segments.

You can look at yield expectations by simply observing the shape of the yield curve. Thus, if the curve is declining sharply, it suggests rates will be decline.

Yield Spread Differences

- Segments, i.e. Treasuries vs corps.
- Sectors of same segments, i.e. industrials vs. utilities.
- Coupons or seasonings.
- End dates within a given segment or sector.

The strength of the direction of a spread can change over time.

Bond Volatility

There is an inverse link between changes in yields and the price of bonds. Importantly, interest rate sensitivity is one factor which affects the amount of price change for a yield change.

Bond Market Price Factors

- Par value,
- Coupon,
- Number of years to end,
- Current market rates.

Link between Yield and Price Change

- Prices move inversely to yields.
- For a given change in yield, longer-term bonds post larger price changes.

- Price volatility increases at a smaller rate as term increases.
- Price movements from equal absolute increases in yield are not square.
- Also, higher coupon issues lose smaller percent price changes.

Interest rate changes trigger different strategies. Thus, bond prices increase during a major decline in rates. Therefore, you want you bonds to have the max rate sensitivity.

The most common measure of rate sensitivity is its duration. As such, it is a composite measure of the timing of a bond's cash flows traits taking into account its coupon and term to maturity.

Duration Types

- Macaulay oldest measure, the time flow of cash from a bond.
- Modified makes small change to Macaulay.
- Effective direct measure where price changes are figured with a value model.
- Empirical measures the real price changes for real changes in rates.

Bond Management

Prior to 1960, bonds were managed by simply buying and holding bonds in a group. At the time, purchases were made based on rate guesses and value models.

The early 1970s were hit by record-breaking inflation and rates. The intro of new finance types were in response to increased return risk. As a result, techniques such as matching funds or contingent portfolio were offered to meet the changing needs of big clients.

Passive Strategies

The simplest strategy is to buy and hold. Thus, these clients do not use active trading to get better returns. Also, a modified version starts with the purchase but still actively looks for ways to trade for stronger holdings.

Some traders opted to build their holdings to match the track record of a major bond index.Therefore, the manager is judged not on risk and return factors but how close the portfolio tracks the index.

Active Strategies

- Interest Rate Anticipation probably the riskiest strategy involves relying on unclear forecasts of future rates.

- Valuation Analysis manager attempts to select bonds based on their intrinsic value.
- Credit Analysis involves detailed analysis of the bond issuer to determine expected changes in its default risk.
- Yield Spread Analysis looks for abnormal spreads within a normal sector spreads and makes swap.
- Bond Swaps involves liquidating a current position and simultaneously buying a different issue in ts place with similar attributes.

Matched Funds Techniques

- Dedicated Portfolio, exact match used to service a prescribed set of liabilities by lining up maturities to liabilities.
- Dedicated Portfolio, optimal cash match and reinvestment matches liability cash flows with interest payments and maturities.
- Immunization Strategies attempts to derive a specified rate of return during a given investment horizon regardless of what happens to market interest rates.
- Horizon Matching is a combination of cash-matching dedications and immunization.

Contingent Procedures

- Contingent Immunization allows managers to pursue the highest returns available through active strategies while relying on classical bond immunization to ensures a given floor return over the time horizon.
- Other Immunization Procedures includes requires an investor to accept a cushion spread and then engaging in various portfolio strategies to increase the ending-wealth value.

Theoretical Implications

The performance of bonds offers total diversification benefits. In an efficient market, neither stocks nor bonds should dominate a portfolio but some combo should provide a superior risk-adjusted return.

Bond returns are linked directly to risk of default and interest rate risk. Although interest rate risk for investment-quality bond is non-diversifiable, some evidence exists default risk is also largely non-diversifiable because default experience is closely related to the business cycle.

Working of Bonds

Bonds are commonly referred to as fixed income securities and are one of three asset classes individual investors are usually familiar with, along with stocks (equities) and cash equivalents. Many corporate and government bonds are publicly traded; others are traded only over-the-counter (OTC) or privately between the borrower and lender.

When companies or other entities need to raise money to finance new projects, maintain ongoing operations, or refinance existing debts, they may issue bonds directly to investors. The borrower (issuer) issues a bond that includes the terms of the loan, interest payments that will be made, and the time at which the loaned funds (bond principal) must be paid back (maturity date). The interest payment (the coupon) is part of the return that bondholders earn for loaning their funds to the issuer. The interest rate that determines the payment is called the coupon rate.

The initial price of most bonds is typically set at par, usually $100 or $1,000 face value per individual bond. The actual market price of a bond depends on a number of factors: the credit quality of the issuer, the length of time until expiration, and the coupon rate compared to the general interest rate environment at the time. The face value of the bond is what will be paid back to the borrower once the bond matures.

Most bonds can be sold by the initial bondholder to other investors after they have been issued. In other words, a bond investor does not have to hold a bond all the way through to its maturity date. It is also common for bonds to be repurchased by the borrower if interest rates decline, or if the borrower's credit has improved, and it can reissue new bonds at a lower cost.

Characteristics of Bonds

Most bonds share some common basic characteristics including:

- Face value is the money amount the bond will be worth at maturity; it is also the reference amount the bond issuer uses when calculating interest payments. For example, say an investor purchases a bond at a premium $1,090 and another investor buys the same bond later when it is trading at a discount for $980. When the bond matures, both investors will receive the $1,000 face value of the bond.
- The coupon rate is the rate of interest the bond issuer will pay on the face value of the bond, expressed as a percentage. For example, a 5% coupon rate means that bondholders will receive 5% x $1000 face value = $50 every year.
- Coupon dates are the dates on which the bond issuer will make interest payments. Payments can be made in any interval, but the standard is semiannual payments.

- The maturity date is the date on which the bond will mature and the bond issuer will pay the bondholder the face value of the bond.
- The issue price is the price at which the bond issuer originally sells the bonds.

Two features of a bond—credit quality and time to maturity—are the principal determinants of a bond's coupon rate. If the issuer has a poor credit rating, the risk of default is greater, and these bonds pay more interest. Bonds that have a very long maturity date also usually pay a higher interest rate. This higher compensation is because the bondholder is more exposed to interest rate and inflation risks for an extended period.

Credit ratings for a company and its bonds are generated by credit rating agencies like Standard and Poor's, Moody's, and Fitch Ratings. The very highest quality bonds are called "investment grade" and include debt issued by the U.S. government and very stable companies, like many utilities. Bonds that are not considered investment grade, but are not in default, are called "high yield" or "junk" bonds. These bonds have a higher risk of default in the future and investors demand a higher coupon payment to compensate them for that risk.

Bonds and bond portfolios will rise or fall in value as interest rates change. The sensitivity to changes in the interest rate environment is called "duration". The use of the term duration in this context can be confusing to new bond investors because it does not refer to the length of time the bond has before maturity. Instead, duration describes how much a bond's price will rise or fall with a change in interest rates.

The rate of change of a bond's or bond portfolio's sensitivity to interest rates (duration) is called "convexity". These factors are difficult to calculate, and the analysis required is usually done by professionals.

Categories of Bonds

There are four primary categories of bonds sold in the markets. However, you may also see foreign bonds issued by corporations and governments on some platforms.

- Corporate bonds are issued by companies. Companies issue bonds rather than seek bank loans for debt financing in many cases because bond markets offer more favorable terms and lower interest rates.
- Municipal bonds are issued by states and municipalities. Some municipal bonds offer tax-free coupon income for investors.
- Government bonds such as those issued by the U.S. Treasury. Bonds issued by the Treasury with a year or less to maturity are called "Bills"; bonds issued with 1 – 10 years to maturity are called "notes"; and bonds issued with more than 10 years to maturity are called "bonds". The entire category of bonds

issued by a government treasury is often collectively referred to as "treasuries." Government bonds issued by national governments may be referred to as sovereign debt.

- Agency bonds are those issued by government-affiliated organizations such as Fannie Mae or Freddie Mac.

Varieties of Bonds

The bonds available for investors come in many different varieties. They can be separated by the rate or type of interest or coupon payment, being recalled by the issuer, or have other attributes.

Zero-coupon bonds do not pay coupon payments and instead are issued at a discount to their par value that will generate a return once the bondholder is paid the full face value when the bond matures. U.S. Treasury bills are a zero-coupon bond. For example, the U.S. Treasury sold 26-week bills with $100 face value for $98.78 on October 18th, 2018. That equates to a total annual yield of 2.479% once the bondholder is repaid the entire $100 at the maturity date.

Convertible bonds are debt instruments with an embedded option that allows bondholders to convert their debt into stock (equity) at some point, depending on certain conditions like the share price. For example, imagine a company that needs to borrow $1 million to fund a new project. They could borrow by issuing bonds with a 12% coupon that matures in 10 years. However, if they knew that there were some investors willing to buy bonds with an 8% coupon that allowed them to convert the bond into stock if the stock's price rose above a certain value, they might prefer to issue those.

The convertible bond may the best solution for the company because they would have lower interest payments while the project was in its early stages. If the investors converted their bonds, the other shareholders would be diluted, but the company would not have to pay any more interest or the principal of the bond.

The investors who purchased a convertible bond may think this is a great solution because they can profit from the upside in the stock if the project is successful. They are taking more risk by accepting a lower coupon payment, but the potential reward if the bonds are converted could make that trade-off acceptable.

Callable bonds also have an embedded option but it is different than what is found in a convertible bond. A callable bond is one that can be "called" back by the company before it matures. Assume that a company has borrowed $1 million by issuing bonds with a 10% coupon that mature in 10 years. If interest rates decline (or the company's credit rating improves) in year 5 when the company could borrow for 8%, they will call or buy the bonds back from the bondholders for the principal amount and reissue new bonds at a lower coupon rate.

A callable bond is riskier for the bond buyer because the bond is more likely to be called when it is rising in value. Remember, when interest rates are falling, bond prices rise. Because of this, callable bonds are not as valuable as bonds that aren't callable with the same maturity, credit rating, and coupon rate.

A Puttable bond allows the bondholders to put or sell the bond back to the company before it has matured. This is valuable for investors who are worried that a bond may fall in value, or if they think interest rates will rise and they want to get their principal back before the bond falls in value.

The bond issuer may include a put option in the bond that benefits the bondholders in return for a lower coupon rate or just to induce the bond sellers to make the initial loan. A puttable bond usually trades at a higher value than a bond without a put option but with the same credit rating, maturity, and coupon rate because it is more valuable to the bondholders.

The possible combinations of embedded puts, calls, and convertibility rights in a bond are endless and each one is unique. There isn't a strict standard for each of these rights and some bonds will contain more than one kind of "option" which can make comparisons difficult. Generally, individual investors rely on bond professionals to select individual bonds or bond funds that meet their investing goals.

Pricing Bonds

The market prices bonds based on their particular characteristics. A bond's price changes on a daily basis, just like that of any other publicly-traded security, where supply and demand in any given moment determine that observed price. But there is a logic to how bonds are valued. Up to this point, we've talked about bonds as if every investor holds them to maturity. It's true that if you do this you're guaranteed to get your principal back plus interest; however, a bond does not have to be held to maturity. At any time, a bondholder can sell their bonds in the open market, where the price can fluctuate, sometimes dramatically.

The price of a bond changes in response to changes in interest rates in the economy. This is due to the fact that for a fixed-rate bond, the issuer has promised to pay a coupon based on the face value of the bond – so for a $1,000 par, 10% annual coupon bond, the issuer will pay the bondholder $100 each year.

Say that prevailing interest rates are also 10% at the time that this bond is issued, as determined by the rate on a short-term government bond. An investor would be indifferent investing in the corporate bond or the government bond since both would return $100. However, imagine a little while later, that the economy has taken a turn for the worse and interest rates dropped to 5%. Now, the investor can only receive $50 from the government bond, but would still receive $100 from the corporate bond.

This difference makes the corporate bond much more attractive. So, investors in the market will bid up to the price of the bond until it trades at a premium that equalizes the prevailing interest rate environment—in this case, the bond will trade at a price of \$2,000 so that the \$100 coupon represents 5%. Likewise, if interest rates soared to 15%, then an investor could make \$150 from the government bond and would not pay \$1,000 to earn just \$100. This bond would be sold until it reached a price that equalized the yields, in this case to a price of \$666.67.

Inverse to Interest Rates

This is why the famous statement that a bond's price varies inversely with interest rates works. When interest rates go up, bond prices fall in order to have the effect of equalizing the interest rate on the bond with prevailing rates, and vice versa.

Another way of illustrating this concept is to consider what the yield on our bond would be given a price change, instead of given an interest rate change. For example, if the price were to go down from \$1,000 to \$800, then the yield goes up to 12.5%. This happens because you are getting the same guaranteed \$100 on an asset that is worth \$800 (\$100/\$800). Conversely, if the bond goes up in price to \$1,200, the yield shrinks to 8.33% (\$100/\$1,200).

Yield-to-Maturity (YTM)

The yield-to-maturity (YTM) of a bond is another way of considering a bond's price. YTM is the total return anticipated on a bond if the bond is held until the end of its lifetime. Yield to maturity is considered a long-term bond yield but is expressed as an annual rate. In other words, it is the internal rate of return of an investment in a bond if the investor holds the bond until maturity and if all payments are made as scheduled. YTM is a complex calculation but is quite useful as a concept evaluating the attractiveness of one bond relative to other bonds of different coupon and maturity in the market. The formula for YTM involves solving for the interest rate in the following equation, which is no easy task, and therefore most bond investors interested in YTM will use a computer:

$$YTM = \sqrt[n]{\frac{\text{Face Value}}{\text{Present Value}}} - 1$$

We can also measure the anticipated changes in bond prices given a change in interest rates with a measure knows as the duration of a bond. Duration is expressed in units of the number of years since it originally referred to zero-coupon bonds, whose duration is its maturity.

For practical purposes, however, duration represents the price change in a bond given a 1% change in interest rates. We call this second, more practical definition the modified duration of a bond.

The duration can be calculated to determine the price sensitivity to interest rate changes of a single bond, or for a portfolio of many bonds. In general, bonds with long maturities, and also bonds with low coupons have the greatest sensitivity to interest rate changes. A bond's duration is not a linear risk measure, meaning that as prices and rates change, the duration itself changes, and convexity measures this relationship.

Bond Example

A bond represents a promise by a borrower to pay a lender their principal and usually interest on a loan. Bonds are issued by governments, municipalities, and corporations. The interest rate (coupon rate), principal amount and maturities will vary from one bond to the next in order to meet the goals of the bond issuer (borrower) and the bond buyer (lender). Most bonds issued by companies include options that can increase or decrease their value and can make comparisons difficult for non-professionals. Bonds can be bought or sold before they mature, and many are publicly listed and can be traded with a broker.

While governments issue many bonds, corporate bonds can be purchased from brokerages. If you're interested in this investment, you'll need to pick a broker. You can take a look at Investopedia's list of the best online stock brokers to get an idea of which brokers best fit your needs.

Because fixed-rate coupon bonds will pay the same percentage of its face value over time, the market price of the bond will fluctuate as that coupon becomes more or less attractive compared to the prevailing interest rates.

Imagine a bond that was issued with a coupon rate of 5% and a $1,000 par value. The bondholder will be paid $50 in interest income annually (most bond coupons are split in half and paid semi annually.) As long as nothing else changes in the interest rate environment, the price of the bond should remain at its par value.

However, if interest rates begin to decline and similar bonds are now issued with a 4% coupon, the original bond has become more valuable. Investors who want a higher coupon rate will have to pay extra for the bond in order to entice the original owner to sell. The increased price will bring the bond's total yield down to 4% for new investors because they will have to pay an amount above par value to purchase the bond.

On the other hand, if interest rates rise and the coupon rate for bonds like this one rise to 6%, the 5% coupon is no longer attractive. The bond's price will decrease and begin selling at a discount compared to the par value until its effective return is 6%.

The bond market tends to move inversely with interest rates because bonds will trade at a discount when interest rates are rising and at a premium when interest rates are falling.

Features of Bonds in Investment

Repayment of Principal

Bonds are issued in denomination of Rs. 1,000 but there are also bonds of values of Rs. 500 and Rs. 100 and of values as high as Rs. 5,000 and Rs. 10,000. Financial institutions are known to buy corporate bonds bearing higher values. The value of the bond is called the 'face value, par value or maturity value'.

The face value of the bond represents the promise to repay the amount to the bondholder at the end of the specified period. This, in other words, may be called the most important feature of bond, return of the principal to the lender on a fixed date specified earlier.

Specified Time Period

The second feature is the maturity date of the bond. The time specified in the bond is called the maturity date or date of repayment of principal amount. The maturity date of bonds varies according to the requirement of each organization. Some organizations issue bonds of a long-term nature. The number of years of these bonds varies from 20 years to 100 years maturity.

Other issues of bonds are for medium term and their maturity is between 5-10 years. Shorter-term bonds are identified as those whose maturity is below 4 years. The bond indenture specifically gives the maturity date of the bond. This is the promise to pay the principal amount on a specified date after the expiry of the number of years for which it is issued.

Call

Bonds have an additional feature of 'call'. This is a privilege to the issuing company to re-purchase bonds at a slightly higher price above the par value. For example, a bond of face value of Rs. 1,000 and maturity of 20 years yields an interest of Rs. 70 annually. After the first 5 years of issue, the market rate of interest on bonds falls considerably.

The ruling rate being 5% the company may choose to use the call feature and buy back the bond for Rs. 1,050. This is a little higher than the face value of Rs. 1,000. By calling the bonds, the company saves money. It may call back the bonds yielding interest of Rs. 70 and issue fresh bonds which will yield Rs. 50 per year.

The firm has been able to save Rs. 20 per year per bond for the next 15 years till the maturity of the bond. By paying Rs. 50 higher than the face value on the bond for early redemption of the bond, the company saves a much higher amount.

The bond holder is on the losing side because he gets the return of the principal amount earlier than he expected. Since, the current market rate of interest is prevailing at a lower rate he cannot buy any other bond which will fetch him an income of Rs. 70 per bond per year. This feature gives a right to the issuing company.

The bondholder should be aware of the call feature before he makes an investment in bonds. He can protect himself by investing in bonds of shorter durations. Although there is risk of fluctuations in interest rates for short durations, a ten year period is considered to be good life of a bond from the point of view of the bondholder.

Pledge of Security

The issuing company sometimes promises to pay to the bondholder by offering some security like property. The pledge of security is a promise to the bondholders in writing and signed under seal and presented to the trustee by the company. A simple promise to pay without the proper formalities is not considered as a pledge of security.

Interest

The rate of interest to be paid to bondholder and the time of payment is recorded in the bond as well as in the indenture, 'interest rate' is also called the 'coupon rate'. Interest on bond may be made by cheque or coupon. When interest is paid to the bondholder by cheque the principal amount on the bond is usually registered to interest value.

The coupons are numbered and every coupon represents, the interest payment period. When the coupon becomes due, the bondholder presents the coupon to the authorized banker and receives interest. The coupons are usually bearer bonds and are negotiable when they become due and payable.

Coupons should be kept safely because it is difficult to recover them if they are lost, since the name of the owner is not required in order to en-cash them. Interest either by coupon or by cheque is paid on the face value of the bond. The rate cannot be changed once it has been fixed. The interest is paid in Rupee Value in India. Gold bonds were issued in India in the early 1950s but now only Rupee Bonds are issued.

Interest on bonds should be paid regularly by the issuing authority. Government bonds are very reliable as they are paid in time. Sometimes, interest is not paid by companies when it is due. The bond issue in this case is considered to be in default and both the interest and principal become due and payable to the bondholder. The trustees of the bondholder at this point of time protect the interest of the bondholders.

In order to be sure that interest and principal sum on the bond will be repaid, it is necessary that the bonds are evaluated and analysed before investing in them.

An investor must look into the net operating profit of the firm as well as its net income after taxes. This will to a great extent determine the quality of the bond. It must be emphasized that bonds will be considered secure when the interest charges are low and the net operating income is high.

Sometimes, the bond issuing companies offer security through assets and in writing, assuring the bondholders of the payment of interest. Sometimes, the company promises to maintain a minimum working capital position or a particular cash position. Interest is guaranteed in assumed bond, guaranteed bond or joint bond.

Interest on bonds is also protected by the 'acceleration clause'. When interest is due but not paid, this clause gives the right to the bondholder to represent himself through the trustee. This clause gives the bondholder the right of a creditor and he can make a claim on his assets but cannot be sure of receiving the principal amount.

The bondholder will be reassured if on an analysis of the company's position. It is found that the company's operating income is sufficient to cover all expenses pertaining to the company's account inclusive of all interest charges made on its issue of debt.

Covenants

Covenants are productive clauses in the bond indenture. They are agreements between the company and the bondholders through the trustees. Through these agreements the company binds itself to the bondholders.

The company agrees to control its operations and in this way offers some protection to bondholders. Sometimes, a company makes an agreement to limit the amount of dividend to be paid to its equity shareholders. Other covenants protect the bondholder by ensuring a minimum, cash balance to be maintained by the firm.

Certain covenants or agreements are specifically used on a particular class of bonds. For example, mortgage bonds may include a covenant to limit the company's expenses or debt position up to a fixed percentage of the value of new purchases of property, for example, 75% of the property.

Covenants are agreements or promises which tone up the quality of the bonds and assure repayment of principal and interest. There are different kinds of bonds based on these special features: Repayment of principal, Maturity date, Call, Pledge of security, Interest and Covenants.

The Basics of Bonds

Ratings

Bonds are rated by popular agencies like Standard and Poor's, and Moody's. Each agency has slightly different ratings scales, but the highest rating is AAA with the lowest being C or D, depending on the agency. The top four ratings are considered safe or investment grade, while anything below BBB for S&P and Baa for Moody's is considered high yield or junk bonds. Although larger institutions are often permitted to purchase only investment grade bonds, high yield or junk bonds have a place in an investor's portfolio as well, but may require more sophisticated guidance.

Pricing

Bonds are generally priced at a face value (also called par) of $1,000 per bond, but once the bond hits the open market, the asking price can be priced lower than the face value, called a discount, or higher, called premium. If a bond is priced at a premium, the investor will receive a lower coupon yield, because they paid more for the bond. If it's priced at a discount, the investor will receive a higher coupon yield, because they paid less than the face value.

Bond pricing isn't as volatile as stocks and often responds more to interest rate changes than other market conditions. This is why investors looking for safety and income often prefer bonds over stocks as they get closer to retirement.

Purchasing

Most bonds are still traded over the counter through electronic markets. Many brokers charge larger commissions for bonds, since the market isn't as liquid and still requires calling bond desks in many buy and sell scenarios. Other times, a broker-dealer may have certain bonds in their inventory and may sell to their investors directly from their inventory. You can often purchase bonds through your broker's website or call with the bond's unique ID number, called the CUSIP number, to get a quote and place a "buy" or "sell" order.

Taxes

Because bonds pay a steady dividend, called the coupon, owners of bonds have to pay dividend taxes on the funds received. For this reason, bonds are best kept in a tax sheltered account, like an IRA, to gain tax advantages not present in a standard brokerage account.

If you purchased a bond at a discount, you'll be required to pay capital gains tax on the difference between the price you paid and the bond's par value, normally $1,000 per bond, but not until the bond matures and you receive the face value of the bond.

Alternatives

If you want the income earning power of a bond, but you don't have the funds or don't want to own individual bonds, consider a bond ETF or bond mutual funds. These are well diversified funds that give you exposure to many different bonds, and pay a monthly or quarterly dividend. Because some bonds have a minimum purchase amount, smaller investors may find these products more appropriate for their smaller amount of capital, while remaining properly diversified.

Most investors, regardless of age, should have at least a small amount of their portfolio allocated to fixed income products like bonds. Bonds add safety and consistency to a portfolio. Although there is a risk that a company may default and cause a large loss, investment grade bonds rarely default, but along with safety comes a lower rate of return.

Types of Bonds

Any bond's single most important characteristic is the entity that issued it, since as an investor you're counting on that issuer to return your money.

There are seven main issuer categories:

1. Treasury bonds,
2. Other U.S. government bonds,
3. Investment-grade corporate bonds (high quality),
4. High-yield corporate bonds (low quality), also known as junk bonds,
5. Foreign bonds,
6. Mortgage-backed bonds,
7. Municipal bonds.

Which one do you want? That depends first of all on your tax bracket. If your tax bill is big enough, it will be worth your while to diversify your stock portfolio with municipal bonds, whose yields are lowest, but for a very good reason: The interest payments are exempt from federal income taxes.

If munis aren't for you, your choice of a taxable category depends on your risk tolerance. Broadly speaking, if you want to hold only as much fixed-income as you need to diversify your stock portfolio, stick with Treasuries, governments or investment-grade corporates. There are important differences between the three, but you don't need more than one to be diversified.

As for the other types, you can't count on them to protect you against downturns in stocks. Case in point: In the third quarter of 1998, when the S&P 500 lost 10.0%, the average long-term Treasury fund, the average U.S. government fund and the average corporate fund investing mostly in high-grade bonds all returned more than 3.6%, according to Lipper Analytical Services. Meanwhile, riskier corporate funds returned less than 2%, the average high-yield fund lost 7.2% and the average emerging market fund lost 27.5%. Other foreign debt funds held up better, and the various classes of mortgage-backed funds didn't do badly; still, these are complicated investments that aren't meant to fill the bond portion of your asset allocation.

Here's what you need to know about each of the seven classes of bonds:

1. Treasury bonds

Treasuries are issued by the federal government to finance its budget deficits. Because they're backed by Uncle Sam's awesome taxing authority, they're considered credit-risk free. The downside: Their yields are always going to be lowest (except for tax-free munis). But in economic downturns they perform better than higher-yielding bonds, and the interest is exempt from state income taxes.

2. Other U.S. government bonds

Also called agency bonds, these bonds are issued by federal agencies, mainly Fannie Mae (FNM) (the Federal National Mortgage Association) and Ginnie Mae (the Government National Mortgage Association). They're different from the mortgage-backed securities issued by those same agencies, and by Freddie Mac (FRE) (the Federal Home Loan Mortgage Corp.). Agency yields are higher than Treasury yields because they are not full-faith-and-credit obligations of the U.S. government, but the credit risk is considered minimal. Interest on the bonds is taxable at both the federal and state levels, however.

3. Investment-grade corporate bonds

Investment-grade corporates are issued by companies or financing vehicles with relatively strong balance sheets. They carry ratings of at least triple-B from Standard & Poor's, Moody's Investors Service or both. (The scale is triple-A as the highest, followed by double-A, single-A, then triple-B, and so on.) For investment-grade bonds, the risk of default is considered pretty remote.

Still, their yields are higher than either Treasury or agency bonds, though like most agencies they are fully taxable. In economic downturns, these bonds tend to underperform Treasuries and agencies.

4. High-yield bonds

These bonds are issued by companies or financing vehicles with relatively weak balance sheets. They carry ratings below triple-B. Default is a distinct possibility.

As a result, high-yield bond prices are more closely tied to the health of corporate balance sheets. They track stock prices more closely than investment-grade bond prices. "High-yield doesn't provide the same asset-allocation benefits you get by mixing high-grade bonds and stocks," observes Charles Schwab Chief Investment Officer Steve Ward.

5. Foreign bonds

These securities are something else altogether. Some are dollar-denominated, but the average foreign bond fund has about a third of its assets in foreign-currency-denominated debt, according to Lipper.

With foreign-currency-denominated bonds, the issuer promises to make fixed interest payments and to return the principal in another currency. The size of those payments when they are converted into dollars depends on exchange rates.

If the dollar strengthens against foreign currencies, foreign interest payments convert into smaller and smaller dollar amounts (if the dollar weakens, the opposite holds true). Exchange rates, more than interest rates, can determine how a foreign bond fund performs.

6. Mortgage-backed bonds

Mortgage-backeds, which have a face value of $25,000 compared to $1,000 or $5,000 for other types of bonds, involve "prepayment risk." Because their value drops when the rate of mortgage prepayments rises, they don't benefit from declining interest rates like most other bonds do.

7. Municipal bonds

Municipal bonds often called "munis" are issued by U.S. states and local governments or their agencies, and they come in both the investment-grade and high-yield varieties. The interest is tax-free, but that doesn't mean everyone can benefit from them.

Taxable yields are higher than muni yields to compensate investors for the taxes, so depending on your bracket, you might still come out ahead with taxable bonds.

Understanding Different Types of Bond Yields

One of the key things to research when performing investment due diligence on a bond is to evaluate the bond's yield or return. This evaluation of a bond's return or yield can be performed in a number of different methods and should be for the different types of bond yields that exist for corporate and government bonds. These different types of bond yields include among others, the so called running yield, nominal yield, yield to maturity (YTM), yield to call (YTC) and yield to worst (YTW).

It is highly important for any investor to know their target return as well as the risk they are willing to take into account (risk/return profile). When determining an approximate target yield for fixed-income investments, it is clearly significant to make sure to understand the various types and measurements of bond yields.

The Different Types of Bond Yields

The running yield is a measurement of a bond's return or yield each year as represented as a percentage of the bond's current market value or price. This is a fairly simple measurement that tells investors what they can expect for a return in the current market. When used to describe a portfolio, a running yield refers to the cumulative return or yield of all investments currently held within that portfolio. This may be somewhat similar to a dividend yield, but instead of describing individual assets, it describes the entire group represented within the portfolio as a whole. Typically, running yields are figured annually, but many investors calculate it more often than this.

The nominal yield is the return of a bond as determined by the percentage of the face value the bond's annual coupon payments amount to. This means the nominal yield is effectively the bond's coupon rate. This rate may or may not change depending on the type of bond:

- Fixed Rate Bonds: The coupon rate or nominal yield will be fixed and will not change over the lifetime of the bond.
- Floating Rate Bonds: The coupon payments/nominal yield will change over the life of the bond as dictated by changes in the referenced rate of interest.
- Indexed Bonds: The coupon payments/nominal yield will change in response to movement within its underlying index.

The YTM (yield to maturity) describes the average yield or return that an investor can expect from an issue each year if they (1) purchase it at its market value and (2) hold it until it matures. This value is determined using the coupon payment, the value of the issue at maturity, and any capital gains or losses that were incurred during the lifetime of the bond. YTM estimates, typically assume that all coupon payments are reinvested (not distributed) within the bond. This figure is typically used to compare different bonds an investor is trying to choose between, and is one of the key figures compared between bonds. This is due to the fact it includes more variable than other comparable figures. For example, comparing the nominal yield of two different bonds is only truly helpful when the bonds have the same cost, same life span and same return. However, if any of these are different, the YTM measure becomes a more effective comparison tool.

The YTC (yield to call) simply refers to the bond's yield at the time of its call date. This value doesn't hold if the bond is kept until maturity, but only describes the value at the call date, which if given, can be found in the prospectus of the bond. This value is determined by the bond's coupon rate, its market price and the length of the call date.

The YTW (yield to worst), as the name suggests, describes the worst possible yield possible for a bond without the issuer of the bond going into default. Investors determine this by imagining worst-case scenarios for the issue. These scenarios include all provisions included in the bond like a call, prepayment or sinking fund—anything that would negatively impact the bond's yield. By knowing the worst yield possible, investors can see how their income will be affected and whether or not it will be sufficient to consider the issue. YTW calculations are determined for all possible call dates in order to provide as much information as possible to investors. It always assumes all conditions or provisions that can be enacted to decrease the yield will be enacted, such as for instance put provisions to lower the coupon rate based upon market conditions. It also assumes no recalculations happen in favor of the investor.

The Bottom Line

Though yield is not the only significant factor to consider when determining which security or issue to invest in, it is nonetheless an important one. The terms and conditions that come with a bond are often not insignificant when it comes to yield and therefore must be examined carefully when performing due diligence before deciding which bond to invest in. Another significant issue that affects the bond's yield is the fact of risk vs. return. As with all financial securities, the trade-off for greater security is less return. Therefore, it will always depend on the investor's risk/return profile when it comes to setting a target yield. In each and every case, if a potential investor chooses to purchase higher-yielding or investment-grade bonds or a mixture of both, a profound professional analysis of each security is required.

Bond Strategies

The returns of bonds are influenced by a number of factors: changes in interest rates, changes in the credit ratings of the issuers, and changes in the yield curve. A bond strategy is the management of a bond portfolio either to increase returns based on anticipated changes in these bond-pricing factors or to maintain a certain return regardless of changes in those factors. Bond strategies can be classified as active, passive, hybrid.

Active strategies usually involve bond swaps, liquidating one group of bonds to purchase another group, to take advantage of expected changes in the bond market, either to seek higher returns or to maintain the value of a portfolio. Active strategies are used to take advantage of expected changes in interest rates, yield curve shifts, and changes in the credit ratings of individual issuers.

Passive strategies are used, not so much to maximize returns, but to earn a good return while matching cash flows to expected liabilities or, as in indexing, to minimize transaction and management costs. Pension funds, banks, and insurance companies use passive strategies extensively to match their income with their expected payouts, especially bond immunization strategies and cash flow matching. Generally, the bonds are purchased to achieve a specific investment objective; thereafter, the bond portfolio is monitored and adjusted as needed.

Hybrid strategies are a combination of both active and passive strategies, often employing immunization that may require rebalancing if interest rates change significantly. Hybrid strategies include contingent immunization and combination matching.

Active Bond Strategies

The primary objective of an active strategy is for greater returns, such as buying bonds with longer durations in anticipation of lower long-term interest rates; buying junk bonds in anticipation of economic growth; buying Treasuries when the Federal Reserve is expected to increase the money supply, which it usually does by buying Treasuries. Active selection strategies are based on anticipated interest rate changes, credit changes, and fundamental valuation techniques.

Interest Rate Anticipation Strategies

A rate anticipation strategy is one that involves selecting bonds that will increase the most in value from an expected drop in interest rates. If a group of bonds are sold so that others can be purchased based on the expected change in interest rates, then it is referred to as a rate anticipation swap. A total return analysis or horizon analysis is conducted to evaluate several strategies using bond portfolios with different durations to see how they would fare under different interest rate changes, based on expected market changes during the investment horizon.

If interest rates are expected to drop, then bonds with longer durations would be purchased, since they would profit most from an interest rate decrease. If rates were expected to increase, then bonds with shorter durations would be purchased, to minimize interest-rate risk. One means of shortening duration is buying cushion bonds, which are callable bonds with a coupon rate that is significantly higher than the current market rate. Cushion bonds generally have a shorter duration because of their call feature and are cheaper to buy, since they generally have a lower market price than a similar bond without the call feature. Rate anticipation strategies generally require a forecast in the yield curve as well since the change in interest rates may not be parallel.

Yield Curve Shifts

Because the yield curve involves a continuum of interest rates, changes in the yield curve can be described as the type of shift that occurs. The types of yield curve shifts that regularly occur include parallel shifts, twisted shifts, and shifts with humpedness. A parallel shift is the simplest kind of shift in which short-, intermediate-, and long-term yields change by the same amount, either up or down. A shift with a twist is one that involves either a flattening or an increasing curvature to the yield curve or it may involve a steepening of the curve where the yield spread becomes either wider or narrower as one progresses from shorter durations to longer durations. A yield shift with humpedness is one where the yields for intermediate durations changes by a different amount from either short- or long-term durations. If the intermediate-term yields increase less than either the short- or long-term durations, then that is considered to be a positive humpedness, or as it is sometimes referred to as a positive butterfly; the obverse, where short-term and long-term yields decline more (meaning that bond prices increase faster) than intermediate term yields is referred to as negative humpedness or a negative butterfly.

Several bond strategies were designed to profit or maintain value due to a specific change in the yield curve. A ladder strategy is a portfolio with equal allocations for each maturity group. A bullet strategy is a portfolio whose duration is allocated to 1 maturity group. For instance, if interest rates were expected to decline, then a profitable bullet strategy would be one with long-term bonds, which would benefit the most from a decrease in interest rates. A barbell strategy is one that has a concentration in both short and long-term bonds if negative humpedness in the yield curve is expected, in which case, short- and long-term bonds will increase in price faster than the intermediate-term bonds.

Credit Strategies

There are 2 types of credit investment strategies: quality swaps and credit analysis strategies. Bonds of a higher quality generally have a higher price than those of lower quality of the same maturity. This is based on the creditworthiness of the bond issuer, since the chance of default increases as the creditworthiness of the issuer declines. Consequently, lower quality bonds pay a higher yield. However, the number of bond issues that default tends to increase in recessions and to decline when the economy is growing. Therefore, there tends to be a higher demand for lower quality bonds during economic prosperity so that higher yields can be earned and a higher demand for high quality bonds during recessions, which offers greater safety and is sometimes referred to as the flight to quality. Hence, as an economy goes from recession to prosperity, the credit spread between high and low quality bonds will tend to narrow; from prosperity to recession, the credit spread widens. Quality swaps usually involve a sector rotation where bonds of a specific quality sector are purchased in anticipation of changes in the economy.

A quality swap profits by selling short the bonds that are expected to decline in price relative to the bonds that are expected to increase in price more, which are bought. A quality swap can be profitable whether interest rates increase or decrease, because profit is made from the spread. If rates increase, the quality spread narrows: the percentage decrease in the price of lower quality bonds will be less than the percentage decrease in the price of higher quality bonds. If rates decrease, then the quality spread expands, because the price percentage increase for the lower quality bonds is greater than the price percentage increase for the higher quality bonds.

Credit Analysis: The Evaluation of Credit Risk

A credit analysis strategy evaluates corporate, municipal, or foreign bonds to anticipate potential changes in credit risk, which will usually result in changes in the issuers' bonds prices. Bonds with forecasted upgrades are bought; bonds with potential downgrades are sold or avoided. Generally, changes in credit risk should be determined before any upgrade or downgrade announcements by the credit rating agencies, such as Moody's, Standard & Poor's, or Fitch; otherwise, it may be too late to take advantage of price changes.

Fundamental Credit Analysis

The credit analysis for corporate bonds includes the following:

- Fundamental analysis:
    - Comparing the company's financial ratios with other firms in the industry, especially the interest coverage ratio, which is earnings before interest and taxes.
    - Leverage, which is long-term debt over total assets.
    - Cash flow, which determines the company's ability to pay interest on debt.
    - Working capital, which is current assets minus current liabilities.
    - Return on equity.
- Asset and liability analysis, which includes assessing:
    - The market values of the company's assets and liabilities.
    - Intangible assets and liabilities, especially unfunded pension liabilities.
    - The age and condition of the plants.
    - Foreign-currency exposures.
- Industrial analysis:
    - Industry and company treads.
    - Assessing the potential growth rate for the industry.
    - Industrial development stage.
    - The cyclicality of the industry.

- Competitiveness.
- Labor and union costs and problems.
- Government regulations.

- Indenture analysis: how protective covenants compare with industry norms.

Foreign corporate bonds are also analyzed in the same way, but additional issues include the foreign exchange rate and any risks that may occur because of political, social, and economic changes in the countries where the bonds are issued or where the company is located.

Indenture analysis and economic analysis are used to gauge the riskiness of municipal bonds.

Economic analysis:

- Debt burden.
- Financial status.
- Fiscal problems:
    - Revenues falling below projections.
    - Declines in debt coverage ratios.
    - Increased use of debt reserves.
    - Project cost overruns or delays.
    - Frequent rate increases.
- And the state of the general and local economy, such as:
    - Decreases in population.
    - Loss of large employers.
    - Increases in unemployment.
    - Declines in property values.
    - The issuance of fewer building permits.

Multiple Discriminate Models and the Altman Z-Score

Multiple discriminate models are statistical models that are used to generate a credit score for a bond so that its overall credit quality can be summarized, much as a credit score is used to summarize a consumer's creditworthiness. Multiple discriminate models generally assess the most important factors that determine the creditworthiness of the issuer by applying appropriate weights to each of the factors. A popular scoring model is the Altman Z-score model, developed by Edward Altman in 1968.

Altman Z-score = 1.2 × W + 1.4 × R + 3.3 × E + 0.6 × M + 1.0 × S:

- W = ratio of working capital to total assets.
- R = ratio of retained earnings to total assets.
- E = ratio of earnings before interest and taxes to total assets.
- M = market value of equity to total liabilities.
- S = ratio of sales to total assets.

The Altman Z-score ranges from -5.0 to +20.0. If a company has a Z score above 3.0, then bankruptcy is considered unlikely; lower values indicate an increased risk of business failure.

Altman's double prime model includes the same factors except that the book value rather than the market value of the company to total liabilities is used and the sales to total assets is excluded.

Altman Z"-score = 6.56 × W + 3.26 × R + 6.70 × E + 1.05 × M.

Scores above 2.6 are considered creditworthy, while scores below 1.1 indicate an increased risk of business failure. Another score that is commonly used is the Hillegeist Z-score (HS), which is an updated estimate of the Altman Z-score.

Hillegeist Z-score = 3.835 + 1.13 × W + 0.0 05 × R + 0.2 69 × E + 0.3 99 × M – 0.033 × S.

The 1 year probability of default = 1 ÷ (exp (HS) +1). Like the Altman Z-score, a higher value indicates a lower probability of bankruptcy.

Passive Bond Management Strategies

In contrast to active management, passive bond management strategies usually involve setting up a bond portfolio with specific characteristics that can achieve investment goals without altering the strategy before maturity. The 3 primary passive bond strategies are index matching, cash flow matching, and immunization.

Bond Indexing

Index matching is constructing a bond portfolio that reflects the returns of a bond index. Some indexes are general, such as the Bloomberg Global Benchmark Bond Indexes or the Barclays Aggregate Indexes; others are specialized, such as the Bloomberg Corporate Bond Indexes. Bond indexing is mainly used to achieve greater returns with lower expenses rather than matching cash flows with liabilities or durations of bonds with liabilities. Because there are several types of indexes, it must 1st be decided which index to replicate. Afterwards, a specific strategy must be selected that best achieves tracking an index, given the resources of the bond fund.

There are several strategies for achieving indexing. Pure bond indexing (aka full replication approach) is to simply buy all the bonds that comprise the index in the same proportions. However, since some indexes consists of thousands of bonds, it may be costly to fully replicate an index, especially for bonds that are thinly traded, which may have high bid/ask spreads. Many bond managers solve this problem by selecting a subset of the index, but the subset may not accurately track the index, thus leading to tracking error.

A cell matching strategy is sometimes used to avoid or minimize tracking error, where the index is decomposed into specific groups with a specific duration, credit rating, sector, and so on and then buying the bonds that have the characteristics of each cell. The quantity of bonds selected for each cell can also mirror the proportions in the bond index.

Rather than taking a sample of a bond index to replicate, some bond managers use enhanced bond indexing, where some bonds are actively selected according to some criteria or forecast, in the hope of earning greater returns. Even if the forecast is incorrect, junk bonds tend to increase in price faster when the economy is improving, because the chance of default declines.

Cash Flow Matching

Cash flow matching involves using dedicated portfolios with cash flows that match specific liabilities. Cash flows include not only coupon payments, but also repayments of principal because the bonds matured or they were called. Cash flow matching is often used by institutions such as banks, insurance companies, and pension funds. Liabilities usually vary as to certainty. For a bank, CD liabilities are certain in both amount and in the timing. In some cases, the liability is certain but the timing is not, such as life insurance payouts and pension distributions. Other liabilities, such as property insurance, are uncertain in both amount and time.

Because most bonds pay semiannual coupons, a cash flow matching strategy is established by 1st constructing a bond portfolio for the last liability, then for the penultimate liability, and so on, working backward. The cash flows for earlier liabilities are modified according to the amount of cash flow received from coupons of the already selected bonds. However, special consideration must be given to callable bonds and lower quality bonds, since their cash flows are more uncertain, although the risk can be mitigated with options or other derivatives.

Because bonds cannot usually be selected to exactly match the cash flow of liabilities, a certain amount of cash must be held on hand to pay liabilities as they come due. Thus, a drawback to cash flow matching over immunization is that the cash is not fully invested.

Bond Immunization Strategies

Bonds have both interest-rate risk and reinvestment risk. Reinvestment is necessary to earn at least a market return. For instance, a 6% coupon bond does not earn a 6% return unless the coupons are reinvested. A 6% 10-year bond with a par value of $1000 earns $600 in interest over the term of the bond. By contrast, $1000 placed in a savings account that earns 6% compounded semiannually would earn $806.11 after 10 years. Hence, to earn a 6% return with a coupon bond, the coupons must be reinvested for at least the 6% rate.

Bond immunization strategies depend on the fact that the interest rate risk and the reinvestment risk are reciprocal: when one increases, the other declines. Increases in interest rates causes increased interest rate risk but lower reinvestment risk. When interest rates decline, bond prices increase, but the cash flows from the bonds can only be reinvested at a lower rate without taking on additional risk. A disadvantage of cash flow matching is that any reinvestment risk cannot be offset by rising bond prices if the bonds are held to maturity.

Classical immunization is the construction of a bond portfolio such that it will have a minimum return regardless of interest rate changes. The immunization strategy has several requirements: no defaults; security prices change only in response to interest rates (for instance, bonds cannot have embedded options); yield curve changes are parallel.

Immunization is more difficult to achieve with bonds with embedded options, such as call provisions, or prepayments made on mortgage-backed securities, since cash flow is more difficult to predict.

The initial value of the bonds must be equal to the present value of the liability using the yield to maturity (YTM) as a discount factor. Otherwise, the modified duration of the portfolio will not match the modified duration of the liability.

Immunization for multiple liabilities is generally achieved by rebalancing, in which bonds are sold, thus freeing up some cash for the current liability, then using the remaining cash to buy bonds that will immunize the portfolio for the later liabilities.

There are several requirements for immunizing multiple liabilities:

- Present value of assets must equal the present value of liabilities.
- The composite portfolio duration must equal the composite liabilities duration.
- The distribution of durations of individual assets must range wider than the distribution of liabilities.

Contingent Immunization

Contingent immunization combines active management with a small portion of invested funds and using the remaining portion for an immunized bond portfolio that ensures a floor on the return, while also allowing for a possibly higher return through active management.

The target rate is the lower potential return that is acceptable to the investor, equal to the market rate for the immunized portion of the portfolio. The cushion spread (aka excess achievable return) is the difference in the rate of return if the entire portfolio was immunized over the rate that will be earned because only part of the portfolio will be immunized; the rest will be actively managed in the hope of achieving a return that is greater than if the entire portfolio was immunized.

The safety margin is the cushion, the part that is actively managed. As long as it is positive, the management can continue to actively manage part of the portfolio. However, if the safety margin declines to 0, then active management ends and only the immunized bond portfolio is maintained. If long-term rates decline, then the safety margin is increased, but any increases in the interest rate will decrease the safety margin, possibly to 0.

The trigger point is the yield level at which the immunization mode becomes necessary in order to achieve the target rate or the target return. At this point, active management ceases.

Rebalancing

Classical immunization may not work if the shifting yield curve is not parallel or if the duration of assets and liabilities diverge, since durations change as interest rates change and as time passes.

Because duration is the average time to receive ½ of the present value of a bond's cash flow, duration changes with time, even if there are no changes in interest rates. If interest rates do change, then duration will shorten if interest rates increase or lengthen if interest rates decrease.

Hence, to maintain immunization, the portfolio must be rebalanced, which involves bond swaps: adding or subtracting bonds to appropriately modify the bond portfolio duration. Risk can also be mitigated with futures, options, or swaps. The primary drawback to rebalancing is that transaction costs are incurred in buying or selling assets. Hence, transaction costs must be weighed against market risk when bond and liability durations diverge.

Rebalancing can be done with a focus strategy, buying bonds with a duration that matches the liability. Another strategy is the bullet strategy, where bonds are selected that cluster around the duration of the liabilities. A dumbbell strategy can also be pursued, in which bonds of both shorter and longer durations than the liabilities are selected, so that any changes in duration will be covered.

To immunize multiple period liabilities, specific bonds can be purchased that match the specific liabilities or a bond portfolio with the duration equal to the average duration of the liabilities can be selected. Although a bond portfolio with an average duration is easier to manage, buying bonds for each individual liability generally works better. If a portfolio requires frequent rebalancing, a better strategy may be matching cash flows to liabilities instead of durations. Some bond managers use combination matching, or horizon matching, matching early liabilities with cash flows and later liabilities with immunization strategies.

Fundamental Valuation Strategies

Another common strategy to benefit from the bond market is to find and buy underpriced bonds and sell overpriced bonds, based on a fundamental analysis of what prices should be. The intrinsic value of the bond is calculated by discounting the cash flows by a required rate of return that generally depends on market interest rates plus a risk premium for taking on the debt. Naturally, the calculations must take into account any embedded options and the credit quality of the issuer and the credit ratings of the bond issue. The required rate of return is equal to the following:

Required Rate of Return = Risk-Free Interest Rate + Default Risk Premium + Liquidity Premium + Option Adjusted Spread.

Bond managers incorporate the basic characteristics of a bond and its market into models, such as multiple discriminate analysis or CDS analysis, to forecast changes in the credit spread. Option pricing models may also be used to determine the value of embedded options or to forecast changes in the option adjusted spread. Note that forecasts are not nearly as important when using fundamental valuation strategies, since buying bonds that are cheaper because of a temporary mispricing by the market and selling the same type of bonds when the market starts pricing the bonds at their intrinsic value will yield better results regardless of how the bond market changes.

A pure yield pickup strategy (aka substitution swap) is based on the yield pickup swap, which takes advantage of temporary mispricing of bonds, buying bonds that are underpriced relative to the same types of bonds held in the portfolio, thus paying a higher yield, and selling those In the portfolio that are overpriced, which, consequently, pay a lower yield. A pure yield pickup strategy can profit from either a higher coupon income or a higher yield to maturity, or both. However, the bonds must be identical in regard to durations, call features, and default ratings and any other feature that may affect its market value; otherwise, the different prices will probably reflect the differences in credit quality or features rather than a mispricing by the market. Nowadays, it is more difficult to profit from yield pickup strategies, since quant firms are constantly scouring the investment universe for mispriced securities.

A tax swap allows an investor to sell bonds at a loss to offset taxes on capital gains and then repurchase the bonds later with similar but not identical characteristics. The bonds cannot be identical because of wash sale rules that apply to bonds as well stocks.

However, the wash sale criteria that apply to bonds are less defined, allowing the purchase of similar bonds with only minor differences.

An intermarket-spread swap is undertaken when the current yield spread between 2 groups of bonds is out of line with their historical yield spread and that the spread is expected to narrow within the investment horizon of the bond portfolio. Spreads exist between bonds of different credit quality, and between differences in features, such as being callable or non-callable, or putable or non-putable. For instance, callable/non-callable bond swaps may be profitable if the spread between the 2 is expected to narrow as interest rates decline. As interest rates decline, callable bonds are limited to their call price, since, if the bonds are called, that is what the bondholder will receive. Hence, the price spread between callable and noncallable bonds is narrower during high interest rates and wider during low interest rates. Thus, as interest rates decline, the callable/noncallable spread increases.

Bond Valuation

Bond valuation is the determination of the fair price of a bond. As with any security or capital investment, the theoretical fair value of a bond is the present value of the stream of cash flows it is expected to generate. Hence, the value of a bond is obtained by discounting the bond's expected cash flows to the present using an appropriate discount rate.

In practice, this discount rate is often determined by reference to similar instruments, provided that such instruments exist. Various related yield-measures are then calculated for the given price.

If the bond includes embedded options, the valuation is more difficult and combines option pricing with discounting. Depending on the type of option, the option price as calculated is either added to or subtracted from the price of the "straight" portion. This total is then the value of the bond.

The fair price of a "straight bond" (a bond with no embedded options;) is usually determined by discounting its expected cash flows at the appropriate discount rate. Although this present value relationship reflects the theoretical approach to determining the value of a bond, in practice its price is (usually) determined with reference to other, more liquid instruments. The two main approaches are, Relative pricing and Arbitrage-free pricing. Finally, where it is important to recognise that future interest rates are uncertain and that the discount rate is not adequately represented by a single fixed number—for example when an option is written on the bond in question—stochastic calculus may be employed. Where the market price of bond is less than its face value (par value), the bond is selling at a discount. Conversely, if the market price of bond is greater than its face value, the bond is selling at a premium. For this and other relationships between price and yield.

Present Value Approach

Below is the formula for calculating a bond's price, which uses the basic present value (PV) formula for a given discount rate: (This formula assumes that a coupon payment has just been made; for adjustments on other dates.)

$$P = \left(\frac{C}{1+i} + \frac{C}{(1+i)^2} + \ldots + \frac{C}{(1+i)^N} \right) + \frac{M}{(1+i)^N}$$

$$= \left(\sum_{n=1}^{N} \frac{C}{(1+i)^n} \right) + \frac{M}{(1+i)^N}$$

$$= C \left(\frac{1-(1+i)^{-N}}{i} \right) + M(1+i)^{-N}$$

where:

F = face values,

i_F = contractual interest rate,

C = F * i_F = coupon payment (periodic interest payment),

N = number of payments

i = market interest rate, or required yield, or observed / appropriate yield to maturity,

M = value at maturity, usually equals face value,

P = market price of bond.

Relative Price Approach

Under this approach—an extension, or application, of the above—the bond will be priced relative to a benchmark, usually a government security. Here, the yield to maturity on the bond is determined based on the bond's Credit rating relative to a government security with similar maturity or duration. The better the quality of the bond, the smaller the spread between its required return and the YTM of the benchmark. This required return is then used to discount the bond cash flows, replacing *i* in the formula above, to obtain the price.

Arbitrage-free Pricing Approach

As distinct from the two related approaches above, a bond may be thought of as a "package of cash flows"—coupon or face—with each cash flow viewed as a zero-coupon instrument maturing on the date it will be received. Thus, rather than using a single discount rate, one should use multiple discount rates, discounting each cash flow at its own rate. Here, each cash flow is separately discounted at the same rate as a zero-coupon bond corresponding to the coupon date, and of equivalent credit worthiness (if possible, from the same issuer as the bond being valued, or if not, with the appropriate credit spread).

Under this approach, the bond price should reflect its "arbitrage-free" price, as any deviation from this price will be exploited and the bond will then quickly reprice to its correct level. Here, we apply the rational pricing logic relating to "Assets with identical cash flows". In detail: (1) the bond's coupon dates and coupon amounts are known with certainty. Therefore, (2) some multiple (or fraction) of zero-coupon bonds, each corresponding to the bond's coupon dates, can be specified so as to produce identical cash flows to the bond. Thus (3) the bond price today must be equal to the sum of each of its cash flows discounted at the discount rate implied by the value of the corresponding ZCB. Were this not the case, (4) the arbitrageur could finance his purchase of whichever of the bond or the sum of the various ZCBs was cheaper, by short selling the other, and meeting his cash flow commitments using the coupons or maturing zeroes as appropriate. Then (5) his "risk free", arbitrage profit would be the difference between the two values.

Stochastic Calculus Approach

When modelling a bond option, or other interest rate derivative (IRD), it is important to recognize that future interest rates are uncertain, and therefore, the discount rate(s) referred to above, under all three cases—i.e. whether for all coupons or for each individual coupon—is not adequately represented by a fixed (deterministic) number. In such cases, stochastic calculus is employed.

The following is a partial differential equation (PDE) in stochastic calculus, which is satisfied by any zero-coupon bond P, over (instantaneous) time t, for corresponding changes in the short rate r.

$$\frac{1}{2}\sigma(r)^2\frac{\partial^2 P}{\partial r^2}+[a(r)+\sigma(r)+\varphi(r,t)]\frac{\partial P}{\partial r}+\frac{\partial P}{\partial t}-rP=0$$

The solution to the PDE is:

$$P[t,T,r(t)]=E_t^*[e^{-R(t,T)}]$$

where E_t^* is the expectation with respect to risk-neutral probabilities, and $R(t,T)$ is a random variable representing the discount rate.

To actually determine the bond price, the analyst must choose the specific short rate model to be employed. The approaches commonly used are:

- The CIR model.
- The Black-Derman-Toy model.
- The Hull-White model.
- The HJM framework.
- The Chen model.

Note that depending on the model selected, a closed-form ("Black like") solution may not be available, and a lattice- or simulation-based implementation of the model in question is then employed.

Clean and Dirty Price

When the bond is not valued precisely on a coupon date, the calculated price, using the methods above, will incorporate accrued interest: i.e. any interest due to the owner of the bond since the previous coupon date. The price of a bond which includes this accrued interest is known as the "dirty price" (or "full price" or "all in price" or "Cash price"). The "clean price" is the price excluding any interest that has accrued. Clean prices are generally more stable over time than dirty prices. This is because the dirty price will drop suddenly when the bond goes "ex interest" and the purchaser is no longer entitled to receive the next coupon payment. In many markets, it is market practice to quote bonds on a clean-price basis. When a purchase is settled, the accrued interest is added to the quoted clean price to arrive at the actual amount to be paid.

Yield and Price Relationships

Once the price or value has been calculated, various yields relating the price of the bond to its coupons can then be determined.

- Buy the bond at price P_0,
- Hold the bond until maturity, and
- Redeem the bond at par.

Coupon Rate

The coupon rate is simply the coupon payment C as a percentage of the face value F.

$$\text{Coupon rate} = \frac{C}{F}$$

Coupon yield is also called nominal yield.

Current Yield

The current yield is simply the coupon payment C as a percentage of the (current) bond price P.

$$\text{Current yield} = \frac{C}{P_0}.$$

Relationship

The concept of current yield is closely related to other bond concepts, including yield to maturity, and coupon yield. The relationship between yield to maturity and the coupon rate is as follows:

- When a bond sells at a discount, YTM > current yield > coupon yield.
- When a bond sells at a premium, coupon yield > current yield > YTM.
- When a bond sells at par, YTM = current yield = coupon yield.

Price Sensitivity

The sensitivity of a bond's market price to interest rate (i.e. yield) movements is measured by its duration, and, additionally, by its convexity.

Duration is a linear measure of how the price of a bond changes in response to interest rate changes. It is approximately equal to the percentage change in price for a given change in yield, and may be thought of as the elasticity of the bond's price with respect to discount rates. For example, for small interest rate changes, the duration is the approximate percentage by which the value of the bond will fall for a 1% per annum increase in market interest rate. So the market price of a 17-year bond with a duration of 7 would fall about 7% if the market interest rate (or more precisely the corresponding force of interest) increased by 1% per annum.

Convexity is a measure of the "curvature" of price changes. It is needed because the price is not a linear function of the discount rate, but rather a convex function of the discount rate. Specifically, duration can be formulated as the first derivative of the price with respect to the interest rate, and convexity as the second derivative. Continuing the above example, for a more accurate estimate of sensitivity, the convexity score would be multiplied by the square of the change in interest rate, and the result added to the value derived by the above linear formula.

Accounting Treatment

In accounting for liabilities, any bond discount or premium must be amortized over the life of the bond. A number of methods may be used for this depending on applicable accounting rules. One possibility is that amortization amount in each period is calculated from the following formula:

$$n \in \{0,1,\ldots,N-1\}$$

a_{n+1} = amortization amount in period number "n + 1"

$$a_{n+1} = |iP - C|(1+i)^n$$

Bond Discount or Bond Premium = $|F - P| = a_1 + a_2 + \ldots + a_N$

Bond Discount or Bond Premium = $F|i - i_F|(\frac{1-(1+i)^{-N}}{i})$

A bond is a debt instrument that provides a steady income stream to the investor in the form of coupon payments. At the maturity date, the full face value of the bond is repaid to the bondholder. The characteristics of a regular bond include:

- Coupon rate: Some bonds have an interest rate, also known as the coupon rate, which is paid to bondholders semi-annually. The coupon rate is the fixed return that an investor earns periodically until it matures.
- Maturity date: All bonds have maturity dates, some short-term, others long-term. When the bond matures, the bond issuer repays the investor the full face value of the bond. For corporate bonds, the face value of a bond is usually $1,000 and for government bonds, face value is $10,000. The face value is not necessarily the invested principal or purchase price of the bond.
- Current Price: Depending on the level of interest rate in the environment, the investor may purchase a bond at par, below par, or above par. For example, if interest rates increase, the value of a bond will decrease since the coupon rate will be lower than the interest rate in the economy. When this occurs, the bond will trade at a discount, that is, below par. However, the bondholder will be paid the full face value of the bond at maturity even though he purchased it for less than the par value.

Bond Valuation in Practice

Since bonds are an essential part of the capital markets, investors and analysts seek to understand how the different features of a bond interact in order to determine its intrinsic value. Like a stock, the value of a bond determines whether it is a suitable investment for a portfolio and hence, is an integral step in bond investing.

Bond valuation, in effect, is calculating the present value of a bond's expected future coupon payments. The theoretical fair value of a bond is calculated by discounting the present value of its coupon payments by an appropriate discount rate. The discount rate used is the yield to maturity, which is the rate of return that an investor will get if s/he reinvested every coupon payment from the bond at a fixed interest rate until the bond matures. It takes into account the price of a bond, par value, coupon rate, and time to maturity.

Coupon Bond Valuation

Calculating the value of a coupon bond factors in the annual or semi-annual coupon payment and the par value of the bond.

The present value of expected cash flows is added to the present value of the face value of the bond as seen in the following formula:

$$V_{\text{coupans}} = \sum \frac{C}{(1+r)^t}$$

$$V_{\text{face value}} = \frac{F}{(1+r)^T}$$

Where C = future cash flows, that is, coupon payments,

r = discount rate, that is, yield to maturity,

F = face value of the bond,

t = number of periods,

T = time to maturity.

For example, let's find the value of a corporate bond with an annual interest rate of 5%, making semi-annual interest payments for 2 years, after which the bond matures and the principal must be repaid. Assume a YTM of 3%.

F = $1000 for corporate bond

Coupon $\text{rate}_{\text{annual}}$ = 5%, therefore, Coupon $\text{rate}_{\text{semi-annual}}$ = 5%/2 = 2.5%

C = 2.5% x $1000 = $25 per period

t = 2 years x 2 = 4 periods for semi-annual coupon payments

T = 4 periods

Present value of semi-annual payments = $25/(1.03)^1 + 25/(1.03)^2 + 25/(1.03)^3 + 25/(1.03)^4$

= 24.27 + 23.56 + 22.88 + 22.21

= 92.93

Present value of face value = $1000/(1.03)^4$

= 888.49

Therefore, value of bond = $92.93 + $888.49 = $981.42.

Zero-Coupon Bond Valuation

A zero-coupon bond makes no annual or semi-annual coupon payments for the duration of the bond. Instead, it is sold at a deep discount to par when issued. The difference between the purchase price and par value is the investor's interest earned on the bond. To calculate the value of a zero-coupon, we only need to find the present value of the face value.

Following our example above, if the bond paid no coupons to investors, its value will simply be:

$\$1000/(1.03)^4 = \$888.49$

Under both calculations, a coupon paying bond is more valuable than a zero-coupon bond.

References

- Bond-analysis-management, issue-selection, clear-investment-approach: simpsoncapital.com, Retrieved 1 February, 2019
- Bond: investopedia.com, Retrieved 4 April, 2019
- Features-of-bonds-investment, bonds-investment, investment: yourarticlelibrary.com, Retrieved 11 June, 2019
- The-basics-of-bonds, financial-edge: investopedia.com, Retrieved 10 August, 2019
- The-different-kinds-of-bonds: thestreet.com, Retrieved 9 January, 2019
- Understanding-different-types-bond-yields, investing: investopedia.com, Retrieved 19 July, 2019
- Bond-strategies, bonds, money: thismatter.com, Retrieved 30 May, 2019
- Bond-valuation: investopedia.com, Retrieved 2 March, 2019

6

Risk and Return on Investment

The probability of the occurrence of a loss relative to the expected return on an investment is known as an investment risk. The efficiency of an investment is evaluated using a performance measure known as Return on Investment (ROI). The topics elaborated in this chapter will help in gaining a better perspective about the branches of different types of investment risks as well as the Risk-Return Ratio.

The expected rate of return of an investment reflects the return an investor anticipates receiving from an investment. The required rate of return reflects the return an investor demands as compensation for postponing consumption and assuming risk. The required rate of return of an investment depends on the risk-free return, premium required for compensating business and financial risks attached with the firm's security.

The required rate of return also reflects the default risk, managerial risk and marketability of a particular security. Investors are generally risk averse. If odds of winning or losing are identical, they are likely to reject the gamble. Why anyone would want to expose himself to a risk without a corresponding return.

A rational investor would have some degree of risk aversion, he would accept the risk if he is compensated adequately for it. The greater the risk, the greater the compensation one would require. This compensation is in the form of increased rate of return. Investments which carry low risks, such as high grade bonds, will offer a lower expected rate of return than those which carry high risk such as common stock of a new unproven company. When one formulates an investment plan, this risk-return trade-off is an important consideration.

In determining the level of expected return one wishes to receive, he will also be determining the level of risk which one will have to accept. Conversely, in accepting a certain level of risk in designing a portfolio, the level of expected return is also get determined.

It may be difficult to quantify these levels, but one would at least have to think on a relative basis; that is a low, medium, or high degree of risk. There is a positive relationship between the amount of risk assumed and the amount of expected return. That is, the greater the risk, the larger the expected return and the larger the chances of substantial loss.

One of the most difficult problems for an investor is to estimate the highest level of risk he is able to assume. Any such estimate is essentially subjective, although attempts to quantify the willingness of an investor to assume various levels of risk can be made, the relationship between the amount of risk assumed in managing a portfolio of securities and the amount of expected return can be graphed as following in figure below.

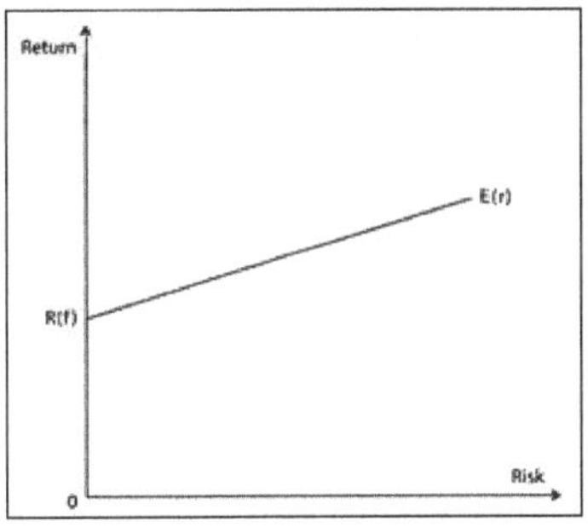

Figure: Relationship risk and return.

Risk is measured along the horizontal axis and increases from left to right. Expected rate of return is measured on the vertical axis and rises from bottom to top, the line from 0 to R (f) is called the rate of return on risk less investments commonly associated with the yield on government securities. The diagonal line from R (f) to E (r) illustrates the concept of expected rate of return increasing as level of risk increases.

The example shows a linear relationship between risk and return, but it need not be linear. Most of the theoretical work on portfolio management assumes a linear relationship between risk and return which may be true for an efficiently run competitive market in developed economies, but in developing countries like ours with administered interest rates and many other restrictive regulations, this linear relationship generally does not hold.

Risk-Return Relationship

The entire scenario of security analysis is built on two concepts of security: return and risk. The risk and return constitute the framework for taking investment decision. Return from equity comprises dividend and capital appreciation.

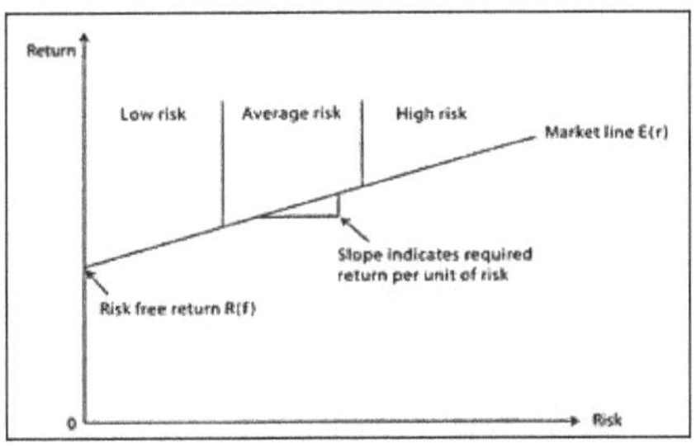

Figure: Risk-return relationship.

To earn return on investment, that is, to earn dividend and to get capital appreciation, investment has to be made for some period which in turn implies passage of time. Dealing with the return to be achieved requires estimate of the return on investment over the time period. Risk denotes deviation of actual return from the estimated return. This deviation of actual return from expected return may be on either side -both above and below the expected return. Figure represents the relationship between risk and return.

However, investors are more concerned with the downside risk. The risk in holding security-deviation of return- deviation of dividend and capital appreciation from the expected return may arise due to internal and external forces. The fact that investors do not hold a single security which they consider most profitable is enough to say that they are not only interested in the maximization of return, but also minimization of risk.

The investors increase their required return as perceived uncertainty increases. The rate of return differs substantially among alternative investments, and because the required return on specific investments change over time, the factors that influence the required rate of return must be considered.

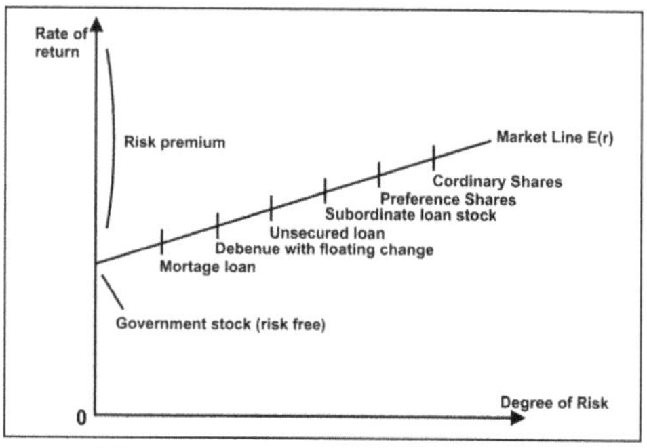

Figure: Risk-return relationship of different stocks.

The slope of the market line in figure indicates the return per unit of risk required by all investors Highly risk- averse investors would have a steeper line, and vice versa. Yields on apparently similar stocks may differ. Differences in price, and therefore yield, reflect the market's assessment of the issuing company's standing and of the risk elements in the particular stocks.

A high yield in relation to the market in general shows an above average risk element. Given the composite market line prevailing at a point of time, investors would select investments that are consistent with their risk preferences. Some will consider low risk investments, while others prefer high risk investments.

Costing and Risk

The word 'costing' relates to the ascertainment of cost of capital from different sources like equity capital, preference capital, debentures, long-term loans etc. The most crucial decision of any company is involved in the formulation of its appropriate capital structure.

The best design or structure of the capital of a company obviously helps the management to achieve its ultimate objectives of minimizing overall cost of capital, maximizing profitability and also maximizing the value of the firm. These will in turn help to maximize the earning per share. It is thus apparent that the design of the capital structure of a company may have some bearing on the profitability of that company.

Capital structure decisions assume vital significance in corporate financial management due to their influence both on return and risk of the shareholders. The close nexus between optimum/judicious use of debt and the market value of the firm is well recognized in literature. Whereas an excessive use of debt may endanger the very survival of the corporate firm, a conservative policy may deprive the corporate firm of its advantages in terms of magnifying the rate of return to its equity owners.

Risk-Return Trade Off

The prime objective of Financial Management is maximize the value of the firm, which is possible only when well balanced financial decisions are taken. The management should try to maximize the average profit while minimizing the risk. The projects promising a high average profit are generally accompanied by high risk.

Managers should accept such projects only if they will induce an increase in stock price. It is known that 'higher the return', other things being equal, 'higher the market value' and vice versa. Hence, it should be kept in view that risk and return go together. The risk-return trade-off is illustrated in figure below.

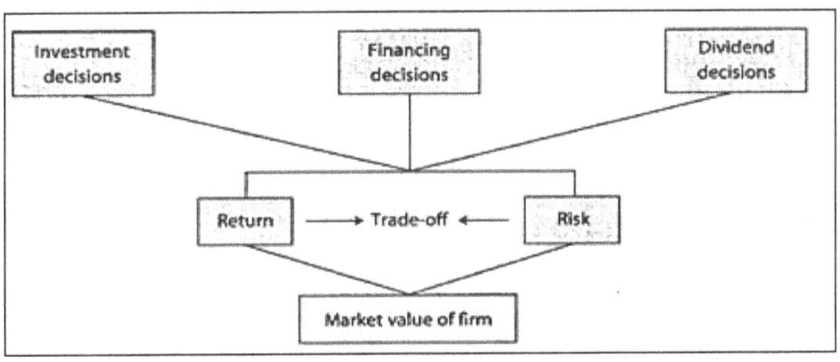

Figure: Risk-return trade off.

Concept of Risk and Returns

After investing money in a project a firm wants to get some outcomes from the project. The outcomes or the benefits that the investment generates are called returns. Wealth maximization approach is based on the concept of future value of expected cash flows from a prospective project.

So cash flows are nothing but the earnings generated by the project that we refer to as returns. Since fixture is uncertain, so returns are associated with some degree of uncertainty. In other words there will be some variability in generating cash flows, which we call as risk.

Concept of Risk

A person making an investment expects to get some returns from the investment in the future. However, as future is uncertain, the future expected returns too are uncertain. It is the uncertainty associated with the returns from an investment that introduces a risk into a project. The expected return is the uncertain future return that a firm expects to get from its project. The realized return, on the contrary, is the certain return that a firm has actually earned.

The realized return from the project may not correspond to the expected return. This possibility of variation of the actual return from the expected return is termed as risk. Risk is the variability in the expected return from a project. In other words, it is the degree of deviation from expected return. Risk is associated with the possibility that realized returns will be less than the returns that were expected. So, when realizations correspond to expectations exactly, there would be no risk.

Elements of Risk

Various components cause the variability in expected returns, which are known as elements of risk. There are broadly two groups of elements classified as systematic risk and unsystematic risk.

Systematic Risk

Business organizations are part of society that is dynamic. Various changes occur in a society like economic, political and social systems that have influence on the performance of companies and thereby on their expected returns. These changes affect all organizations to varying degrees. Hence the impact of these changes is system-wide and the portion of total variability in returns caused by such across the board factors is referred to as systematic risk. These risks are further subdivided into interest rate risk, market risk, and purchasing power risk.

Unsystematic Risk

The returns of a company may vary due to certain factors that affect only that company. Examples of such factors are raw material scarcity, labour strike, management inefficiency, etc. When the variability in returns occurs due to such firm-specific factors it is known as unsystematic risk. This risk is unique or peculiar to a specific organization and affects it in addition to the systematic risk. These risks are subdivided into business risk and financial risk.

Measurement of Risk

Quantification of risk is known as measurement of risk.

Two approaches are followed in measurement of risk:

i. Mean-variance approach,

ii. Correlation or regression approach.

Mean-variance approach is used to measure the total risk, i.e. sum of systematic and unsystematic risks. Under this approach the variance and standard deviation measure the extent of variability of possible returns from the expected return and is calculated as:

$$\sigma^2 = \sum_{i=1}^{n}\left[\left(X_i - \overline{X}\right)^2 p\left(X_i\right)\right]$$

Where, X_i = Possible return,

P = Probability of return,

n = Number of possible returns.

Correlation or regression method is used to measure the systematic risk. Systematic risk is expressed by β and is calculated by the following formula:

$$\beta_i = \frac{r_{im}\sigma_i\sigma_m}{\sigma_m^2}$$

Where, r_{im} = Correlation coefficient between the returns of stock i and the return of the market index,

σ_m = Standard deviation of returns of the market index,

σ_i = Standard deviation of returns of stock i.

Using regression method we may measure the systematic risk.

The form of the regression equation is as follows:

$$Y = \alpha + \beta X$$

It is used in the following form:

Or $\alpha + \overline{Y} - \beta\overline{X}$

And $\beta = \dfrac{n\sum XY - \left(\sum X\right)\left(\sum Y\right)}{n\sum X^2 - \left(\sum X\right)^2}$

Where, n = Number of items,

Y = Mean value of the company's return,

X = Mean value of return of the market index,

α = Estimated return of the security when the market is stationary, and

β = Change in the return of the individual security in response to unit change in the return of the market index.

Concept of Return

Return can be defined as the actual income from a project as well as appreciation in the value of capital. Thus there are two components in return—the basic component or the periodic cash flows from the investment, either in the form of interest or dividends; and the change in the price of the asset, commonly called as the capital gain or loss.

The term yield is often used in connection to return, which refers to the income component in relation to some price for the asset. The total return of an asset for the holding period relates to all the cash flows received by an investor during any designated time period to the amount of money invested in the asset.

It is Measured as:

Total Return = Cash payments received + Price change in assets over the period /Purchase price of the asset. In connection with return we use two terms—realized return and expected or predicted return. Realized return is the return that was earned by the firm, so it is historic. Expected or predicted return is the return the firm anticipates to earn from an asset over some future period.

Investment Risk

By understanding investment risk and how it relates to potential returns, investors can help strengthen their portfolios and improve their chances for greater wealth.

Defining Risk

Many investors view risk as the possibility of losing money, but it's really much more complex. Because of its multifaceted nature, risk can affect your investment in a number of ways.

Market/Downside Risk

Economic factors, such as recession, inflation or changing interest rates, can all influence the overall movement of the markets, thus affecting the value of your investment.

Also, stock values may fluctuate in response to the activities and financial prospects of an individual company. Because the financial markets are so dynamic, it's normal for your investment value to change on a daily basis. The degree to which your investment value can fluctuate determines how volatile it is.

Some individuals—even those with long-term investment horizons—dislike volatility because they are uncomfortable with short-term swings in value. As a general rule, the greater the volatility of an investment, the greater its potential for higher returns.

The most significant downside risk to your mutual fund investment is not short-term price changes, but that its value will decline at the point you need to sell. So, as you approach your investment goal, it may make sense to shift your portfolio to investments that seek to conserve principal, rather than to grow principal. This can lessen your downside risk in the short run.

Interest Rate Risk

Bond funds are generally perceived to be "safer" than stock funds because they have historically experienced less price volatility. However, individual bonds are issued with a fixed rate of interest, so their values fluctuate in response to changes in current interest rates. When interest rates increase, the value of an existing bond goes down, because it is paying a lower rate than what investors could earn elsewhere. When interest rates decrease, bonds increase in value because they are earning a higher rate than what investors could earn from newly issued bonds. Generally, the longer the maturity of a bond, the greater its degree of interest rate risk.

Credit Risk

If the company that issues a bond experiences financial difficulty or fails, bondholders may not be paid the promised interest or the full amount of their principal. This is referred to as credit risk. To help investors understand the extent of credit risk associated with different bonds, third-party organizations such as Moody's Investors Services evaluate and rate bonds. The higher the rating, the higher the quality of the bond. In exchange for greater safety though, higher quality bonds have less return potential. Likewise, lower quality bonds generally pay a higher interest rate to compensate investors for greater credit risk.

Inflation Risk

Some investors choose investments with fixed or guaranteed interest rates, such as bonds or certificates of deposit, because they desire security of principal. But inflation poses a risk to these investors, because there is a chance that the fixed rate may not keep pace with the rising cost of goods and services over time.

International Risk

There are a variety of risks involved with international investing. Foreign markets may be less mature and less regulated than US financial markets; the issuer of an international security may be subject to greater political or economic uncertainty, and foreign securities can gain or lose value when converted from one currency to another. However, international investing gives investors the opportunity to participate in a broader range of companies and economies. In many cases, these companies may offer greater potential than US-only investments. Also, a fund that is invested in several different countries can reduce risk through greater diversification.

Managing Risk

While awareness of risk can lead an investor to make prudent decisions, it is possible to be overly cautious. "Safe," low-interest cash investments, like money market funds, for example, are excellent choices for preserving assets once you approach or achieve your goal. But over the long-term, they generally cannot provide the capital appreciation needed to meet a significant investment goal. All investments involve risk—but there are strategies that you can follow to manage these risks and pursue your financial goals with more confidence.

Stay the Course

Some investors rush into the market when it is doing well and then unload their shares at the first hint of decline. While it is important to be knowledgeable about market movements, attempting to chase returns can be a risky business. If you have a significant investment goal, you must be willing to commit for the long term. The longer you remain with an investment, the greater its ability to withstand the market's normal fluctuations.

Diversify

You can offset the risks unique to one investment by simultaneously spreading your dollars among others. This way, you can balance the greater price volatility of stocks, for example, with the more stable, income-generating nature of bonds. This is called diversification. Diversification can also be accomplished by investing broadly within a particular asset—such as exposing the stock portion of your portfolio to different types of stock funds: an international stock fund, a large company stock fund and mid-size company stock fund.

Invest Regularly

Another effective method of managing risk is to invest regularly—that is, invest a consistent amount every month or quarter, regardless of what is happening in the markets.

As prices fall, your regular investment will buy more shares, and when prices rise again, your existing shares will increase in value. Many working individuals have the opportunity to participate in this approach—also called dollar cost averaging—through their company's retirement plan. Those who contribute with each payroll deduction are already familiar with the discipline and benefits derived from regular investing.

Put Risk in Perspective

Whether you're sampling a cup of steaming coffee or beginning the first day of a new job, you are encountering some form of risk. In the final analysis, only you can decide what you are willing to chance for meaningful rewards. Certainly no one should build an investment portfolio that causes one to lose sleep—you must feel comfortable about your investment objectives and the methods you've chosen to achieve them. Regardless of your investment goals, you can benefit from an understanding of risk. Use proven risk management techniques and commit to your chosen investment plan, and you may find risk to be a valuable ally.

Types of Investment Risk

Types of Risk

Systematic Risk: It refers to that portion of variability in return which is caused by the factors affecting all the firms. It refers to fluctuation in return due to general factors in the market such as money supply, inflation, economic recessions, interest rate policy of the government, political factors, credit policy, tax reforms, etc. these are the factors which affect almost all firms. The effect of these factors is to cause the prices of all securities to move together. This part of risk arises because every security has a built in tendency to move in line with fluctuations in the market. No investor can avoid or eliminate this risk, whatever precautions or diversification may be resorted to. The systematic risk is also called the non-diversifiable risk or general risk.

Types of Systematic Risk

1. Market Risk: Market prices of investments, particularly equity shares may fluctuate widely within a short span of time even though the earnings of the company are not changing. The reasons for this change in prices may be varied. Due to one factor or the other, investors' attitude may change towards equities resulting in the change in market price. Change in market price causes the return from investment to very. This is known as market risk. The market risk refers to variability in return due to change in market price of investment. Market risk appears because of reaction of investors to different events. There are different social, economic, political and firm specific events which affect the market price

of equity shares. Market psychology is another factor affecting market prices. In bull phases, market prices of all shares tend to increase while in bear phases, the prices tend to decline. In such situations, the market prices are pushed beyond far out of line with the fundamental value.

2. Interest-rate Risk: Interest rates on risk free securities and general interest rate level are related to each other. If the risk free rate of interest rises or falls, the rate of interest on the other bond securities also rises or falls. The interest rate risk refers to the variability in return caused by the change in level of interest rates. Such interest rate risk usually appears through the change in market price of fixed income securities, i.e., bonds and debentures. Security (bond and debentures) prices have an inverse relationship with the level of interest rates. When the interest rate rises, the prices of existing securities fall and vice-versa.

3. Purchasing power or Inflation Risk: The inflation risk refers to the uncertainty of purchasing power of cash flows to be received out of investment. It shows the impact of inflation or deflation on the investment. The inflation risk is related to interest rate risk because as inflation increases, the interest rates also tend to increase. The reason being that the investor wants an additional premium for inflation risk (resulting from decrease in purchasing power) Thus, there is an increase in interest rate. Investment involves a postponement in present consumption. If an investor makes an investment, he forgoes the opportunity to buy some goods or services during the investment period. If, during this period, the prices of goods and services go up, the investor losses in terms of purchasing power. The inflation risk arises because of uncertainty of purchasing power of the amount to be received from investment in future.

4. Unsystematic Risk: The unsystematic risk represents the fluctuation in return from an investment due to factors which are specific to the particular firm and not the market as a whole. These factors are largely independent of the factors affecting market in general. Since these factors are unique to a particular firm, these must be examined separately for each firm and for each industry. These factors may also be called firm-specific as these affect one firm without affecting the other firms. For example, a fluctuation in price of crude oil will affect the fortune of petroleum companies but not the textile manufacturing companies. As the unsystematic risk results from random events that tend to be unique to an industry or a firm, this risk is random in nature. Unsystematic risk is also called specific risk or diversifiable risk.

Types of Unsystematic Risk

1. Business Risk: Business risk refers to the variability in incomes of the firms and expected dividend there from, resulting from the operating condition in which

the firms have to operate. For example, if the earning or dividends from a company are expected to increase say, by 6%, however, the actual increase is 10% or 12 %. The variation in actual earnings than the expected earnings refers to business risk. Some industries have higher business risk than others. So, the securities of higher business risk firms are more risky than the securities of other firms which have lesser business risk.

2. Financial Risk: It refers to the degree of leverage or degree of debt financing used by a firm in the capital structure. Higher the degree of debt financing, the greater is the degree of financial risk. The presence of interest payment brings more variability in the earning available for equity shares. This is also known as financial leverage. A firm having lesser or no risk financing has lesser or no financial risk.

3. Measurement of risk: No investor can predict with certainty whether the income from an investment increase or decrease or by how much. Statistical measures can be used to make precise measurement of risk about the estimated returns, to gauge the extent to which the expected return and actual return are likely to differ.

The expected return, standard deviation and variance of outcomes can be computed as:

$$R = \sum_{i\ L}^{n} P_i\ Q_i$$

$$\sigma = \sqrt{\sum_{i\ L}^{n} P_i (O_i - R)^2}$$

Variance is σ^2

Where,

R = expected return,

σ^2 = variance of expected return,

σ = standard deviation of expected return,

P = Probability,

O = Outcome,

n = total number of different outcomes.

Beta Coefficient: There is another measure of risk known as β which measures the risk of one security/portfolio in relation to market risk. The market risk is represented by fluctuation in the market benchmark, i.e., market index, e.g., SENSEX. Shares whose β factor is more than 1 are considered less risky. It may be noted that β is a measure of systematic risk which cannot be diversified away.

The total risk of an investment consists of two components: diversifiable (unsystematic) risk and non diversifiable (systematic) risk.

The relationship between total risk, diversifiable risk, and non diversifiable risk can be expressed by the following equation:

Total risk = Diversifiable risk + Non Diversifiable risk.

Return on Investment

Return on Investment (ROI) is a performance measure used to evaluate the efficiency of an investment or compare the efficiency of a number of different investments. ROI tries to directly measure the amount of return on a particular investment, relative to the investment's cost. To calculate ROI, the benefit (or return) of an investment is divided by the cost of the investment. The result is expressed as a percentage or a ratio.

The return on investment formula:

ROI = (Current Value of Investment - Cost of Investment) / Cost of Investment

In the above formula, "Current Value of Investment" refers to the proceeds obtained from the sale of the investment of interest. Because ROI is measured as a percentage, it can be easily compared with returns from other investments, allowing one to measure a variety of types of investments against one another.

ROI is a popular metric because of its versatility and simplicity. Essentially, ROI can be used as a rudimentary gauge of an investment's profitability. This could be the ROI on a stock investment, the ROI a company expects on expanding a factory, or the ROI generated in a real estate transaction. The calculation itself is not too complicated, and it is relatively easy to interpret for its wide range of applications. If an investment's ROI is net positive, it is probably worthwhile. But if other opportunities with higher ROIs are available, these signals can help investors eliminate or select the best options. Likewise, investors should avoid negative ROIs, which imply a net a loss.

For example, suppose Joe invested $1,000 in Slice Pizza Corp. in 2017 and sold his stock shares for a total of $1,200 one year later. To calculate his return on his investment, he would divide his profits ($1,200 - $1,000 = $200) by the investment cost ($1,000), for a ROI of $200/$1,000, or 20 percent.

With this information, he could compare his investment in Slice Pizza with his other projects. Suppose Joe also invested $2,000 in Big-Sale Stores Inc. in 2014 and sold his shares for a total of $2,800 in 2017. The ROI on Joe's holdings in Big-Sale would be $800/$2,000, or 40 percent.

Limitations of ROI

Examples like Joe's (above) reveal some limitations of using ROI, particularly when comparing investments. While the ROI of Joe's second investment was twice that of his first investment, the time between Joe's purchase and sale was one year for his first investment and three years for his second.

Joe could adjust the ROI of his multi-year investment accordingly. Since his total ROI was 40 percent, to obtain his average annual ROI, he could divide 40 percent by 3 to yield 13.33 percent. With this adjustment, it appears that although Joe's second investment earned him more profit, his first investment was actually the more efficient choice.

ROI can be used in conjunction with Rate of Return, which takes in account a project's time frame. One may also use Net Present Value (NPV), which accounts for differences in the value of money over time, due to inflation. The application of NPV when calculating rate of return is often called the Real Rate of Return.

Developments in ROI

Recently, certain investors and businesses have taken an interest in the development of a new form of the ROI metric, called "Social Return on Investment," or SROI. SROI was initially developed in the early 2000s and takes into account broader impacts of projects using extra-financial value (i.e. social and environmental metrics not currently reflected in conventional financial accounts). SROI helps understand the value proposition of certain ESG (Environmental Social & Governance) criteria used in socially responsible investing (SRI) practices. For instance, a company may undertake to recycle water in its factories and replace its lighting with all LED bulbs. These undertakings have an immediate cost which may negatively impact traditional ROI - however, the net benefit to society and the environment could lead to a positive SROI.

There are several other new flavors of ROI that have been developed for particular purposes. Social media statistics ROI pinpoints the effectiveness of social media campaigns - for example how many clicks or likes are generated for a unit of effort. Similarly, marketing statistics ROI tries to identify the return attributable to advertising or marketing campaigns. So-called learning ROI relates to amount of information learned and retained as return on education or skills training. As the world progresses and the economy changes, several other niche forms of ROI are sure to be developed in the future.

Purpose of ROI

In business, the purpose of the return on investment (ROI) metric is to measure, per period, rates of return on money invested in an economic entity in order to decide whether or not to undertake an investment. It is also used as an indicator to compare different investments within a portfolio. The investment with the largest ROI is usually prioritized, even though the spread of ROI over the time period of an investment should also be taken into account. Recently, the concept has also been applied to scientific funding agencies' (e.g., National Science Foundation) investments in research of open source hardware and subsequent returns for direct digital replication.

ROI and related metrics provide a snapshot of profitability, adjusted for the size of the investment assets tied up in the enterprise. ROI is often compared to expected (or required) rates of return on money invested. ROI is not time-adjusted (unlike e.g. net present value).

Marketing decisions have an obvious potential connection to the numerator of ROI (profits), but these same decisions often influence assets' usage and capital requirements (for example, receivables and inventories). Marketers should understand the position of their company and the returns expected. In a survey of nearly 200 senior marketing managers, 77 percent responded that they found the "return on investment" metric very useful.

Return on investment may be extended to terms other than financial gain. For example, social return on investment (SROI) is a principles-based method for measuring extra-financial value (i.e., environmental and social value not currently reflected in conventional financial accounts) relative to resources invested. It can be used by any entity to evaluate the impact on stakeholders, identify ways to improve performance and enhance the performance of investments.

Risk with ROI usage

As a decision tool, it is simple to understand. The simplicity of the formula allows users to freely choose variables, e.g., length of the calculation time, whether overhead cost is included, or which factors are used to calculate income or cost components. To use ROI as an indicator for prioritizing investment projects is risky since usually the ROI figure is not accompanied by an explanation of its make-up.

For long-term investments, the need for a Net Present Value adjustment is great. Similar to Discounted Cash Flow, a Discounted ROI should be used instead.

One of greatest risks associated with the traditional ROI calculation is that it does not fully "capture the short-term or long-term importance, value, or risks associated with natural and social capital" because it does not account for the environmental, social and governance performance of an organization. Without a metric for measuring the short- and long-term environmental, social and governance performance of a firm, decision makers are planning for the future without considering the extent of the impacts associated with their decisions.

ROI Calculation and Formula

ROI = (Net Profit / Cost of Investment) x 100.

The ROI calculation is flexible and can be manipulated for different uses. A company may use the calculation to compare the ROI on different potential investments, while an investor could use it to calculate a return on a stock.

For example, an investor buys $1,000 worth of stocks and sells the shares two years later for $1,200. The net profit from the investment would be $200 and the ROI would be calculated as follows:

ROI = (200 / 1,000) x 100 = 20%.

The ROI in the example above would be 20%. The calculation can be altered by deducting taxes and fees to get a more accurate picture of the total ROI.

The same calculation can be used to calculate an investment made by a company. However, the calculation is more complex because there are more inputs. For example, to figure out the net profit of an investment, a company might need to track exactly how much cash went into the project and the time spent by employees working on it.

Calculating ROI

Because ROI can be made as complex or as simple as the measurer wants it to be, it can be used by a variety of different professionals or companies.

A marketing professional could calculate the ROI of a marketing campaign by dividing the campaign's revenue by the marketing expenses directly involved in that campaign.

So if the marketing department spent a total of $1,000 on material costs and labor hours on the campaign, and it generated $5,000 in revenue for the year, then the campaign had an ROI of 500% or ($5,000 in revenue / $1,000 in cost) X 100 = 500% ROI.

A homeowner could calculate the ROI of a given home renovation, too. Let's say the homeowner spent $30,000 to update their kitchen. If the homeowner had the home appraised just before and after the renovation, and found the house gained $45,000 in value, that would mean the renovation yielded a 50% ROI or ($15,000 in profit / $30,000 in cost) X 100= 50% ROI.

Good ROI

ROI is one of the most used profitability ratios because of its flexibility. That being said, one of the downsides of the ROI calculation is that it can be manipulated, so results may vary between users. When using ROI to compare investments, it's important to use the same inputs to get an accurate comparison.

Also, it's important to note that the basic ROI calculation does not take time into consideration. Obviously, it's more desirable to get a +15% return over one year than it is over two years.

Common Mistakes in Calculating ROI

ROI can be used for any type of investment. The only variation in investments that must be considered is how costs and profits are accounted for. Two examples how return on investment can be commonly miscalculated.

- Stocks: Investors commonly fail to incorporate transaction costs and dividend payouts into the ROI of stocks. Transaction costs are a cost to your investment while dividend payouts are a gain to your investment. The investor must take into account both the transaction cost and dividend gain to get an accurate return calculation. If this is not done, the ROI would be misrepresented.

- Real Estate: Investors commonly fail to incorporate rental income, taxes, insurance, and upkeep in the return on investment calculation of real estate. Rental income is a gain to your investment while taxes, insurance, and upkeep are costs to your investment.

It is important to account for the costs and gains of your investment throughout its entire lifespan, instead of merely taking the end of investment value and dividing it by initial cost.

ROI Calculator in Excel

Download CFI's free ROI Calculator in Excel to perform your own analysis. The calculator uses the examples explained and is designed so you can easily input your own numbers and see what the output is under different scenarios.

The calculator covers four different methods: net income, capital gain, total return, and annualized return.

ROI Calculator	
Net Income Method	
Original Investment Value	$1,000,000
Net Income	$125,500
ROI	12.6%
Capital Gain Method	
Original Share Price	$12.50
Current Share Price	$15.20
ROI	21.6%
Total Return Method	
Original Share Price	$12.50
Total Dividends Received	$1.25
Current Share Price	$15.20
ROI	31.6%
Annualized ROI	
Original Share Price	$12.50
Current Share Price	$15.20
Purchase Date	1/1/2017
Sale Date	8/24/2017
Annualized ROI	35.5%

The best way to learn the difference between each of the four approaches is to input different numbers and scenarios and see what happens to the results.

Risk-Return Tradeoff

The risk-return tradeoff states that the potential return rises with an increase in risk. Using this principle, individuals associate low levels of uncertainty with low potential returns, and high levels of uncertainty or risk with high potential returns. According to the risk-return tradeoff, invested money can render higher profits only if the investor will accept a higher possibility of losses.

The risk-return tradeoff is the trading principle that links high risk with high reward. The appropriate risk-return tradeoff depends on a variety of factors including an investor's risk tolerance, the investor's years to retirement and the potential to replace lost funds. Time also plays an essential role in determining a portfolio with the appropriate levels of risk and reward. For example, if an investor has the ability to invest in equities over the long term, that provides the investor with the potential to recover from the risks of bear markets and participate in bull markets, while if an investor can only invest in a short time frame, the same equities have a higher risk proposition.

Investors use the risk-return tradeoff as one of the essential components of each investment decision, as well as to assess their portfolios as a whole. At the portfolio level, the risk-return tradeoff can include assessments of the concentration or the diversity of holdings and whether the mix presents too much risk or a lower-than-desired potential for returns.

Measuring Singular Risk in Context

When an investor considers high-risk-high-return investments, the investor can apply the risk-return tradeoff to the vehicle on a singular basis as well as within the context of the portfolio as a whole. Examples of high-risk-high return investments include options, penny stocks and leveraged exchange-traded funds (ETFs). Generally speaking, a diversified portfolio reduces the risks presented by individual investment positions. For example, a penny stock position may have a high risk on a singular basis, but if it is the only position of its kind in a larger portfolio, the risk incurred by holding the stock is minimal.

Risk-Return Tradeoff at the Portfolio Level

That said, the risk-return tradeoff also exists at the portfolio level. For example, a portfolio composed of all equities presents both higher risk and higher potential returns. Within an all-equity portfolio, risk and reward can be increased by concentrating investments in specific sectors or by taking on single positions that represent a large percentage of holdings. For investors, assessing the cumulative risk-return tradeoff of all positions can provide insight on whether a portfolio assumes enough risk to achieve long-term return objectives or if the risk levels are too high with the existing mix of holdings.

Risk–Return Spectrum

The risk–return spectrum (also called the risk–return tradeoff or risk–reward) is the relationship between the amount of return gained on an investment and the amount of risk undertaken in that investment. The more return sought, the more risk that must be undertaken.

The Progression

There are various classes of possible investments, each with their own positions on the overall risk-return spectrum. The general progression is: short-term debt; long-term debt; property; high-yield debt; equity. There is considerable overlap of the ranges for each investment class.

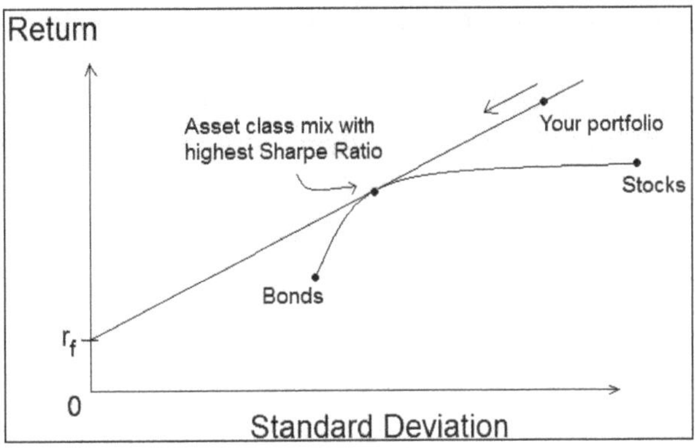

Sharpe Ratio.

All this can be visualised by plotting expected return on the vertical axis against risk (represented by standard deviation upon that expected return) on the horizontal axis. This line starts at the risk-free rate and rises as risk rises. The line will tend to be straight, and will be straight at equilibrium.

For any particular investment type, the line drawn from the risk-free rate on the vertical axis to the risk-return point for that investment has a slope called the Sharpe ratio.

Short-Term Loans to Good Government Bodies

On the lowest end is short-dated loans to government and government-guaranteed entities (usually semi-independent government departments). The lowest of all is the risk-free rate of return. The risk-free rate has zero risk (most modern major governments will inflate and monetise their debts rather than default upon them), but the return is positive because there is still both the time-preference and inflation premium components of minimum expected rates of return that must be met or exceeded if the funding is to be forthcoming from providers. The risk-free rate is commonly approximated by the return paid upon 30-day or their equivalent, but in reality that rate has more to do with the monetary policy of that country's central bank than the market supply conditions for credit.

Mid- and Long-Term Loans to Good Government Bodies

The next types of investment is longer-term loans to government, such as 3-year bonds. The range width is larger, and follows the influence of increasing risk premium required as the maturity of that debt grows longer. Nevertheless, because it is debt of good government the highest end of the range is still comparatively low compared to the ranges of other investment types

Also, if the government in question is not at the highest jurisdiction (i.e., is a state or municipal government), or the smaller that government is, the more along the risk-return spectrum that government's securities will be.

Short-Term Loans to Blue-Chip Corporations

Following the lowest-risk investments are short-dated bills of exchange from major blue-chip corporations with the highest credit ratings. The further away from perfect the credit rating, the higher up the risk-return spectrum that particular investment will be.

Mid- and Long-Term Loans to Blue-Chip Corporations

Overlapping the range for short-term debt is the longer term debt from those same well-rated corporations. These are higher up the range because the maturity has increased. The overlap occurs of the mid-term debt of the best rated corporations with the short-term debt of the nearly perfectly, but not perfectly rated corporations.

In this arena, the debts are called investment grade by the rating agencies. The lower the credit rating, the higher the yield and thus the expected return.

Rental Property

A commercial property that the investor rents out is comparable in risk or return to a low-investment grade. Industrial property has higher risk and returns, followed by residential (with the possible exception of the investor's own home).

High-Yield Debt

After the returns upon all classes of investment-grade debt come the returns on speculative-grade high-yield debt (also known derisively as junk bonds). These may come from mid and low rated corporations, and less politically stable governments.

Equity

Equity returns are the profits earned by businesses after interest and tax. Even the equity returns on the highest rated corporations are notably risky. Small-cap stocks are generally riskier than large-cap; companies that primarily service governments, or provide basic consumer goods such as food or utilities, tend to be less volatile than those in other industries. Note that since stocks tend to rise when corporate bonds fall and vice versa, a portfolio containing a small percentage of stocks can be less risky than one containing only debts.

Options and Futures

Option and futures contracts often provide leverage on underlying stocks, bonds or commodities; this increases the returns but also the risks. Note that in some cases, derivatives can be used to hedge, decreasing the overall risk of the portfolio due to negative correlation with other investments.

Progression

The existence of risk causes the need to incur a number of expenses. For example, the more risky the investment the more time and effort is usually required to obtain information about it and monitor its progress. For another, the importance of a loss of X amount of value is greater than the importance of a gain of X amount of value, so a riskier investment will attract a higher risk premium even if the forecast return is the same as upon a less risky investment. Risk is therefore something that must be compensated for, and the more risk the more compensation required.

If an investment had a high return with low risk, eventually everyone would want to invest there. That action would drive down the actual rate of return achieved, until it reached the rate of return the market deems commensurate with the level of risk. Similarly, if an investment had a low return with high risk, all the present investors would want to leave that investment, which would then increase the actual return until again it reached the rate of return the market deems commensurate with the level of risk. That part of total returns which sets this appropriate level is called the risk premium.

Leverage Extends the Spectrum

The use of leverage can extend the progression out even further. Examples of this include borrowing funds to invest in equities, or use of derivatives.

If leverage is used then there are two lines instead of one. This is because although one can invest at the risk-free rate, one can only borrow at an interest rate according to one's own credit-rating. This is visualised by the new line starting at the point of the riskiest unleveraged investment (equities) and rising at a lower slope than the original line. If this new line were traced back to the vertical axis of zero risk, it will cross it at the borrowing rate.

Domination

All investment types compete against each other, even though they are on different positions on the risk-return spectrum. Any of the mid-range investments can have their performances simulated by a portfolio consisting of a risk-free component and the highest-risk component. This principle, called the separation property, is a crucial feature of modern portfolio theory. The line is then called the capital market line.

If at any time there is an investment that has a higher Sharpe ratio than another then that return is said to dominate. When there are two or more investments above the spectrum line, then the one with the highest Sharpe ratio is the most dominant one, even if the risk and return on that particular investment is lower than another. If every mid-range return falls below the spectrum line, this means that the highest-risk investment has the highest Sharpe Ratio and so dominates over all others.

If at any time there is an investment that dominates then funds will tend to be withdrawn from all others and be redirected to that dominating investment. This action will lower the return on that investment and raise it on others. The withdrawal and redirection of capital ceases when all returns are at the levels appropriate for the degrees of risk and commensurate with the opportunity cost arising from competition with the other investment types on the spectrum, which means they all tend to end up having the same Sharpe Ratio.

Efficient Frontier

The efficient frontier is the set of optimal portfolios that offer the highest expected return for a defined level of risk or the lowest risk for a given level of expected return. Portfolios that lie below the efficient frontier are sub-optimal because they do not provide enough return for the level of risk. Portfolios that cluster to the right of the efficient frontier are sub-optimal because they have a higher level of risk for the defined rate of return.

The efficient frontier rates portfolios (investments) on a scale of return (y-axis) versus risk (x-axis). Compound Annual Growth Rate (CAGR) of an investment is commonly used as the return component while standard deviation (annualized) depicts the risk metric. The efficient frontier theory was introduced by Nobel Laureate Harry Markowitz in 1952 and is a cornerstone of modern portfolio theory (MPT).

The efficient frontier graphically represents portfolios that maximize returns for the risk assumed. Returns are dependent on the investment combinations that make up the portfolio. The standard deviation of a security is synonymous with risk. Ideally, an investor seeks to populate the portfolio with securities offering exceptional returns but whose combined standard deviation is lower than the standard deviations of the individual securities. The less synchronized the securities (lower covariance) then the lower the standard deviation. If this mix of optimizing the return versus risk paradigm is successful then that portfolio should line up along the efficient frontier line.

A key finding of the concept was the benefit of diversification resulting from the curvature of the efficient frontier. The curvature is integral in revealing how diversification improves the portfolio's risk / reward profile. It also reveals that there is a diminishing marginal return to risk. The relationship is not linear. In other words, adding more risk to a portfolio does not gain an equal amount of return. Optimal portfolios that comprise the efficient frontier tend to have a higher degree of diversification than the sub-optimal ones, which are typically less diversified.

Optimal Portfolio

One assumption in investing is that a higher degree of risk means a higher potential return. Conversely, investors who take on a low degree of risk have a low potential return. According to Markowitz's theory, there is an optimal portfolio that could be designed with a perfect balance between risk and return. The optimal portfolio does not simply include securities with the highest potential returns or low-risk securities. The optimal portfolio aims to balance securities with the greatest potential returns with an acceptable degree of risk or securities with the lowest degree of risk for a given level of potential return. The points on the plot of risk versus expected returns where optimal portfolios lie are known as the efficient frontier.

Selecting Investments

Assume a risk-seeking investor uses the efficient frontier to select investments. The investor would select securities that lie on the right end of the efficient frontier. The right end of the efficient frontier includes securities that are expected to have a high degree of risk coupled with high potential returns, which is suitable for highly risk-tolerant investors. Conversely, securities that lie on the left end of the efficient frontier would be suitable for risk-averse investors.

Limitations

The efficient frontier and modern portfolio theory have many assumptions that may not properly represent reality. For example, one of the assumptions is that asset returns follow a normal distribution. In reality, securities may experience returns that are more than three standard deviations away from the mean in more than 0.03% of the observed values. Consequently, asset returns are said to follow a leptokurtic distribution or heavy-tailed distribution.

Additionally, Markowitz posits several assumptions in his theory, such as that investors are rational and avoid risk when possible; there are not enough investors to influence market prices; and investors have unlimited access to borrowing and lending money at the risk-free interest rate. However, reality proves that the market includes irrational and risk-seeking investors, there are large market participants who could influence market prices, and there are investors who do not have unlimited access to borrowing and lending money.

Capital Asset Pricing Model (CAPM)

The Capital Asset Pricing Model (CAPM) describes the relationship between systematic risk and expected return for assets, particularly stocks. CAPM is widely used throughout finance for pricing risky securities and generating expected returns for assets given the risk of those assets and cost of capital.

Understanding the Capital Asset Pricing Model (CAPM)

The formula for calculating the expected return of an asset given its risk is as follows:

$$ER_i = R_f + \beta_i\left(ER_m - R_f\right)$$

ER_i = Expected return of investment

R_f = Risk-free rate

β_i = Beta of the investment

ER_m = Expected return of market

$(ER_m - R_f)$ = Market risk premium

Investors expect to be compensated for risk and the time value of money. The risk-free rate in the CAPM formula accounts for the time value of money. The other components of the CAPM formula account for the investor taking on additional risk.

The beta of a potential investment is a measure of how much risk the investment will add to a portfolio that looks like the market. If a stock is riskier than the market, it will have a beta greater than one. If a stock has a beta of less than one, the formula assumes it will reduce the risk of a portfolio.

A stock's beta is then multiplied by the market risk premium, which is the return expected from the market above the risk-free rate. The risk-free rate is then added to the product of the stock's beta and the market risk premium. The result should give an investor the required return or discount rate they can use to find the value of an asset.

The goal of the CAPM formula is to evaluate whether a stock is fairly valued when its risk and the time value of money are compared to its expected return.

For example, imagine an investor is contemplating a stock worth $100 per share today that pays a 3% annual dividend. The stock has a beta compared to the market of 1.3, which means it is riskier than a market portfolio. Also, assume that the risk-free rate is 3% and this investor expects the market to rise in value by 8% per year.

The expected return of the stock based on the CAPM formula is 9.5%.

$$9.5\% = 3\% + 1.3\left(8\% - 3\%\right)$$

The expected return of the CAPM formula is used to discount the expected dividends and capital appreciation of the stock over the expected holding period. If the discounted value of those future cash flows is equal to $100 then the CAPM formula indicates the stock is fairly valued relative to risk.

Problems with the CAPM

There are several assumptions behind the CAPM formula that have been shown not to hold in reality. Despite these issues, the CAPM formula is still widely used because it is simple and allows for easy comparisons of investment alternatives.

Including beta in the formula assumes that risk can be measured by a stock's price volatility. However, price movements in both directions are not equally risky. The look-back period to determine a stock's volatility is not standard because stock returns (and risk) are not normally distributed.

The CAPM also assumes that the risk-free rate will remain constant over the discounting period. Assume in the previous example that the interest rate on U.S. Treasury bonds rose to 5% or 6% during the 10-year holding period. An increase in the risk-free rate also increases the cost of the capital used in the investment and could make the stock look overvalued.

The market portfolio that is used to find the market risk premium is only a theoretical value and is not an asset that can be purchased or invested in as an alternative to the stock. Most of the time, investors will use a major stock index, like the S&P 500, to substitute for the market, which is an imperfect comparison.

The most serious critique of the CAPM is the assumption that future cash flows can be estimated for the discounting process. If an investor could estimate the future return of a stock with a high level of accuracy, the CAPM would not be necessary.

The CAPM and the Efficient Frontier

Using the CAPM to build a portfolio is supposed to help an investor manage their risk. If an investor were able to use the CAPM to perfectly optimize a portfolio's return relative to risk, it would exist on a curve called the efficient frontier, as shown on the following graph.

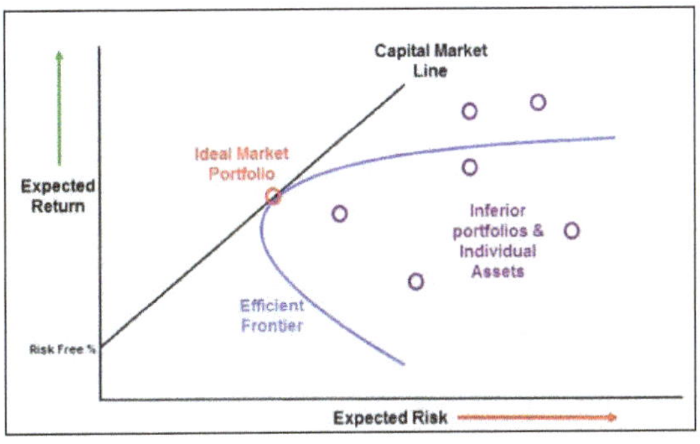

The graph shows how greater expected returns (y-axis) require greater expected risk (x-axis). Modern Portfolio Theory suggests that starting with the risk-free rate, the expected return of a portfolio increases as the risk increases. Any portfolio that fits on the Capital Market Line (CML) is better than any possible portfolio to the right of that line, but at some point, a theoretical portfolio can be constructed on the CML with the best return for the amount of risk being taken.

The CML and efficient frontier may be difficult to define, but it illustrates an important concept for investors: there is a trade-off between increased return and increased risk. Because it isn't possible to perfectly build a portfolio that fits on the CML, it is more common for investors to take on too much risk as they seek additional return.

In the following chart, you can see two portfolios that have been constructed to fit along the efficient frontier. Portfolio A is expected to return 8% per year and has a 10% standard deviation or risk level. Portfolio B is expected to return 10% per year but has a 16% standard deviation. The risk of portfolio B rose faster than its expected returns.

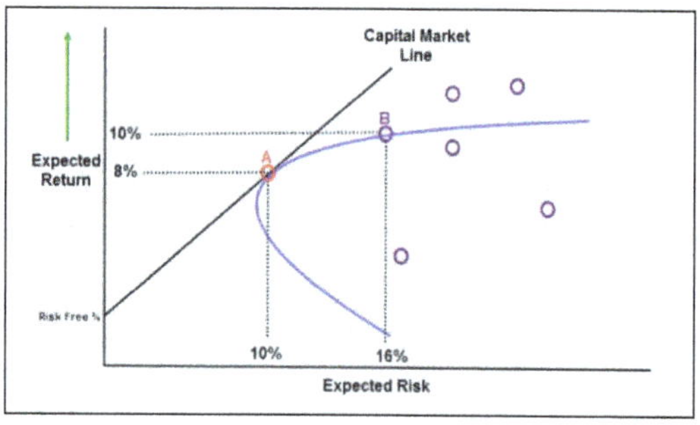

The efficient frontier assumes the same things as the CAPM and can only be calculated in theory. If a portfolio existed on the efficient frontier it would be providing the maximal return for its level of risk. However, it is impossible to know whether a portfolio exists on the efficient frontier or not because future returns cannot be predicted.

This trade-off between risk and return applies to the CAPM and the efficient frontier graph can be rearranged to illustrate the trade-off for individual assets. In the following chart, you can see that the CML is now called the Security Market Line (SML). Instead of expected risk on the x-axis, the stock's beta is used. As you can see in the illustration, as beta increases from one to two, the expected return is also rising.

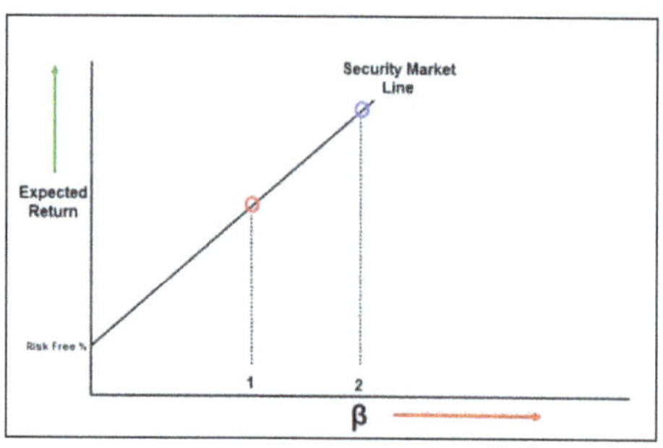

The CAPM and SML make a connection between a stock's beta and its expected risk. A higher beta means more risk but a portfolio of high beta stocks could exist somewhere on the CML where the trade-off is acceptable, if not the theoretical ideal.

The value of these two models is diminished by assumptions about beta and market participants that aren't true in the real markets. For example, beta does not account for the relative riskiness of a stock that is more volatile than the market with a high frequency of downside shocks compared to another stock with an equally high beta that does not experience the same kind of price movements to the downside.

Practical Value of the CAPM

Considering the critiques of the CAPM and the assumptions behind its use in portfolio construction, it might be difficult to see how it could be useful. However, using the CAPM as a tool to evaluate the reasonableness of future expectations or to conduct comparisons can still have some value.

Imagine an advisor who has proposed adding a stock to a portfolio with a $100 share price. The advisor uses the CAPM to justify the price with a discount rate of 13%. The advisor's investment manager can take this information and compare it to the company's past performance and its peers to see if a 13% return is a reasonable expectation.

Assume in this example that the peer group's performance over the last few years was a little better than 10% while this stock had consistently underperformed with 9% returns. The investment manager shouldn't take the advisor's recommendation without some justification for the increased expected return.

An investor can also use the concepts from the CAPM and efficient frontier to evaluate their portfolio or individual stock performance compared to the rest of the market. For example, assume that an investor's portfolio has returned 10% per year for the last three years with a standard deviation of returns (risk) of 10%. However, the market averages have returned 10% for the last three years with a risk of 8%.

The investor could use this observation to reevaluate how their portfolio is constructed and which holdings may not be on the SML. This could explain why the investor's portfolio is to the right of the CML. If the holdings that are either dragging on returns or have increased the portfolio's risk disproportionately can be identified, the investor can make changes to improve returns.

The CAPM uses the principles of Modern Portfolio Theory to determine if a security is fairly valued. It relies on assumptions about investor behaviors, risk and return distributions, and market fundamentals that don't match reality. However, the underlying concepts of CAPM and the associated efficient frontier can help investors understand the relationship between expected risk and reward as they make better decisions about adding securities to a portfolio.

Risk-Return Ratio

The risk-return-ratio is a measure of return in terms of risk for a specific time period. The percentage return (R) for the time period is measured in a straightforward way:

$$R = \left(P_{end} - P_{start}\right) / P_{start}$$

where P_{start} and P_{end} simply refer to the price by the start and end of the time period.

The risk is measured as the percentage maximum drawdown (MDD) for the specific period:

$$MDD = Max_{t \in (start,\, end)}\left(DD_t\right) \text{ where } DD_t = \begin{cases} 1 - DD_{t-1}\dfrac{P_t}{P_{t-1}} & \text{if } P_t - P_{t-1} < 0 \\ 0 & \text{otherwise} \end{cases}$$

where DD_t, DD_{t-1}, P_t and P_{t-1} refer the drawdown (*DD*) and prices (*P*) at a specific point in time, *t*, or the time right before that, *t*-1.

The risk-return-ratio is then defined and measured, for a specific time period, as:

RRR = R/MDD

Note that dividing a percentage numerator by a percentage denominator renders a single number. This RRR number is a measure of the return in terms of risk. It is fully comparable, i.e. it's possible to compare the RRR for one share with the RRR of another share, just as long as it's the same time period.

The RRR as defined here is formally the same as the so-called MER ratio, and shares some similarities with the Calmar ratio, the Sterling ratio and the Burke ratio. However, the RRR can arguably be regarded as more general than the MER ratio since it can be used for any time interval even daily or intra-day prices, while the MER ratio seems to be confined to measuring only the risk and return of a fund since inception until the current date. It is also less ad hoc than the Calmar, the Sterling and the Burke ratios.

Factors Influencing the Return-Rate on an Investment

When you decide to invest your finances, the chances are good that the estimated return of the investment asset (which could be stocks, bonds, real estate, mutual funds, etc.) has factored significantly into your decision. The rate of return on an investment asset can be defined as the income and capital appreciation over a measurement period divided by the cost of acquisition, expressed as a percentage. Not surprisingly, the rates of return depend on several factors, such as the portfolio composition and macroeconomic conditions, among others. These return rates will largely determine the extent to which you, the investor, can meet your financial objectives.

Factors that influence your rate of return include the mix of assets, the business's strategy and operations, the state of the economy, political stability, fiscal policy and regulations.

The Ideal Asset Mix

The asset mix of an investment portfolio determines its overall return. There is a risk-return tradeoff with every asset – the higher the risk, the higher the volatility and return potential. For example, stocks are generally riskier and more volatile than bonds, but the rates of return on stocks have exceeded those of bonds over the long term.

An investment portfolio fully invested in stocks is likely to suffer in a down economy and during periods of high market volatility. On the other hand, a conservative portfolio invested mainly in high-quality bonds is likely to have lower, although more predictable and stable returns.

Strategic and Operational Fundamentals

The strategic and operational fundamentals of the underlying businesses affect investment returns. Strategy involves positioning a company to take advantage of opportunities and responding effectively to competitive threats. Operational execution involves managing costs, expanding into new markets and continually innovating to stay ahead of the competition.

Companies that consistently meet sales and profit expectations generally see their stock prices outperform market averages. Conversely, companies that lose market share and miss earnings expectations almost always underperform the market.

The General Economy

Macroeconomic conditions affect investment rates of return. A growing economy means that more people have jobs, which means they spend more. For businesses, this leads to increases in sales, profits and investments in new employees and equipment. However, rapid economic growth can lead to higher interest rates. This makes credit more expensive, thus dampening consumer spending and business investments.

Economic slowdowns lead to low employment, which usually means lower profits and stock prices. The resulting weakness in the stock markets could improve bond prices as investors move funds to the relative safety of bonds.

Government and Political Factors

Fiscal policy, regulations and political stability also affect investment rates of return. Large fiscal deficits reduce government flexibility and may result in higher borrowing costs for businesses. An arduous regulatory approval process can hamper business investments in the resource and energy sectors. Political stability creates investor and business confidence because there is more visibility into possible investment returns. Investors tend to avoid countries that change governments frequently or have civil strife.

Risk Premium

The risk premium is the rate of return on an investment over and above the risk-free or guaranteed rate of return.

To calculate risk premium, investors must first calculate the estimated return and the risk-free rate of return. The estimated return, or the expected return, on a stock refers to the amount of profit or loss that an investor expects from a particular investment.

The estimated return is a projection and is not a guaranteed return. Investors can calculate the estimated return by multiplying the potential outcomes by the percent chance of them occurring and then adding those calculations together.

Calculating the estimated return is one way for investors to assess the risk of an investment.

The risk-free rate is the rate of return on an investment when there is no chance of financial loss. For example, the U.S. government backs Treasury bills, which makes them low risk. However, because the risk is low, the rate of return is also lower than other types of investments.

If the estimated rate of return on the investment is less than the risk-free rate, then the result is a negative risk premium. In these instances, investors would be better off investing in a Treasury bill because the return is both greater and guaranteed.

Basics of Risk Premia

Think of a risk premium as a form of hazard pay for your investments. Just as employees who have relatively dangerous jobs receive hazard pay as compensation for the risks they undertake, risky investments must provide an investor with the potential for larger returns to compensate for the risks of the investment.

Investors expect to be properly compensated for the amount of risk they undertake in the form of a risk premium, or additional returns above the rate of return on a risk-free investment such as U.S. government-issued securities. In other words, investors risk losing their money because of the uncertainty of a potential investment failure on the part of the borrower in exchange for receiving extra returns as a reward if the investment is profitable. Therefore, the prospect of earning a risk premium does not mean investors can actually get it because it is possible the borrower may default absent a successful investment outcome.

A risk premium can also be construed as a true earnings reward as some risky investments are inherently more profitable when and if they come through as an investment success. Investments with certainties and predictable outcomes are not likely to become business breakthroughs when already operating in well-penetrated markets. Only novel and risky business and investment initiatives could potentially offer above-average returns the borrower may then use as an earnings reward for investors. This is one underlying incentive that has encouraged some investors to seek riskier investments, knowing there could be potentially bigger payoffs.

Premium Cost

A risk premium can be costly for borrowers, especially when their investments are not potentially the most prosperous ones. The more risk premium they pay investors as risk compensation, the more financial burden they may take on, which likely hurts the very success of their investments and increases the chance of a default. With this perspective in mind, it is in the best interest of investors themselves to reconsider the level of risk premium they demand, or else they must be prepared to fight over debt collections in the event of a default. In many borrowing-laden bankruptcies, for example, investors only receive back cents on the dollar on their investment, despite prior promises of a risk premium.

The Equity Risk Premium

The equity risk premium refers to the excess return that investing in the stock market provides over a risk-free rate. This excess return compensates investors for taking on the relatively higher risk of equity investing. The size of the premium varies depending on the level of risk in a particular portfolio and also changes over time as market risk fluctuates. As a rule, high-risk investments are compensated with a higher premium. A majority of economists agree that the concept of an equity risk premium is valid: over the long term, markets compensate investors more for taking on the greater risk of investing in stocks.

The equity risk premium is can be computed in several ways, but is most often estimated using the capital asset pricing model (CAPM):

$$CAPM\left(Cost\ of\ equity\right) = R_f + beta\left(R_m - R_f\right)$$

where the cost of equity is effectively the equity risk premium. R_f is the risk-free rate of return, and R_m-R_f is the excess return of the market, multiplied by the stock market's beta coefficient.

The second half of the 20th century saw a relatively high equity risk premium, over 8% by some calculations, versus just under 5% for the first half of the century. Given that the century ended at the height of the dot-com bubble, however, this arbitrary window may not be ideal.

Market Risk Premium

The market risk premium is the additional return an investor will receive (or expects to receive) from holding a risky market portfolio instead of risk-free assets.

The market risk premium is part of the Capital Asset Pricing Model (CAPM) which analysts and investors use to calculate the acceptable rate of return. At the center of the CAPM is the concept of risk (volatility of returns) and reward (rate of returns). Investors always prefer to have the highest possible rate of return combined with the lowest possible volatility of returns.

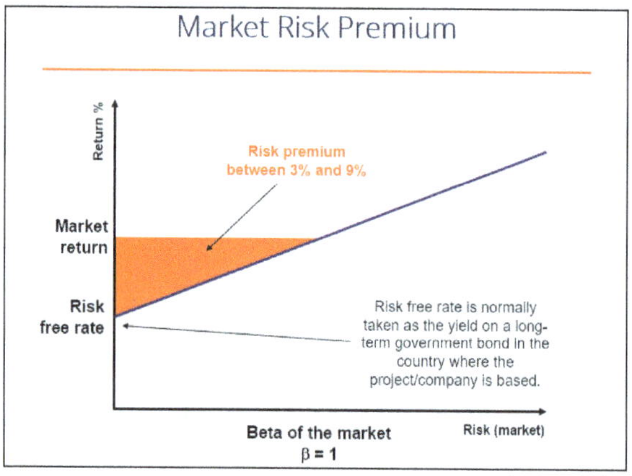

Concepts used to Determine Market Risk Premium

There are three concepts related to the market risk premium:

1. Required market risk premium: The minimum amount investors should accept. If an investment's rate of return is lower than that of the required rate of return, then the investor will not invest. It is also called hurdle rate of return.
2. Historical market risk premium: A measurement of the return's past investment performances taken from an investment instrument that is used to determine

the premium. The historical premium will produce the same result for all investors as the value's calculation is based on past performances.

3. Expected market risk premium: Based on the investor's return expectation.

The required and expected market risk premiums would differ from one investor to another. During the calculation, the investor needs to take the cost of equity it takes to acquire the investment into consideration.

With a historical market risk premium, the return will differ depending on what instrument the analyst uses. Most analysts use S&P 500 as a benchmark for calculating past performance.

Usually, a government bond yield is the instrument used to calculate risk-free assets as it has little to no risk.

Market Risk Premium Formula and Calculation

The formula for Market Risk Premium is:

Market Risk Premium = Expected Rate of Return – Risk-Free Rate.

Example:

S&P 500 generated a return of 8% the previous year, and the current rate of the Treasury bill is 4%. The premium is 8% – 4% = 4%.

Market Risk Premium		
Example		
Expected Rate of Return	S & P 500 Return	8%
Risk-Free Rate	Treasury Bill Rate	4%
Market Risk Premium =		4%

Use of Market Risk Premium

As stated above, the market risk premium is part of the Capital Asset Pricing Model. In the CAPM, the return of an asset is the risk-free rate plus the premium multiplied by the beta of the asset. The beta is the measure of how risky an asset is compared to the market, and as such, the premium is adjusted for the risk of the asset. An asset with zero.

An asset with zero risk, and therefore zero beta, for example, would have the market risk premium canceled out. On the other hand, a highly risky asset, with a beta would 0.8, would take on almost the full premium. At 1.5 beta, the asset is 150% more volatile than the market.

Volatility

It's important to reiterate that the relationship between risk and reward is the main premise behind market risk premiums. If a security returns 10% every time period without fail, it has zero volatility of returns. If a different security returns 20% in period one, 30% in period two, and 15% in period three, it has a higher volatility of returns and is therefore considered "risker", even though it has a higher average return profile.

References

- Risk-and-return-on-investment, firm-financial-management, investment: businessmanagementideas.com, Retrieved 15 March, 2019
- Risk-and-returns-concept-of-risk-and-returns, financial-management: yourarticlelibrary.com, Retrieved 5 June, 2019
- Understanding-investment-risk: columbiathreadneedleus.com, Retrieved 20 March, 2019
- Concept-of-Return-and-Risk: scribd.com, Retrieved 11 February, 2019
- Joshua M. Pearce. (2015) Return on Investment for Open Source Hardware Development. Science and Public Policy. DOI :10.1093/scipol/scv034 open access
- Returnoninvestment: investopedia.com, Retrieved 18 May, 2019
- Return-investment-roi: investinganswers.com, Retrieved 8 January, 2019
- What-is-return-on-investment-roi, finance: corporatefinanceinstitute.com, Retrieved 19 January, 2019
- Riskreturntradeoff: investopedia.com, Retrieved 3 April, 2019
- Efficientfrontier: investopedia.com, Retrieved 20 July, 2019
- Factors-influence-rates-return-investment: zacks.com, Retrieved 23 April, 2019
- Risk-premium: bankrate.com, Retrieved 17 February, 2019
- Riskpremium: investopedia.com, Retrieved 8 August, 2019
- Market-risk-premium, finance: corporatefinanceinstitute.com, Retrieved 3 May, 2019

Permissions

All chapters in this book are published with permission under the Creative Commons Attribution Share Alike License or equivalent. Every chapter published in this book has been scrutinized by our experts. Their significance has been extensively debated. The topics covered herein carry significant information for a comprehensive understanding. They may even be implemented as practical applications or may be referred to as a beginning point for further studies.

We would like to thank the editorial team for lending their expertise to make the book truly unique. They have played a crucial role in the development of this book. Without their invaluable contributions this book wouldn't have been possible. They have made vital efforts to compile up to date information on the varied aspects of this subject to make this book a valuable addition to the collection of many professionals and students.

This book was conceptualized with the vision of imparting up-to-date and integrated information in this field. To ensure the same, a matchless editorial board was set up. Every individual on the board went through rigorous rounds of assessment to prove their worth. After which they invested a large part of their time researching and compiling the most relevant data for our readers.

The editorial board has been involved in producing this book since its inception. They have spent rigorous hours researching and exploring the diverse topics which have resulted in the successful publishing of this book. They have passed on their knowledge of decades through this book. To expedite this challenging task, the publisher supported the team at every step. A small team of assistant editors was also appointed to further simplify the editing procedure and attain best results for the readers.

Apart from the editorial board, the designing team has also invested a significant amount of their time in understanding the subject and creating the most relevant covers. They scrutinized every image to scout for the most suitable representation of the subject and create an appropriate cover for the book.

The publishing team has been an ardent support to the editorial, designing and production team. Their endless efforts to recruit the best for this project, has resulted in the accomplishment of this book. They are a veteran in the field of academics and their pool of knowledge is as vast as their experience in printing. Their expertise and guidance has proved useful at every step. Their uncompromising quality standards have made this book an exceptional effort. Their encouragement from time to time has been an inspiration for everyone.

The publisher and the editorial board hope that this book will prove to be a valuable piece of knowledge for students, practitioners and scholars across the globe.

Index